Maik Fielitz, Nick Thurston (eds.)
Post-Digital Cultures of the Far Rig

Political Science | Volume 71

Maik Fielitz, Nick Thurston (eds.)

Post-Digital Cultures of the Far Right

Online Actions and Offline Consequences in Europe and the US

[transcript]

With kind support of

Bibliographic information published by the Deutsche Nationalbibliothek
The Deutsche Nationalbibliothek lists this publication in the Deutsche Nationalbibliografie; detailed bibliographic data are available in the Internet at http://dnb.d-nb.de

© 2019 transcript Verlag, Bielefeld

Cover layout: Kordula Röckenhaus, Bielefeld
Typeset by Alexander Masch, Bielefeld
Printed by Majuskel Medienproduktion GmbH, Wetzlar
Print-ISBN 978-3-8376-4670-2
PDF-ISBN 978-3-8394-4670-6
https://doi.org/10.14361/9783839446706

Contents

Introduction

Stephen Albrecht, Maik Fielitz and Nick Thurston

THE RIGHTWARDS PRESSURE

Web 2.0 and the proliferation of social media platforms enable user-generated content to be shared instantly via networks that record their own searchable archives. This advent has accelerated and deepened the effective reach of activists and organizations from across the political spectrum. However, in the neoliberal democracies of Europe and the US the most alarming surge of online political pressure in recent years has come from the far right and been felt in the centerground. Far-right movements from around the world have relentlessly intervened in both the private and public spheres of our digital worlds, from the deep web to the surface net, from public chat rooms to multi-player gaming environments. Digital platforms that bypass traditional editorial and governmental controls yet overlay our traditional political milieus have empowered such groups to directly broadcast their content globally to witting and unwitting audiences alike. What this extent of fluid connectivity generates is the dream of all digital marketeers: it motivates reciprocation and sharing among users who become communities bonded in tribal ways (Roberts 2017; Seemann 2017). Those communities have digitally-driven ecosystems whose filters favor the reinforcement of shared terms yet facilitate inter-community collaboration at any level. Those levels range from the local and interpersonal spaces that we inhabit to the imagined communities and coalitions that we can create across cyberspace.

  With growing confidence, bolstered by the electoral successes of right-wing politicians across both continents and beyond (India, Russia, Brazil and Turkey), far-right activists online now openly share offensive content and promote incitements to violence against vulnerable people. They use a range of harassment methods, from the blunt to the innovative, harnessing the pooled click-power of such communities to loosely coordinate propaganda and intimidation campaigns. Not only do these "tactical media" (Raley 2009) publishing strategies normalize access to far-right ideas, they also normalize the ideas themselves. These ideas blur into, or sometimes brazenly constitute, 'dangerous speech', which are expressions that go beyond the fuzzy category of 'hate speech' because they increase the risk that audiences will condone or participate in violence against the targeted group (Benesch 2018). They typically exploit a fear of the unknown to build on a patriarchal foundation of anti-feminist, anti-LGBTQ+, racist and anti-minority scapegoating.

The quantity, sophistication and inter-connectedness of both unofficial activists and official party channels online has made it more and more difficult to carry forwards established academic categories to explain the far-right's renewal. Virtual activists celebrate their transgressive behavior while political parties veil their ideological agendas with rhetorical trickery (Feldman/Jackson 2014), both blurring their traditional roles. The categorization of these actor positions on a spectrum running from the socially accepted and legally protected 'radical right' to an anti-constitutional and violent 'extreme right' is now obsolete. To avoid exhausting debates about terminological essentialism, throughout the chapters that follow, contributors work on or under the umbrella idea that the far right is a "political space whose actors base their ideology and action on the notion of inequality among human beings, combining the supremacy of a particular nation, 'race' or 'civilization' with ambitions for an authoritarian transformation of values and styles of government" (Fielitz/Laloire 2016: 17–18).

Many far-right groups were early adopters of the internet as a space in which they could create their own ideological publishing frames (Foxman/Wolf 2013). For example, the world's largest white supremacist website, Stormfront, was established in 1996 and preceded by a bulletin board system that operated during the early 1990s. Indeed, the development of early online far-right subcultures forecasted political changes in the organized far right (Kaplan/Weinberg 1998). We have witnessed the potency of their new operational models on the streets and in parliaments since the financial crisis of 2007-8 and the so-called 'migration crisis' of 2015. These changes are measurable in terms of their policy impacts, including the pressure to close borders in Greece and Germany, the ongoing rightward shift of political cultures in Italy and Austria, the installation of authoritarian regimes in Hungary and elsewhere, and explicit collusions between governments and far-right influencers that have become common knowledge in the US.

Having expanded on to the world wide web, far-right activism evolved from the grounded street marches of previous protest eras to take on different characteristics. Generally speaking, early accounts stress how it became more individualized, anonymized and geographically scattered (Köhler 2014; Bennett 2012). Too often these accounts ignore how the networking aspects of the technology empowered the creation of broad-brush alliances with pan-national ambitions (Margetts et al. 2018). Terms like 'clicktivism' and 'slacktivism' became popular in the early 2010s as a way of dismissing the credibility of online campaigning. We now know that these atomization arguments created blind spots in mainstream thinking and power vacuums online, both with dangerous repercussions.

The Berlin-based Amadeu Antonio Foundation has come to call what has heated up since the 2010s a conflict over digital civil society (2017). This book goes further by thinking holistically about contemporary civil society as a context that is being re-defined by the normalization of digital networked technologies in everyday life, a context that demands we take online actions seriously if we are going to better understand their offline consequences and vice versa.

Social media tools like Twitter and Facebook are now considered indispensable by protest groups from across the spectrum (Gerbaudo 2012) and have generated (or at least significantly intensified) their own playbooks, led by click-swarm tactics like trolling and doxing (Bartlett 2015). On the far right in particular, at a macro level, the symbols and icons that anchored such communities have shifted from the tropes of National Socialism to re-coded hipster emblems (Miller-Idriss 2018) and humorous memes (Lovink/Tuters 2018). Just as the means of communication were brought up-to-date, so too were the vocabularies and outreach agendas of the larger far-right movements and parties (Mammone 2009). At a micro level, time and again we can trace the planning of anti-migrant protests, vigilantism and anti-Muslim squads back to social media crusades (Awan/Zempi 2016; Busher 2016). These evolved macro and micro tactical changes demonstrate that there is no longer a simple distinction between online and offline campaigning practices – in fact, that the two are now evermore inter-effecting and that contemporary protest politics is fundamentally post-digital.

THE POST-DIGITAL FAR RIGHT

In the social sciences, much has been written about why the far right has tipped the balance of online political discourse rightwards, away from the supposed 'liberal hegemony' they rail against, including, for example, several publications on the use of the internet by far-right extremists (Caiani 2018; Caiani/Parenti 2013). Such studies tend to focus on the communication potential of digital networks as something subsequent to the politics of the actors using that channel, thus reducing the digital to a 'means to an end'. Relatively little has been written in accessible terms to explain how the far right is tipping that balance. Less still has been published to explain how or why such technologies have transformed the very nature of contemporary far right political action and discourse. This book offers thirteen perspectives on these developments, exploring the ways in which their entwinement is reciprocal and urgent in different national contexts with ramifications that are felt around the world. It re-casts official and unofficial far-right groups, movements and parties as activists in a post-digital world, one where they seem to be winning many of the ideological battles.

Most media historians agree that we are living in an era in which so-called 'new media' are ever-present and no longer new in the sense that theoretically sustained the category distinctions of old and new media. Our technical era is intermedia and digitally driven – one in which old and new interact – and our intermedia tools run software that allow multiple simultaneous user-tool and user-user interactions with "glocal scope" (Hampton/Wellman 2002). This connectivity makes the online and offline responsive to one another, and their growing augmentation makes them increasingly inter-dependent. This book introduces the concept of the 'post-digital' to social science discussions about the resurgent far right, re-contextualizing their shocking power to mobilize online and offline in terms of this pervasive inter-effectivity. It therefore promotes a network-oriented, sociological account of the nearing far right.

The term post-digital was coined in 2000 by American composer Kim Cascone to describe an aesthetic tendency in contemporary computer music that champions processing glitches as a source of unique sounds (Cascone 2000). That tendency is now more commonly labelled by the pan-arts term "glitch aesthetic" (Applegate 2016), and media theorists including Geert Lovink and Florian Cramer have re-directed post-digital to describe a bigger, deeper phenomenon: "'Post-digital' ... refers to a state in which the disruption brought upon by digital information technology has already occurred. This can mean, as it did for Cascone, that this technology is no longer perceived as 'disruptive'" (Cramer 2014: 12–13). Here, the prefix 'post-' signifies a dependent break from the word it precedes, in much the way we might talk about the post-modern or post-human. The post-digital names a technical condition that followed the so-called digital revolution and is constituted by the naturalization of pervasive and connected computing processes and outcomes in everyday life, such that digitality is now inextricable from the way we live while its forms, functions and effects are no longer necessarily perceptible.

This 'naturalization' has been accelerated by the growth in computing power, internet-enabled mobile devices, the low participation barriers to internet culture, as well as the push within that culture towards an emphasis on mass postproduction, compressed expression, images and "circulationism" (Steyerl 2013). For those post-digital far-right actors leading the current resurgence, intermedia systems are not neutral communication tools. Rather, they are a catalyst for highly social processes and forums where political opinions are created, expressed and practiced. These media are mediating politics. They connect larger audiences more quickly and widely, allow for autonomous spreading, circumvent regional and national restrictions, can host parallel channels that range from open access to the encrypted, and use overlapping frames, feeds and windows to keep politics, digital citizenship and users' personal lives in constant contact. Every contributor to this book has tried to analyze these dizzying layers of relationships through a real and recent case study, contextualizing the national and historical frame of their sample in an engaging narrative, and doing all of this in a medium-length essay.

MAINSTREAMING THE EXTREME

A general climate of fear and political despondency seems to be percolating through societies in Europe and the US, which must play some intangible role in making both contexts amenable to reactionary extremisms, especially of the conservative sort that promises to restore some mythic version of proper order. In traditional political milieus, this despondency has been coupled with a failure on the part of civil society and the Left to act collectively. In non-traditional milieus, the far right has excelled, heeding Breitbart's often-quoted maxim that "politics is downstream from culture" (Meyers 2011). As well as the ease with which different far-right subcultures can share news using the internet, it has also proven a rich playground for the adaptation of propaganda material (Whine 2012) and visual content (Doerr 2017) across contexts, flattening circumstantial differences in favor of general ideological alignment. For example, memes have become one of the most common ways that far-right content gets shared, often playing with a cynical or ironic stance relative to current affairs to recruit new sympathizers and make its messages attractive (Miller-Idriss 2018). Through forceful play and distributed action the far right, as a political space, has established unity in difference, in ways that the liberal center and Left have failed.

In an always-connected content-saturated era, attention becomes distracted. Understanding the attention economy and designing campaigns responsively to manage audiences' attention has become a hallmark of successful far-right movements. This typically involves offering an array of content-type choices simultaneously, which mimic variety, even disagreement, but actually all share the same narrow ideological range. Compressed and dogmatic forms of social media posting have risen in importance alongside public message boards such as 4chan that were a hotbed for the American Alt-Right when it was organizing in support of Donald Trump's 2016 election bid (Nagle 2017; Wendling 2018).[1] Yet other, semi-discrete publishing platforms like moderated web forums can accommodate public and private exchanges. As such, they are the tip of an iceberg of more invisible communication channels used by far-right activists on the dark web (Bartlett 2015) and encrypted messenger services (Ebner 2017). What has become abundantly clear is that the far right has a core of tech-savvy participants who are willing to teach and advise, and their post-digital strategy is flexible enough to migrate from one platform to the next (Donovan et al. in this volume). The Alt-Tech movement is an important example of how and why this works. Its aim is to provide a self-sufficient safe haven for right-wing communities to freely express their opinions, as a response to what they

---

1 | The convention of bracketing the name 'Alt-Right' in speech marks to question that group's status claim is one we support, and is discussed in this volume by both Fledman/May and Miller-Idriss. However, unless it is a subject of discussion, in this book we have chosen not to follow that convention for the sake of clarity.

consider the unjust censorship of their right to free speech by mainstream providers. Alt-Tech works to achieve that goal by creating its own technological infrastructure (Roose 2017).

The startling result of this attention management approach – its fake variety, constant multiple channels, and mix of content types – is the gradual mainstreaming of ideas, expressions and behaviors that would have previously been considered extremist. Here this active verb, 'main-streaming', describes a confluence of processes that together cultivate sympathy amongst large portions of the general public for social attitudes that would otherwise be considered beyond the pale, then tries to mobilize that sympathy to institutionalize those attitudes in policies, legislation and public opinion about what is considered normal. Although the factors at play and their success are always difficult to pinpoint, their impact does not need to be complete or explicit for the strategy to have influence. The payoffs from shifting the frame of what is acceptable in mainstream discourse are demonstrated by the frailties of hate speech legislation. If the range of what is considered normal can change, and change differently in different contexts simultaneously, then so can its opposite, the range of what is considered prejudicial and unacceptable. This contextual dynamism, plus the complicated issue of free speech in democratic countries and the global reach of online media, make it incredibly difficult to define and enforce what constitutes hate within national jurisdictions.

Across Europe and the US, this gradual rightwards shift in the frame of what is normal has also had an array of knock-on effects (Davey et al. 2018). A strange mix of subcultures have been absorbed by the far right, from particular fashion brands (Idriss-Miller 2018) to anonymous and pseudonymous sections of the deep web (Tuters in this volume). The far right has its own internet stars and social media influencers, including Lauren Southern and Milo Yiannopoulos, who use their accounts like independent media channels that blur the distinction between lone actor activism and strategic movement campaigning in a manner best described as "post-organizational" (Mulhall 2018). Such ideologues often publish shock-tactic content as click-bait to compete for audience attention – the more controversial the better. In a highly politicized climate like ours, no matter how independent or distasteful these accounts are, they seed ideas and hyperlinks that attract more attention to local far-right organizations in the real world, often becoming a news story in themselves and so serving as a gateway to radicalized cultural spaces. The scope of other, more collective efforts has also been stretched by the technical affordances of overlapping networks. Militant far-right groups have become more agile and are quicker to re-organize after their websites are deleted or banned (Hess 2018). InfoWars, Rebel Media and Breitbart represent the growing importance of alternative right-wing news platforms, while book presses like Arktos give a semblance of intellectual credibility to the European New Right's worldview (de Keulennar 2018).

COUNTER-THOUGHT AND COUNTER-ACTION

No book can exhaustively catalogue let alone solve these problems. In fact, a hero politics based on strongmen who save their people through sovereign action is a recurring feature of our current mess. This book has been developed in the opposite spirit. It is a collaborative attempt to pay close critical attention to a complex tangle of urgent problems, and to share the informed research of a range of academics, policy advisers and activists who want to communicate with broad readerships. The main body is organized into two sections, yet all of the contributors use grounded examples and try to offer actionable advice.

Section One gathers seven chapters that focus on 'Analyzing' various far-right strategies and collaborations that have involved a blend of virtual- and actual-reality campaigning, which are either little known in themselves or have had an under-discussed impact on national or international debates. Understanding exactly how online communities function requires a kind of double literacy: a technical appreciation of how the media operate has to be paired with a cultural awareness of what the content it mediates is trying to represent.

Rob May and Matthew Feldman together unpick the online strategies of the infamous Alt-Right. They explain how the apparent breadth and lightheartedness of the US-based movement has allowed fascists and neo-Nazis to hide in plain sight among its ranks. They trace the links between the supposedly jovial culture of online LOLs, their sharpened derivative lulz, and the booming popularity of pseudo-comic shaming tactics used by activists including Richard Spencer. Closely tied to all of this is the Alt-Right's weaponized use of irony and subcultural idioms, which Marc Tuters takes up in a detailed account of the connections between gamer culture, fan culture, the deep web and the far right. Tuters introduces his concept of the "deep vernacular web" to explain the affinity or sense of existential threat shared by some online subcultures with white supremacists. He also deftly explains how the gatekeeping practices common to the former have been adapted by the latter, such that inclusion and exclusion are constantly reinforced through "live action role play" or LARPing protests that distinguish those 'in the know' from the enemy. Joan Donovan, Becca Lewis and Brian Friedberg critique the free-speech and market-disruption claims of the Alt-Tech movement. They unpack how its participants have created and stabilized new tools by cloning and consolidating popular features from corporate platforms that have blocked extremist users and advertisers. While platforms might be sociotechnical infrastructure that adapt to the norms of their users, ideological bubbles like Gab show that the moral values of their design teams are encoded in each system.

One of the most thriving platform types is, of course, social media, and two further contributions take up case-studies that concentrate on how European far-right political parties have successfully innovated social media strategies that enhance their offline authority. Philipp Karl investigates the post-digital promotion of a family-friendly, youth-oriented nationalist message that elevated Jobbik into position as Hungary's main opposition party. He explains the simple but consistent messaging that framed Jobbik's annual Nationalist May festival. These celebrations of Hungarian culture mobilized food, drink and music in support of a populist agenda, but relied on Facebook and Twitter to cash their lasting symbolic impact as political capital. Lynn Berg presents a damning assessment of the anti-feminist views and standards expressed by Germany's far-right AfD party through speeches, adverts and constant micro-aggressions online. She shows how the perpetual reinforcement of regressive gender roles by male and female party representatives and supporters typifies the tandem bond between far-right ideology and a patriarchal understanding of gender norms. Further, she connects this to an on-going ethnicization of sexism in the culture war being waged by far-right actors across Germany and elsewhere.

Caterina Froio's and Bharath Ganesh's co-authored chapter reminds us that far-right activism has always had a transnational dimension, but shows how Twitter has opened up new opportunities for parties, movements and organizations with cross-border interests. They use a dataset of re-tweets by far-right parties in France, Germany, Italy and the UK to assess what does and does not garner international attention. Their findings are surprising in many ways, especially at the level of take up. Yet they also re-affirm some sadly familiar trends, including the importance of hash-tags and issues-led posting for international circulation, and the ubiquity of anti-Muslim prejudice among such groups. Kaja Marczewska flips our focus to consider the booming zine culture amongst factions of the far right in contemporary Poland. She contrasts the pseudo-slick stylistic features of her examples against the traditional cut-and-paste aesthetic that was a signature of zine-making in its leftwing origins. Rather than dismiss the limited online presence of this strange boom as a failure to migrate to 'new media', Marczewska credits the offline limited circulation of such zines with being generative of a powerful safe space for community building.

Section Two has the intentionally ambiguous title 'Unmasking' because the six chapters it gathers try, in various ways, to draw the background practices and convictions of far-right communities into the foreground so that we can think critically about what actually unifies their memberships. Much of what unfolds in this section involves sensitive forms of disentangling and disambiguation. These are critical skills that are becoming all the more necessary in an era when digital networking makes the propagation of obfuscation, misinformation and 'fake news' a media strategy in itself for those who care more about power than truth.

Processes of meaning-making are always contextually specific and depend on shared terms and tools for understanding. Deciphering meanings, particularly of the symbolic sort, connect individuals to specific collective histories. They can fortify a community against the unversed, and also encourage a sense of belonging among the versed. As Cynthia Idriss-Miller explains in her chapter on youth culture and fashion, both of those payoffs make the symbology of far-right cultures a powerful aspect of how they define themselves, caricature their enemies and perpetuate the anxieties and obsessions that give them (positive and negative) continuity. She shows how iconography is adapted, commercialized and traded, and how consumer goods can become a symbolic force for political messaging on image-driven platforms like Instagram. Lisa Bogerts and Maik Fielitz study the power of visual memes used by the German far-right project Reconquista Germanica, which mobilizes troll armies by remixing generic tropes of white nationalism. Cartoons, the crusades, nature and motherhood get spun through Vaporwave visual distortions or neo-Romantic collage techniques. Bogerts and Fielitz find a "humorous ambiguity" to be so consistently deployed that it qualifies as a strategy, one that continues the long history of fascist movements aestheticizing politics. Alina Darmstadt, Mick Prinz and Oliver Saal survey a disinformation campaign that hijacked the tragic murder of a 14-year-old girl in Berlin in 2018 to fuel xenophobic fear about migrants and to stage overtly racist rumours about refugees. Politicians and citizens swarmed to echo the misleading claims that were drip-fed via social media about the ethnicity of the perpetrator. Darmstadt, Prinz and Saal show how this case is sadly typical of the politics of fear being sown by the far right in Germany and beyond, whereby suspicion becomes a racialized social lens. They also offer a clear-sighted list of everyday counter-actions that civil society can engage in to offer some push back.

The question of counter-action is central to the last three chapters in this book. Julia Ebner develops an analysis of far-right communication tactics and the ecosystem they create for cyber content, focusing on the use of satire, their odd claims to alterity, and the scary impact they are having amongst Generation Z digital natives. She maps out four pillars on which an international community could collaboratively build a framework to protect those who are targeted by radicalization, manipulation and intimidation practices. Gregory Sholette draws upon his long history as a participant and teacher in activist art communities to give a theoretical overview of the challenges now facing socially-engaged arts practice. Situating these challenges relative to capitalism's precarious prevalence, he contrasts two rebel impulses. One is an essentialist push towards a homogenous, white concept of identity. The other faction are bonded by the long struggle for equality, which demands some space for uncertainty so that more equal futures can be imagined, a space that art might be well-suited to creating. Lastly, Nick Thurston loops this book project back to its starting point, an artwork called *Hate Library* (2017). His chapter connects the importance of sociable settings for reading, like libraries, with the value of pausing fluid streams of online language in print. Drawing on documentary poetry, file-sharing practices and the choreography of installation art, he outlines some of the roles that the arts might play when societies are faced by fundamental questions about who is responsible for the consequences of public expressions.

ENGAGING APPROACHES

One paradox of editing any collection of new essays is that there is always more to say and more people who deserve to be read, but you have to stop somewhere to publish the book. A second paradox of the form, exacerbated by a topic like ours, is that in an era of accelerated change grounded analyses are outdated pretty quickly by real life events. This book has been developed reactively, with the aim of sharing some informed opinions about a growing problem that has been all-too-easily ignored by people with power. Those opinions bridge art, activism, policy research and political science. As such, the editors and authors who have worked quickly and ambitiously to create this book have chosen to engage with the post-digital cultures of the resurgent far right – from a range of novel perspectives – rather than bury their heads in the sand, against the academic trend for quietism or socially-detached scholarship.

We are sensitive to the many problems that come with an engaged approach to researching global issues. Publishers face economic struggles, sensationalist media coverage about current affairs circulates everywhere, and attention spans of readers are supposedly decreasing. Social science literature is trying to keep up with these trends, as is research funding, but what sells is policy-oriented studies of causes, consequences and best practices. Similarly in art, so-called socially-engaged approaches have to accept their complicity with the structural inequalities that underwrite their industry. For example, discussing the co-option of artists' critical conscience by institutions who have different priorities is now a platitude. Nonetheless, we hope that the many original insights offered by this book will strengthen the great work already being done by civil society campaigners and contribute to a more sophisticated common understanding of how the personal and public, micro-action and macro-repercussions, online and offline behavior, are all tied-up in contemporary politics whether we like it or not.

As mentioned above, this book stemmed from the research into, and conversations about, an artwork by Nick Thurston called *Hate Library*, which was commissioned by Foksal Gallery in Warsaw where it was first exhibited in 2017. The advisory support of Matthew Feldman and curatorial trust of Katarzyna Krysiak on that exhibition were invaluable, as was the support of Inga Seidler and her colleagues for its next showing at transmediale 2018 in Berlin. We are sincerely grateful to all of them for helping to develop this project. However, this book is worth reading because of the quality and intellectual generosity of the international mix of specialists who have contributed to it, to all of whom we owe endless thanks. Our editors at transcript Verlag recognized the importance of our topic and have supported us with great enthusiasm to start and finish this publication in less than 10 months, which would not have been possible without Florian Eckert's editorial care. We have remained determined to the end to make sure the length, variety and tone of this book makes it engaging and useful for specialist and non-specialist readers. To that end, it has been released in a post-digital manner, in a print edition and for Open Access download. Neither version would have been possible without the generous support of the Rosa Luxemburg Foundation and the Amadeu Antonio Foundation, and we owe special thanks to Research Institute for Societal Development (FGW) for ensuring the digital edition would be available for free to readers anywhere in the world.

REFERENCES

Amadeu Antonio Foundation (2017): "Digital Streetwork. Pädagogische Intervention im Web 2.0", (https://www.amadeu-antonio-stiftung.de/w/files/pdfs/digital_streetwork_web.pdf).

Applegate, Matt (2016): "Glitched in Translation: Reading Text and Code as Play of Spaces", (http://amodern.net/article/glitched-in-translation/).

Awan, Imran/Zempi, Irene (2016): "The Affinity Between Online and Offline Anti-Muslim Hate Crime. Dynamics and Impacts." In: Aggression and Violent Behavior 27, pp. 1–8.

Bartlett, Jamie (2015): The Dark Net. Inside the Digital Underworld, New York: Melville House.

Benesch, Susan (2018): "What is Dangerous Speech?", 28 August 2018 (https://dangerousspeech.org/the-dangerous-speech-project-preventing-mass-violence/).

Bennett, Lance W. (2012): "The Personalization of Politics. Political Identity, Social Media, and Changing Patterns of Participation." In: The Annals of the American Academy of Political and Social Science 644/1, pp. 20–39.

Busher, Joel (2016): The Making of Anti-Muslim Protest. Grassroots Activism in the English Defence League. London, New York: Routledge.

Caiani, Manuela (2018): "Radical Right Cross-National Links and International Cooperation." In: Rydgren, Jens (ed.): The Oxford Handbook of the Radical Right, Oxford: Oxford University Press, pp. 394–411.

Caiani, Manuela/Parenti, Linda (2013): European and American Extreme Right Groups and the Internet, Farnham, Surrey and Burlington: Ashgate.

Cascone, Kim (2000): "The Aesthetics of Failure: 'Post-Digital' Tendencies in Contemporary Computer Music." In: Computer Music Journal 24/4, pp. 12–18.

Cramer, Florian (2015): "What is 'Post-Digital'?" In: Berry, David M./Dieter, Michael (eds.) (2014): Postdigital Aesthetics. Art, Computation And Design, London: Palgrave Macmillan, pp. 12–26.

Davey, Jacob/Salman Erin M./Birdwell, Jonathan (2018): "The Mainstreaming of Far-Right Extremism Online and how to Counter it: A Case Study on UK, US and French Elections." In: Herman, Lise Esther/Muldoon, James B. (eds), Trumping the Mainstream. The Conquest of Mainstream Democratic Politics by the Populist Radical Right, Abingdon, Oxon and New York, NY: Routledge.

de Keulennar, Emillie V. (2018): "Arktos' Reformulation of the Far Right", 16 March 2018 (https://oilab.eu/arktos-reformulations-of-far-right-ideas/).

Doerr, Nicole (2017): "Bridging Language Barriers, Bonding Against Immigrants. A Visual Case Study of Transnational Network Publics Created by Far-Right Activists in Europe." In: Discourse & Society 28/1, pp. 3–23.

Ebner, Julia (2017): The Rage. The Vicious Circle of Islamist and Far-Right Extremism, London and New York: I.B. Tauris.

Feldman, Matthew/Jackson, Paul (eds.) (2014): Doublespeak. The Rhetoric of the Far Right since 1945, Stuttgart: Ibidem.

Fielitz, Maik/Laloire, Laura L. (eds.) (2016): Trouble on the Far Right. Contemporary Right-Wing Strategies and Practices in Europe, Bielefeld: transcript.

Foxman, Abraham H./Wolf, Christopher (2013): Viral Hate. Containing its Spread on the Internet, New York, Basingstoke and Hampshire: Palgrave Macmillan.

Gerbaudo, Paolo (2012): Tweets and the Streets. Social Media and Contemporary Activism, London, Berlin: Pluto Press.

Hampton, Keith/Wellman, Barry (2002): "The not so Global Village of Netville." In: Wellman, Barry/Haythornthwaite, Caroline (eds.), The Internet in Everyday Life, Oxford: Blackwell, pp. 345–371.

Hess, Amanda (2018): "The Far Right has a New Digital Safe Space", 22 December 2017 (https://www.nytimes.com/2016/11/30/arts/the-far-right-has-a-new-digital-safe-space.html).

Kaplan, Jeffrey/Weinberg, Leonard (1998): The Emergence of a Euro-American Radical Right, New Brunswick: Rutgers University Press.

Köhler, Daniel (2014): The Radical Online: Individual Radicalization Processes and the Role of the Internet. In: Journal for Deradicalization 1, pp. 116–134.

Lovink, Geert/Tuters Marc (2018): "They Say we Can't Meme: Politics of Idea Compression", 11 February 2018 (https://non.copyriot.com/they-say-we-cant-meme-politics-of-idea-compression/).

Mammone, Andrea (2009): "The Eternal Return? Faux Populism and Contemporarization of Neo-Fascism across Britain, France and Italy." In: Journal of Contemporary European Studies 17/2, pp. 171–192.

Margetts, Helen/John, Peter/Hale, Scott A./Yasseri, Taha (2017): Political Turbulence. How Social Media Shape Collective Action. First paperback printing, Princeton and Oxford: Princeton University Press.

Meyers, Lawrence (2011): "Politics Really Is Downstream From Culture – Breitbart", 22 August 2011 (http://www.breitbart.com/big-hollywood/2011/08/22/politics-really-is-downstream-from-culture/).

Miller-Idriss, Cynthia (2018): The Extreme Gone Mainstream. Commercialization and Far Right Youth Culture in Germany, Princeton: Princeton University Press.

Mulhall, Joe (2018): "A Post-Organisational Far Right?", (https://www.hopenothate.org.uk/research/state-of-hate-2018/online-radicalisation/post-organisational-far-right/).

Nagle, Angela (2017): Kill All Normies. The Online Culture Wars from Tumblr and 4chan to the Alt-Right and Trump, Winchester and Washington: Zero Books.

Raley, Rita (2009): Tactical Media, Minneapolis: University of Minnesota Press.

Roberts, David (2017): "Donald Trump and the Rise of Tribal Epistemology", (https://www.vox.com/policy-and-politics/2017/3/22/14762030/donald-trump-tribal-epistemology).

Roose, Kevin (2017): "The Alt-Right Created a Parallel Internet. It's an Unholy Mess", (https://www.nytimes.com/2017/12/11/technology/alt-right-internet.html).

Seemann, Michael (2017): "Digital Tribalism – The Real Story about Fake News", (http://ctrl-verlust.net/DigitalTribalism.pdf).

Steyerl, Hito (2013): "Too Much World: Is the Internet Dead?", (https://www.e-flux.com/journal/49/60004/too-much-world-is-the-internet-dead/).

Wendling, Mike (2018): Alt-Right. From 4chan to the White House, London: Pluto Press.

Whine, Michael (2012): "Trans-European Trends in Right-Wing Extremism." In: Godin, Emmanuel/Jenkins, Brian/Mammone, Andrea (eds.), Mapping the Extreme Right in Contemporary Europe. From Local to Transnational, Hoboken: Taylor & Francis, pp. 317–333.

Analyzing

Understanding the Alt-Right

Ideologues, 'Lulz' and Hiding in Plain Sight

Rob May and Matthew Feldman

The Alt-Right has perhaps performed the most successful rebranding of fascist ideology since the Axis dénouement of 1945. Fascist ideology has been a vexatious term for almost as long as fascism has existed, resistant to definition and typically used as either an insult or political hyperbole. Yet the utility of the term as a definitional starting point for understanding fascists past and present has changed markedly over the last generation. There has come to be a notable confluence of scholarly views on this forward-looking, revolutionary and even cultic form of (usually ethnically-based) integral nationalism:

"Since it first emerged in the wake of World War One, fascism can be profitably conceptualised as a specifically modern form of secular 'millenarianism' constructed culturally and politically, not religiously, as a revolutionary movement centring upon the 'renaissance' of a given people (whether perceived nationally, ethnically, culturally, or religiously) through the total reordering of all perceivedly 'pure' collective energies towards a realisable utopia; an ideological core implacably hostile to democratic representation and socialist materialism, equality and individualism, in addition to any specific enemies viewed as alien or oppositional to such a program" (Feldman 2008: xviii).

Not all groups falling under the umbrella term 'Alt-Right', fit this view; for instance, the arch-reactionary racists of the League of the South take their inspiration from the Civil War-era Confederate States of America. Yet most of the ideologues who self-identify with the Alt-Right movement do fit this understanding, like hand in glove.

The Alt-Right's 'hand', in the analogy above, is its explicit ideological extremism. In keeping with historic fascism, despite savvy use of social media, this is a movement that seeks ethno-national 'purity' through revolution. Such revolutionary change is directed against social and political 'sickness'; like a patient dying in the emergency room, fascists believe that only a defibrillating shock can return the race (and often synonymously, nation) to mythic glory and dominance. While this zap would undoubtedly be violent – and, as in the past, target leftists, ethnic and religious minorities – the emergent society is invariably cast in utopian terms. For the Alt-Right, this means reactionary gender roles; a militant state focussed on dynamic expansion, even colonization; and above all, a top-down policing of ethics and politics putting the collective above any and all individuals, save a charismatic leader. The latter also helps to explain the importance of Alt-Right ideologues today, in both charting this 'regenerative' course, and in embodying the 'healthy' nation, giving it a renewed sense of self belief and, in a Nietzschean sense, a racist will to power capable of eradicating weakness and opposition from all quarters – internally and externally.

To pursue this simile a bit further, far from the jackbooted paramilitaries who marched across the 'fascist epoch' between 1919 and the end of World War Two, the Alt-Right's 'glove' – that is, its identifying feature and way of displaying its beliefs – has typically been the defence of mere 'lulz'. A distortion of 'LOL', or 'Laugh out Loud', lulz are a sharper form of offensive humour directed by online activists. Exemplified by Pepe the Frog avatars and targeted 'humour' about ethnic and religious minorities in Europe and North America, lulz provide ironic distance where necessary. In this way, the public response of 'just joking' is used as a 'frontstage' mechanism; or better, a shield to protect against charges of racism and their potential consequences, like falling foul in Europe of anti-racist legislation, including Holocaust denial. This characteristic feature is candidly described in Andrew Anglin's *Normie's Guide to the Alt-Right* for the neo-Nazi Daily Stormer online site, which has swiftly become one of the most popular Alt-Right websites today:

"While racial slurs are allowed/recommended, not every reference to non-white should not be a slur and their use should be based on the tone of the article. Generally, when using racial slurs, it should come across as half-joking – like a racist joke that everyone laughs at because it's true. This follows the generally light tone of the site. It should not come across as genuine raging vitriol. That is a turnoff to the overwhelming majority of people" (Anglin 2016).

A subsequent section of this *Normie's Guide* is still more explicit:

"Lulz

The tone of the site should be light. Most people are not comfortable with material that comes across as vitriolic, raging, non- ironic hatred. The unindoctrinated should not be able to tell if we are joking or not. There should also be a conscious awareness of mocking stereotypes of hateful racists. I usually think of this as self-deprecating humor – I am a racist making fun of stereotype of racists, because I don't take myself super-seriously. This is obviously a ploy and I actually do want to gas kikes. But that's neither here nor there" (Anglin 2016).

Speaking in forked tongues to a wider public while signalling a fealty to committed activists has long been a tactic for the postwar far right, eager to counter the stigma of wartime totalitarianism and genocide committed by the Axis. Fully a generation earlier, Roger Eatwell (1996: 100) raised a distinction between the neo-fascist British National Party's 'esoteric' nods-and-winks to hardcore members and their more populist 'exoteric' appeal intended for the general public. In a book examining this phenomenon across a range of different countries and groups, Chip Berlet termed this persistent feature "coded rhetoric" (Berlet 2014), while Graham Macklin described this frontstage-backstage dynamic as 'ideological bifurcation':

"ideological bifurcation functions as an innate component of the operating system of post-war fascist ideology. It serves as a mode of communication and as a 'coping strategy' enabling far right groups to organize themselves around certain forms of 'rejected knowledge' which, since the Second World War, have been profoundly out of step with the values of the societies in which they organize. This duality co-exists without contradiction, resulting in an 'exoteric' articulation of its ideology for public consumption and an 'esoteric' truth understood by an initiated hardcore of political activists" (Macklin 2014: 123–124).

To take just one Alt-Right example – chosen simply by reading the comments on the Daily Stormer about a mainstream new story current at the time of writing – in response to a child who was bullied for being gay and then committed suicide, Andrew Anglin's (2018) headline is *LOL: 9-Year-*

Old Mulatto Niglet Commits Suicide After Bullying! God Bless the USA! The opening of this account then proclaims: "It's a proud day for all Americans. Things like this don't happen in Europe, you know – because they love sucking cock and actually encourage little boys to do it, instead of bullying them into suicide for saying they like doing it. This heart-warming tale reminds me of my favorite patriotic song..." Further racist and homophobic content is then cossetted in just enough lulz to provide a semblance of ironic distance, just as the Daily Stormer's *Normie's Guide* advocates.

Put simply, leopards do not change their spots. 'Ironic misdirection' is vital for understanding the mainstream push by Alt-Right ideologues and online activists. It is but one of the key techniques deployed in the Alt-Right's rise to prominence over the last five years. The panoramic glimpse provided by this chapter, emphasizing recurrent themes and leading figures in this still-nascent movement, also serves as a salutary reminder that the revolutionary goals of fascist socio-cultural 'purity' – especially in the previously hostile terrain of mainstream politics in Europe and North America, the most familiar stamping grounds for the Alt-Right to date – has many paths toward this goal. 'Joking' about the Holocaust is but one of them.

Although not all far-right trolls are as gratuitously offensive as the Daily Stormer and its stable of online neo-Nazis, normalizing fascism, and above all Hitler's Third Reich and its Axis partners' genocidal crimes, remains the principal tollbooth through which every Alt-Right group and ideologue must pass. As this chapter underscores, it is Alt-Right ideologues that frame, justify and often direct the growing online army of so-called 'shitposters'. The idealogues are the self-appointed ringmasters of this racist circus, even if they often disagree and sometimes directly clash with one another. Richard Spencer, perhaps their most influential and sophisticated ambassador, demonstrated this shockingly when speaking to a roomful of Nazi saluters shortly after Donald Trump's shock election to the presidency: "For us, it is either conquer or die ... Let's party like its 1933 ... Hail Trump! Hail our people! Hail victory!, accompanied by an English version of Nazism's *Sieg Heil!*"[1]

---

1 | See a video recording of this speech, alongside commentary with cited quotations, in NZ Herald (2016): "The Big Read: Insight the Alt-Right world of Richard

KEY ALT-RIGHT IDEOLOGUES

It was Richard Spencer who first popularized the term 'Alternative-Right' in 2008. Son of an heiress to cotton farms in Louisiana, Spencer is educated to MA level – having read English Literature and Music as an undergraduate and Humanities as a postgraduate – before dropping out of a Ph.D. in History "to pursue a life of thought-crime" (Burghart 2014). Perhaps tellingly, Spencer's entrance essay for the Ph.D. examined the German judicial theorist and onetime Nazi, Carl Schmitt. Thereafter, Spencer became an Assistant Editor at The American Conservative, a magazine led by the noted paleoconservative Pat Buchanan who was White House Director of Communications under the Reagan administration. Spencer was dismissed for his extremist views (Lyons 2017: 2; Wood 2017). After a two-year period as Executive Editor at the fringe publication Taki's Magazine, Spencer founded the now-defunct www.AlternativeRight.com in 2010, which he defined as "an online magazine of radical traditionalism [which] marks an attempt to forge an intellectual right wing that is independent of and outside the American conservative establishment" (quoted in Hartzell 2018: 19). As far back as 2010, the Southern Poverty Law Centre described the website as extreme right and "loaded with contributors who, like Spencer, have long lamented the white man's decline" (Keller 2010).

The success of AlternativeRight.com opened up various new avenues for Spencer. He accepted the role of President and Director at the National Policy Institute (NPI), a racialist organization dedicated to the "heritage, identity, and future of people of European descent in the United States and around the world."[2] On its website, the NPI continues to describe itself as "a central and indispensable component of the international Alt-Right" while boasting that "Richard Spencer and NPI are at the forefront of Alt-Right activism."[3] Spencer is also the Executive Director at Washington Summit Publishers, a white nationalist publisher specializing in eugenics, anthropology, and human biodiversity. As an offshoot of Washington Summit Publishers, Spencer also launched the online Radix journal

Spencer", 23 November 2016 (https://www.nzherald.co.nz/world/news/article.cfm?c_id=2&objectid=11753791).

2 | National Policy Institut: "About", (https://www.nationalpolicy.institute/who arewe).

3 | Ibid.

which, according to its website, produces "original work on culture, race, tradition, meta-politics, and critical theory."[4]

Most recently, Spencer launched www.Alt-Right.com, an 'academic' think-tank seeking "to give a platform to dissident opinions within the right." Its thinly-veiled racist aim is to "promote information and discourse in support of Western civilization and draw attention to the imminent demographic threat of mass immigration which is on course to completely erase the unique cultures and peoples of the Occident."[5] Notwithstanding the sanitized language above, a legal complaint by civil rights groups claimed that the white supremacist site was actively promoting violence and hatred against racial and ethnic minorities. In response, the internet domain registrar GoDaddy.com, which hosted Alt-Right.com, shut down the website in May 2018 (see Murdock 2018; Sharwood 2018). In recent weeks, however, www.Alt-Right.com has re-emerged online.

As a self-identified white nationalist, Spencer's vision for a utopian United States is a place for whites only. He claims that "European America is being demographically dispossessed [and therefore] we are losing our culture [and] our sense of being." Spencer's aim is to influence politics and culture by "raising consciousness and influencing people", which he claims to be engaged in daily. Spencer insists that he has an "amazing" opportunity to achieve this with Donald Trump in the Oval Office. Although conceding that Trump is not Alt-Right himself, he sees Trump's presidency the first step towards white nationalist policies in the US.[6] For his part, though one of many Alt-Right ideologues, Spencer can rightly claim the mantle of *primus inter pares* given his editorial undertakings, media savvy engagements and long-standing activism for an 'Alternative Right'.

However, the most repulsive and (at least publicly) extreme devotee to the Alt-Right is Andrew Anglin. In 2006, Anglin launched the conspiratorial website, Outlaw Journalism, which was modelled on the works of Infowars founder Alex Jones and gonzo journalism (journalism without objectivity) originator Hunter Thompson, who he greatly admired. Before forming his first neo-Nazi website Total Fascism in 2012, Anglin went

---

4 | Radix: "About", (www.radixjournal.com/about/).

5 | Alt-Right.com: "Who We Are", (www.Alt-Right.com/who-we-are/).

6 | *Los Angeles Times:* "Richard Spencer, Chairman of the National Policy Institute", 18 November 2016 (www.youtube.com/watch?v=jm4DNMNEZM0&t=29s).

on a spiritual and psychological journey resulting in his conversion to 'full Nazi'. He worked as an English teacher in Asia where, according to Anglin, "all the White people you meet are outcast sorts who you can usually connect with easily" (Anglin 2015). In comments that must again be treated with large helpings of salt, Anglin claims that "having been raised mostly without exposure to non-Whites, this was when I first started thinking seriously about race as a biological concept. Eventually, I got fed up and realized that I couldn't live in a jungle with a bunch of 80 IQ jungle people" (ibid.). Combined with his continental experience was his obsession with the uncensored imageboard, 4chan, where anyone can post anonymously. Anglin explains how he had latched on to the less overtly fascist 'brand' of the Alt-Right, helping to give his patch a more explicitly neo-Nazi inflection:

"I had always been into 4chan, as I am at heart a troll. This is about the time [I k]new [I]was going full-Nazi, and so I got into Hitler, and realized that through this type of nationalist system, alienation could be replaced with community in a real sense while the authoritarianism would allow for technology to develop in a direction that was beneficial rather than destructive to the people" (Anglin 2015).

Due to its lengthy articles, Anglin replaced Total Fascism a year later with Daily Stormer, named after the infamous antisemitic weekly newspaper *Der Stürmer* run by a Nazi called Julius Streicher, which vehemently attacked Jews. With shorter and more provocative pieces, Anglin hoped his new platform would appeal to a broader audience. Central to Anglin's website is extreme racism, misogyny, homophobia, Holocaust Denial and, above all, antisemitism. According to traffic statistics website Alexa, Daily Stormer is ranked 5,722 most viewed in the US and 17,558 globally, making it one of the most popular Alt-Right websites.[7] The success of Daily Stormer has established Anglin to one of the most influential ideologues in the Alt-Right, resulting in his inclusion (along with Spencer) in a leaders' pact to unite the Alt-Right in December 2016.[8]

---

7 | Alexa: "dailystormer.name Traffic Statistics", (www.alexa.com/siteinfo/daily stormer.name).

8 | SPLC: "Andrew Anglin", (www.splcenter.org/fighting-hate/extremist-files/indi vidual/andrew-anglin).

Anglin's mission is to create a Nazi world (2015). As a proud Hitler-worshipper, he admits to philosophizing over "what [would] Hitler do if he'd been born in 1984 [the year of Anglin's birth]?" Unsurprisingly, given his adoration of Hitler, Anglin harbours an innate hatred of Jews. In his vital 78-page primer, *A Normie's Guide to the Alt-Right*, Anglin defines the Alt-Right thus: "The core concept of the movement, upon which all else is based, is that Whites are undergoing an extermination, via mass immigration into White countries which was enabled by a corrosive liberal ideology of White self-hatred, and that the Jews are at the center of this agenda" (Anglin 2016: 2).

Through the *Daily Stormer*, Anglin has created an ad hoc group of followers called 'The Stormer Troll Army' who perpetrate harassment on his behalf, mostly directed towards Jews. In December 2016, Anglin targeted Tanya Gersh, a Jewish woman who had a disagreement with Richard Spencer's mother. Anglin uploaded photographs of Gersh and her contact details along with a rally cry to his readers: "Are y'all ready for an old-fashioned Troll Storm?" (quoted in Stevens 2017). Subsequently, Gersh received "more than 700 threatening, hateful, harassing, antisemitic communications from Anglin's followers at all hours of the day and night". This included harassing telephone calls, asserting that she should have been murdered in the Holocaust "with the rest of your people" (Beckett 2017). As the SPLC has stated: "Anglin is infamous for the crudity of his language and his thinking, a contrast to his sophistication as a prolific Internet troll and serial harasser."[9]

While there is no doubt that the Alt-Right was originally, and remains predominantly, an American phenomenon, there is more to it than that. Needless to say, the internet connects across national borders, and Alt-Rights white supremacism is similarly transnational (if heavily weighted toward Anglophone countries like the US and Britain, together responsible for more than half of the global site visitors to The Daily Stormer).[10] Notwithstanding this English-as-first-language propensity, Daniel Friberg is the most prominent Alt-Right figure in Europe. The Swede has a background in neo-Nazism and convictions for criminality, including possession of illegal arms. He has also been involved with several fascist

---

9 | Ibid.

10 | Alexa: "dailystormer.name Traffic Statistics", (www.alexa.com/siteinfo/daily stormer.name).

parties in Sweden, including Sweden's National Alliance and the violently extreme Swedish Resistance.[11] In 2009, Friberg formed the publishing company Arktos in Sweden, which has evolved into "the most important purveyor of European New Right and Alt-Right material, publishing works by the likes of de Benoist and Dugin."[12] With over 150 titles translated into 14 different languages, Arktos publishes "literature that dares to challenge the current paradigm of liberal democracy."[13] In January 2017, in an attempt to unite the Alt-Right, Spencer's NPI, the Alt-Right's Scandinavian Independent media company, Red Ice Creations, and Friberg's Arktos merged to form the AltRight Corporation, with Friberg sitting on the Board of Directors as its European Editor.[14] Relatedly, Friberg is the organizer of a prominent Alt-Right conference series in Europe, known as 'Identitarian Ideas', where he and his fellow Alt-Rightists deliver lectures.[15]

Friberg is a vocal supporter of Spencer and shares many of his perspectives. He describes Spencer as "a great guy [and] a great advocate of our viewpoints", further revealing that "I share a lot of viewpoints with Richard Spencer [...] we come from the same ideological background". Like Spencer, with the phrases 'White guilt' and 'White dispossession', Friberg similarly claims that European civilization is under threat of extinction (Kovacs 2017). The latter differentiates between the 'real right [the Alt-Right]', to which he claims allegiance, and the 'false right', which some call the 'Alt-Lite' and is fronted by such non-fascist radical right figures as Milo Yiannopolous and even onetime special advisor and chief strategist to President Donald Trump, Stephen K. Bannon. According to Friberg, unlike the more reform-minded reactionaries of the 'Alt-Lite', the 'real right' adheres to traditional values, ethnic consciousness and the preservation of European civilization, while the 'false right' believes in civic nationalism and liberal economics, bringing together old-style American

---

11 | AltRight.com: "Daniel Friberg Annihilates BBC Journalists in Interview", 4 February 2018 (https://www.youtube.com/watch?v=OetLTAFu1Po&bpctr=153 7382158).

12 | Hope Not Hate: "Daniel Friberg", (https://alternativeright.hopenothate. com).

13 | Arktos: "About Arktos", (www.arktos.com/about/).

14 | Hope Not Hate: "Daniel Friberg", (https://alternativeright.hopenothate.com).

15 | Ibid.

Republicans and even fringe figures like the provocateurs from Breitbart. In separating the Alt-Right from even far-right groups like UKIP or the Tea Party, Friberg argues that a strong meta-political basis and theory is crucial for the Alt-Right to triumph. In sum, he claims that controlling culture is pivotal to political success. It is only a matter of time, according to Friberg, before the 'false right' are replaced by the 'real right' – that is, proud fascists – in all western European countries.[16]

HIDING IN PLAIN SIGHT

It is no coincidence that all the key ideologues cited above are male. The sociologist Hannah Bergman (2018) conducted an extensive analysis of rank-and-file supporters of the Alt-Right to explore the preponderance of white men in the movement. Bergman argues that the Alt-Right promotes a sense of "male entitlement" which, in turn, is "easily radicalized and connected to white nationalism and white supremacy" (2018). By attacking feminism and liberal notions of gender equality, the Alt-Right has "created a culture of vitriolic defensiveness among young white males, which aims to establish a common belief in white male victimhood". Importantly, Bergman points out that the Alt-Right's existence, in part, relies upon a "rejection of the accomplishments of feminism". This negation raises the spectre of the 'f' word for uniting revolutionary-minded white men around a core of misogynistic disgruntlement, which licences the Alt-Right to "view the subordination of women as both part of a functional society and a stepping stone to a larger movement: one steeped in fascist ideology and willing to openly champion a politics of hate and violence" (ibid.).

This misogyny is but one of the indelible features of the Alt-Right's fascism. Given the commitment of chief ideologues of the movement, like Anglin and Spencer in the US, and Friberg in Europe, it is a phenomenon which shows little sign of abating. This is despite the washout of the second Unite the Right rally in Washington D.C. in August 2018 – a year after the Charlottesville Unite the Right rally in 2017, which saw one protester killed by and many more injured, some severely – underscoring the

---

16 | AltRight.com: "Daniel Friberg Annihilates BBC Journalists in Interview", 4 February 2018 (https://www.stormfront.org/forum/t1240745/).

fact that this is a movement much more at home in the eddies of online extremism. This is in no small part due to the way digital networks allow them, on one hand, to mobilize fluid groups of activists, especially for online trolling and 'pile-ons'; but on the other, to hide behind the 'lulz' of alleged irony and defence of hateful incitement as free speech. More than anything, it is these strategies that allow the fascists of the Alt-Right to hide in plain sight, ever like leopards ready to pounce on their prey.

REFERENCES

Anglin, Andrew (2015): "Andrew Anglin Exposed", 14 March 2015 (http://dailystormer.name/andrew-anglin-exposed/).

Anglin, Andrew (2016): "A Normie's Guide to the Alt-Right", 31 August 2016 (https://katana17.files.wordpress.com/2016/09/daily-stormer-a-normies-guide-to-the-Alt-Right-ver-31.pdf).

Beckett, Lois (2017): "I was the Target of a Neo-Nazi 'Troll Storm'", 20 April 2017 (www.theguardian.com/us-news/2017/apr/20/tanya-gersh daily-stormer-richard-spencer-whitefish-montana).

Bergman, Hannah (2018): "White Men's Fear of Women: Anti-Feminism and the Rise of the Alt-Right", 31 March 2018 (https://mathias-nil ges.com/student-projects-the-new-culture-wars/2018/4/1/white-mens-fear-of-women-anti-feminism-and-the-rise-of-the-Alt-Right).

Berlet, Chip (2014): "Heroes Know Which Villains to Kill: How Coded Rhetoric Incites Scripted Violence." In: Feldman, Matthew/Jackson, Paul (eds.), Doublespeak: The Rhetoric of the Far-Right since 1945, Stuttgart: Ibidem, pp. 303–330.

Burghart, Devin (2014): "Who is Richard Spencer?", 27 June 2014 (https://www.irehr.org/2014/06/27/who-is-richard-spencer/).

Eatwell, Roger (1996): "Contemporary Fascism in the Local Arena: The British National Party and 'Rights for Whites.'" In: Cronin, Mike (ed.), The Failure of British Fascism Basingstoke: Palgrave, pp. 99–117.

Feinberg, Ashley (2017): "This is the Daily Stormer's Playbook", 13 December 2017 (https://www.huffingtonpost.co.uk/entry/daily-stormer-nazi-style-guide_us_5a2ece19e4b0ce3b344492f2).

Feldman, Matthew (2008): "Editorial Introduction." In: Griffin, Roger/Feldman, Matthew (eds.), A Fascist Century: Essays by Roger Griffin, New York: Palgrave, pp. XII–XXVII.

Hartzell, Stephanie L. (2018): "Alt-White: Conceptualizing the 'Alt-Right' as a Rhetorical Bridge between White Nationalism and Mainstream Public Discourse." In: Journal of Contemporary Rhetoric 8/1–2, pp. 6–25.

Keller, Larry (2010): "Paleocon Starts New Extreme-Right Magazine", 15 March 2010 (www.splcenter.org/hatewatch/2010/03/15/paleocon-starts-new-extreme-right-magazine).

Kovacs, Kasia (2017): "Richard Spencer Quotes: 12 Things White Nationalist Leader of Alt-Right Movement Has Said About Race, Immigration and Trump", 25 February 2017 (www.ibtimes.com/richard-spencer-quotes-12-things-white-nationalist-leader-Alt-Right-movement-has-said-2497495).

Lyons, Matthew N. (2017): CTRL-ALT-DELETE: The Origins and Ideology of the Alternative Right, Oakland: Kersplebedeb Publishing.

Macklin, Graham (2014): "'Teaching the Truth to the Hardcore': The Public and Private Presentation of BNP Ideology." In: Feldman, Matthew/Jackson, Paul (eds.), Doublespeak: The Rhetoric of the Far-Right since 1945, Stuttgart: Ibidem Verlag, pp. 123–146.

Murdock, Jason (2018): "Richard Spencer's 'White Supremacist' Website Alright.com Taken Offline", 5 April 2018 (www.newsweek.com/richard-spencers-white-supremacist-website-altrightcom-goes-offline-910320).

Sharwood, Simon (2018): "GoDaddy Exiles Altright.com after Civil Rights Group Complaint", 4 May 2018 (https://www.theregister.co.uk/2018/05/04/whackanazi_resumes_as_godaddy_exiles_altrightcom/).

Stevens, Matt (2017): "Lawsuit Accuses Alt-Right Leader of 'Terror Campaign' Against a Jewish Woman", 19 April 2017 (https://www.nytimes.com/2017/04/19/us/splc-neo-nazi-lawsuit.html?smid=fb-nytimes&smtyp=cur).

Wood, Graeme (2017): "His Kampf", June 2017 (www.theatlantic.com/magazine/archive/2017/06/his-kampf/524505/).

LARPing & Liberal Tears

Irony, Belief and Idiocy in the Deep Vernacular Web

Marc Tuters

In the summer of 2017, the American Alt-Right gained international recognition following the violence at their Unite the Right rally in Charlottesville, North Carolina, which left one counter-protester dead and dozens
of others injured. Unwilling to condemn this act of far-right violence, the
American president Donald Trump instead spoke of violence having occurred "on many sides" (Peters 2017). As exemplified by this response,
over the course of his election campaign and early days in office Trump's
reluctance to distance himself from the far right had the effect of normalizing the public expression of their ideas to an extent that seemed unprecedented to many (Mulhall et al. 2018; Marwick/Lewis 2017). Beyond the sixty
million Americans that voted for him, Trump's inflammatory political style
also appealed to heretofore little known elements of internet subculture for
whom he also appeared as an avatar of their indignation at feeling somehow
demographically displaced. This source of indignation, however imaginary,
is what accounts for the resonance between bizarre internet subcultures and
the global insurgency of far-right populism, and is the subject of this chapter.

Although Trump's initial rebellious appeal was somewhat diminished
in the eyes of radicals by the time of Charlottesville, a significant number
of those at the rally still saw themselves as the loyal foot soldiers of the
world's first meme president, who they imagined themselves as having
helped elect through their skillful deployment of "meme magic". While
self described "internet trolls" were pleased to publicly pronounce such
ridiculous sounding claims in the media (Shreckinger 2017), one may rea-
sonably ask if they actually believed it to be true? While there are those
who have attempted to seriously grapple with such claims (Lachman
2018), the standard fallback response from most of these figures when

pushed to explain their actions is that they are 'trolling', which is to say they are just playing around. To put it in the jargon of computer game culture, they are 'live action role playing' or *LARPing*. This explanation offers those involved with a convenient excuse if and when things get out of hand. It is based on the core belief that "teh Internet is serious business", an ironic slogan whose meaning is its opposite, which is to say that the internet is *not* serious business, and anyone who thinks otherwise should be corrected and is, essentially, undeserving of pity.

The Identitarian Movement (in Germany), LARPing at Pepe.[1]

For many this dualistic outlook was, however, no longer sustainable in the face of the bloody violence in Charlottesville. Indeed, in the aftermath of that event the apparently inexorable rise of the Alt-Right was, for the first time since Trump's rise, brought into question. A year later, on the anniversary of the rally, the movement's momentum appears rather diminished. It seems that there has been a softening of the Alt-Right as many who had been flirting with its explicit white-racial supremacist elements have fallen back to the more 'mainstream' position of contemporary far-right populism, with its reactionary suspicion of 'migrants' and celebration of 'Western culture'. But while the disturbing spectacle of violence in

---

1 | Source: https://blog.identitaere-bewegung.de/pepe-und-identitaere-aktivis ten-waren-heute-in-mecklenburg-vorpommern-unterwegs/.

Charlottesville may have tested the commitment of many to 'real-world' political organizing, from an online audience perspective the rally nevertheless seemed like the culmination of a trend which had been consistently developing for some time and which continues unabated.

If the Alt-Right can be said to have accomplished anything, besides briefly normalizing 'ironic' expressions of intolerance and hate, it would be in their innovative infusion and deployment of elements of high concept fan culture in the form of political tactics. It would seem that many continue to see themselves as engaged in an online culture war whose primary battlefield is social media (in particular Youtube), and in which they appear to have the upper hand, in spite of an apparent disenchantment with the Alt-Right's more ideologically extreme propositions. While the European far right, unlike its American counterpart, has a long and established tradition of organized street protest, it would seem that they, too, are learning from the Alt-Right playbook.

THE DEEP VERNACULAR WEB

While much has been made of the Alt-Right's supposedly ironical stance (Neiwert 2017), their ideological core lies in an essentialist vision of identity politics developed by the European New Right, which has been referred to as "differentialist racism" (Taguieff 2001). Many radical right populist parties in Europe have embraced these same ideas, seeing themselves as engaged in a civilizational struggle. This worldview implores supposedly autochthonous Europeans to prevent the "great replacement": waves of immigrants overtaking Europe, all orchestrated according to the nefarious multicultural agenda of the "globalist" class. Like some of the radical right populists, there is an expressed feeling amongst these long-established denizens of the web that *their web* is being encroached upon and gentrified. The rise of social media platforms that have corporatized the experience of the web has led these otherwise disparate and marginal niches of what I call *the deep vernacular web* to see themselves as an oppositional subculture tasked with keeping alive what they perceive to be the original spirit of the web. Due in part to the cleverly strategic amplification of these antagonisms via platforms such as Twitter and Youtube, in practice this has manifested as an online culture war, the opening battle of which was the notorious Gamergate that I unpack below.

The concept of the deep vernacular web can be understood as a heuristic intended to historicize these online antagonistic communities as antecedent to social media and even to the web itself. The deep vernacular web is characterized by anonymous or pseudonymous subcultures that largely see themselves as standing in opposition to the dominant culture of the surface web. Identified to an extent with the anonymous 4chan image board – which hosts one million posts per day, three quarters of which are made by visitors from English-speaking countries[2] – these subcultures tend to imagine themselves as a faceless mass. In direct contrast to the individualized culture of the selfies associated with social media, we might thus characterize the deep vernacular web as a *mask culture* in which individual identity is effaced by the totemic deployment of memes. Insofar as this mask culture constructs an image of itself as an autochthonous culture whose integrity is under threat, we can perhaps begin to understand how grievances of the deep vernacular web have been capitalized upon by those espousing a far-right ideology. Conversely we can also see how the *vernacular innovations* of these often bizarre subcultures, such as Pepe the Frog, have themselves been absorbed in the service of far-right populism.

The reasons why 4chan is productive of vernacular innovation have to do, in part, with the affordances of the platform. 4chan 'moves' very quickly – threads are quickly purged from the website, meaning the website does not offer a way to 'catch up' with the latest developments (notwithstanding external archival websites or wikis like *Encyclopedia Dramatica*). Furthermore, 4chan is anonymous, which means that if one wants to participate in the conversation one has to demonstrate a degree of subcultural literacy. Although there are other 4chan boards which operate differently, on its most popular board, /pol/ – which has, since about 2015, increasingly been viewed as a point of convergence been online subculture and Alt-Right ideas (Heikkilä 2017) – if you speak out of turn you are likely to be either brutally insulted or else, even worse, simply ignored. As a result of this blend of affordances and practices, /pol/ drives many away while exhibiting a strong socialization effect on those remain – one byproduct of which is that sensationalist behavior helps one to be noticed on /pol/. Combined with an ironic relationship with the idea of belief, discussed below, these factors help to account for why 4chan is so productive of ver-

---

2 | Anon (2018): "Advertise", (http://www.4chan.org/advertise).

nacular innovation and arguably why /pol/, a board devoted to 'politically incorrect' discussion, appears so productive of far-right hate speech.

The adepts of the deep vernacular web engage in gatekeeping processes to mark-off and maintain its boundaries from the surface web. In spite of the familiar purist tendencies of the hard core that wish to remain resolutely underground, the broader influence of their subcultural imaginary can be seen as extending rather deeply into aspects of corporate social media. As an example of such an incursion we might consider the Kekistan meme that had its origins in 4chan but which came to prominence on Youtube as a kind of imaginary homeland for trolls (de Keulenaar 2018). In a series of videos posted on Youtube over the course of 2017, the Kekistan meme developed the mythology of an imaginary country with its own flag and history, a kind of 'ethnostate' in the language of the European New Right, whose people imagined themselves to be engaged in a civilizational conflict against the forces of 'political correctness.'

Initially functioning as a kind of in-group slang expression for gamers, in 4chan the term 'kek' (at the root of Kekistan) became a conceptual marker for the concept of 'meme magic'. As such 'kek', often symbolized by Pepe, signifies the peculiarly postmodern idea that an empty symbol can itself be used as a tool to create belief in which its 'adepts' bear witness to effects of that idea without necessarily believing in any sort of truth, as one would normally expect from 'believers'. Since expressions of sincerely political belief would be dismissed as 'causefagging' on 4chan, any political memes that it generated were thus veiled in layer upon layer of irony. As a keyword, 'kek' spread from 4chan to other parts of the deep vernacular web, such as /r/The_Donald, a popular discussion board on the aggregator site Reddit devoted to Donald Trump's insurgent candidacy. On the Facebook page *God Emperor Trump*, the candidate was envisioned as a figure of divine chaos, the embodiment of the 'cult of kek'. On Youtube the Kekistan meme was developed in a number of directions by a variety of channels including some associated with Youtube's so-called "intellectual dark web" (Weiss 2018). Common to most of these channels were videos which staged confrontational encounters with liberal protesters, so-called social justice warriors or SJWs. Following a well established technique of internet trolls, the objective of these Youtube videos was to 'trigger' an emotional reaction from the SJWs, who are considered to exhibit an embarrassing and predictable lack of composure – connected to this, for example, was a whole new genre of 'liberal tears' videos.

THE IDIOTIC ADJACENT

The Kekistani flag became emblematic of Alt-Right trolling tactics. It was 'iconically' modeled on the Nazi *Reichskriegsflagge*, an echo that was intended to 'trigger' SJWs into accusing their opponents of being Nazis. While the ironic use of Nazi iconography may appear baffling, the logic deployed is that, as memes, even the most taboo symbols can be disconnected from their fixed historical meaning and made to function as *floating signifiers* for those who understand the rules of memes. As with Trump's own populism, we can think of the essential formlessness of the Kekistan meme as having created a kind of "equivalential chain" across an otherwise disaffected group of people, thereby uniting them (Laclau 2005). As opposed to SJWs, trolls thus perceived the flag of Kekistan as being governed by the first and second laws of the internet: that all discussions find their end in a fallacious comparison with the Nazis (Godwin's Law) and that, in any case, it is impossible to distinguish between sincerity and parody online (Poe's Law). These videos thus staged a conflict not only between Alt-Right Kekistanis and liberal SJWs but also between the imagined depths of authentic web subculture and its superficial surface. We could call this LARPing deployment of 4chan 'meme magic' in the sphere of protest politics a kind of idiocy, in the sense that Isabelle Stengers discusses "the idiot" as someone who takes a kind of stand against objective reality (Stengers 2005). To this end, self-described Kekistani's imagined themselves as staging a kind of counter-protest against what 60s counter-culturalists sometimes referred to as "consensus reality", represented in this case by all the "'normies' and 'basic bitches' who 'don't get' the countercultural styles of the amoral subculture" (Nagle 2017: 107).

But while this ethnographic perspective may offer some insights, and in spite of how adamantly or articulately some self-described Kekistanis may protest their ideological innocence, as the Kekistan flag should make clear, the meme also draws its transgressive appeal from its *subjunctive adjacency* to actual violence – violence made possible thanks to the deep vernacular web's digital dualism. Although the digital dualist notion that the online world is somehow distinct from 'real life' is a relic of an earlier era of 1990s 'cyber-theory', there is residue of its effects in the deep vernacular web. Given its roots in the pre-web era internet, the deep vernacular web's subcultural imaginary may be understood as predating the current *social media dispensation* of the surface web, pre-dating Facebook's global imposition of a "real name policy". As articulated by 90s libertarian media theorists with roots in the 60s counter-cultural movements, the earlier *cyberspace dispensation* promised to be a "new home of Mind", of disembodied avatars exempt from the laws and constraints of the physical world (Barlow 1996). For all of Facebook's hegemony, the frontier ideology of this earlier cyberspace dispensation has continued in the pseudonymous and anonymous cultures of the deep vernacular web, in particular in the thriving parallel reality of online multiplayer gaming.

Trump supporter in New York 2017 with a Kekistan flag. Photo by Alec Perkins from Hoboken, USA.[3]

As has been well explored elsewhere (Massanari 2016), the current reactionary populist moment in online culture can be traced back to the convo-

---

3 | Source: https://commons.wikimedia.org/wiki/File:Trump_supporters_May_Day_2017_in_New_York_City(34430306665).jpg, CC BY 2.0.

luted narrative of "Gamergate", which was essentially an anti-feminist protest movement bewilderingly disguised as a moral outrage against "ethics
in game journalism". Gamergate may be understood as having pioneered
a new model of right-wing activism centred around a fundamentalist defence of free speech, neo-reactionary and traditionalist notions of identity
politics and a series of online harassment tactic referred to as 'brigading'.
What is of particular significant for our purposes is how Gamergate served
to politicize a cross-section of previously relatively politically unengaged
internet users in the service of a cause. (In a rare instance of such censure
on an otherwise uncensored platform, discussions of Gamergate were in
fact banned from 4chan since they violated its 'causefagging' prohibition.)
In apparent violation of *4chan's irony imperative*, Gamergate created true
believers. Through a process they referred to as 'red pilling', coverts came
to see themselves as part of a collective quasi-religious community. While
this awakening had none of the individual piety of prior American religious revivals, it did draw its strength from the Thomist idea of the just
war against the infidel, who were in this case the dreaded SJWs. Alongside
the globalist and the so-called Cultural Marxist, the figure of the SJW
served to unite these online antagonistic communities. While originally
derived from the famous psychedelic scene in the 1999 film *The Matrix*,
the 'red pill' became a metaphor for revealing and overcoming false ideology through The Dark Enlightenment – a quasi-philosophical movement
that may be considered as a precursor to the Alt-Right – which posits the
existence of a hegemonic, unconscious consensus between powerful figures within academia and the media who use the concept of "political correctness" as a tool of oppression (see Sandifer 2017). Dark Enlightenment
thinkers thus advocated embracing the most extreme elements of trolling
as an antidote to, and violent rejection of, insidious attempts at mind-con-
trol by these unholy forces. Thus, it is by way of fan culture and conspiracy
ideology that we may we come to understand the newfound appeal of reactionary post-digital activism.

DARK FANDOM

It would be a mistake to claim that the Alt-Right pioneered this relationship to fan culture. American media studies scholarship has for some
years sought to study how online fan culture might inform new forms of

liberal protest politics. Building on the celebration the 'agency' of active audiences in 90s cultural studies scholarship, Henry Jenkins argued that fandom represented not only a source of cultural innovation but a new model for citizenship and even activist politics (Jenkins 2006). In contrast to the anti-consumerist culture jamming practices of earlier activists, with their fatalistic and purist vision of commercial culture, Jenkins champions the notion of the empowered consumer: co-creation versus co-optation. In this new model, which has been referred to as "transmedia organizing" (Costanza-Chock 2014), activists thus come to resemble the active audience of fan culture by engaging in the co-creation of world-building leading to narratives or story elements dispersing across multiple delivery channels. We can find striking examples of Jenkins' model on the American progressive left, notably the #MyHungerGames protests in 2014 in which the Twitter hashtag allowed young adult sci-fi fans to show solidarity with low paid service employees (Ashoka 2014). While such progressive examples continue, it would however appear that in the aftermath of Gamergate, and especially since the rise of Trump, the new vanguard has become "toxic fandom" (Parham 2018). Indeed, at a structural level reactionary memes like Kekistan seem more innovative and original than their politically-progressive counterparts: As instances of world-building they can be understood as the autopoetic creations of the deep vernacular web.

The argument developed above is that the deep vernacular web, long the source of memetic innovation, has recently become a staging ground and recruitment center for the new-right. In contrast, however, to the post-critical argument (so forcefully articled by Henry Jenkins), it would appear that what makes the new-right so appealing to so many in these subcultures is how this ideology seems to offer a critique of the dominant hegemonic system which they perceive as threatening their enjoyment (Lovink/Tuters 2018). Whatever we call them, these online antagonistic communities appear to be here to stay. Part of the reason for this is indeed their capacity to world-build by drawing from the abundant 'lore' of gamer culture. Although equally significant is the *schadenfreude* of triggering SJW. These innovations come together in the deployment of 'meme magic' in the sphere of protest politics. However idiotic such protest-LARPing may appear to 'normies', those who consider themselves to be 'in on the joke' may perceive their actions to be a kind of avant-garde activism, which aims to disrupt 'consensus reality'. We may even consider the former in terms of an anarchistic protest against what Jacques Rancière (2004) refers to as the dominant "partition of the sensible," according to which aesthetic conventions are used to disguise the essentially arbitrary nature of political domination. Insofar as protest-LARPing does not exhibit an accompanying "desire to engage in reasoned discourse", by this same measure one may say that it fails to meet the normative standard of a genuinely activist "disruption effect" (Rancière cited in Bennett 2009: 109).

In spite of all the ironic posturing, what we should not overlook is the extent to which these communities also represent the concerns of those who perceive their identities as under threat. Given the demographic make-up of the culture of 4chan and of 'hard core' computer gamers, this political movement has appeared as a backlash spurred by an aggrieved 'silent majority'. While one may not necessarily sympathize with the substance of these grievances, in terms of political strategy it would be an oversight to dismiss them out of hand. Given the degree of their entrenchment in the broader political discourse, it is not obvious how to respond to this situation. In a simplification of Gramscian meta-politics, the New-Right in both Europe and America would have us believe that "politics is downstream from culture" (Griffin 2000; Meyers 2011). While these online antagonistic communities appear to have occupied the high ground in the current online culture war – figuratively speaking of course – it has also been argued that "this supposed new and revolutionary countercultural influence hasn't produced any original cultural artefacts of note beyond a few frog memes" (Wendling 2018). If, as the red pill metaphor would seem to suggest, there is a deep desire on the part of many to see beneath the ideological superstructure, then the left can gain advantage by shifting the theatre of conflict from half-baked pop culture to the conventional political sphere and issues like economics and social justice. On that terrain, we might say the left still has all the best memes.

REFERENCES

Ashoka (2014): "Hunger Games Salute Used by Black Friday Protesters Fighting for Higher Wages", 5 December 2014 (https://www.forbes.com/sites/ashoka/2014/12/05/hunger-games-salute-used-by-black-friday-pro testers-fighting-for-higher-wages/#6b953b1a712e).

Barlow, John P. (1996): "A Declaration of the Independence of Cyberspace", 8 February 1996 (https://projects.eff.org/~barlow/Declaration-Final. html).

Bennett, Jane (2009): Vibrant Matter: A Political Ecology of Things, Durham and London: Duke University Press.

Costanza-Chock, Sasha (2014): Out of the Shadows, Into the Streets! Transmedia Organizing and the Immigrant Rights Movement, Cambridge: MIT Press.

de Keulenaar, Emillie V. (2018): "The Rise and Fall of Kekistan: a Story of Idiomatic Animus as Told Through Youtube's Related Videos", 6 April 2018 (https://oilab.eu/the-rise-and-fall-of-kekistan-a-story-of-idiomatic-animus-as-told-through-the-youtube-recommender-system/).

Griffin, Roger (2000): "Interregnum or Endgame? the Radical Right in the 'Post-Fascist' Era." In: Journal of Political Ideologies 5/2, pp. 163–178.

Heikkilä, Niko (2017): "Online Antagonism of the Alt-Right in the 2016 Election." In: European Journal of American Studies 12/2, pp. 1–23.

Jenkins, Henry (2006): Convergence Culture: Where Old and New Media Collide, New York: NYU Press.

Lachman, Gary (2018): Dark Star Rising: Magick and Power in the Age of Trump, New York: Tarcher Perigee.

Laclau, Ernesto (2005): On Populist Reason, London: Verso.

Lovink, Geert/Tuters, Marc (2018): "Memes and the Reactionary Totemism of the Theft of Joy", 12 August 2018 (https://non.copyriot.com/memes-and-the-reactionary-totemism-of-the-theft-of-joy/).

Marwick, Alice/Lewis, Rebecca (2017): "Media Manipulation and Disinformation Online," 15 May 2017 (https://datasociety.net/pubs/oh/DataAndSociety_MediaManipulationAndDisinformationOnline.pdf).

Massanari, Adrienne (2016): "#Gamergate and the Fappening: How Reddit's Algorithm, Governance, and Culture Support Toxic Technocultures." In: New Media & Society 19/3, pp. 329–346.

Meyers, Lawrence (2011): "Politics Really Is Downstream From Culture – Breitbart", 22 August 2011 (http://www.breitbart.com/big-hollywood/2011/08/22/politics-really-is-downstream-from-culture/).

Mulhall, Joe/Lawrence, David/Murdoch, Simon/Simmonds, Abigail (2018): The International Alternative Right, London: Hope Not Hate.

Nagle, Angela (2017): Kill All Normies. The Online Culture Wars from Tumblr and 4chan to the Alt-Right and Trump, Winchester and Washington: Zero Books.

Neiwert, David (2017): Alt-America: The Rise of the Radical Right in the Age of Trump, New York: Verso.

Parham, Jason (2018): "The Ultimate Toxic Fandom Lives in Trumpworld", 23 July 2018 (https://www.wired.com/story/trump-fandom/).

Peters, Jeremy W. (2017): "One Theory Over Meaning of Trump's 'Many Sides' Remark", 15 August 2017 (https://www.nytimes.com/2017/08/15/us/politics/theories-meaning-trump-many-sides-remark.html).

Rancière, Jacques (2004): The Politics of Aesthetics, London and New York: Continuum.

Sandifer, Elizabeth (2017): Neoreaction a Basilisk: Essays on and Around the Alt-Right, London: Eruditorum Press.

Shreckinger, Ben (2016): "At Trump's Victory Party, Hints of Vengeance to Come", 11 September 2016 (https://www.politico.com/story/2016/11/trump-vengeance-victory-speech-2016-231084).

Stengers, Isabelle (2005): "The Cosmopolitical Proposal." In: Latour, Bruno/Weibel, Peter (eds.), Making Things Public: Atmospheres of Democracy, Cambridge, and Karlsruhe: MIT Press & Center for Art and Media, pp. 994–1003.

Taguieff, Pierre-André (2001): The Force of Prejudice: on Racism and Its Doubles, Minneapolis: Minnesota University Press.

Weiss, Ben (2018): "Meet the Renegades of the Intellectual Dark Web", 8 May 2018 (https://www.nytimes.com/2018/05/08/opinion/intellectual-dark-web.html).

Wendling, Mike (2018): Alt-Right: From 4chan to the White House, Chicago: University of Chicago Press.

Parallel Ports

Sociotechnical Change from the Alt-Right to Alt-Tech

Joan Donovan, Becca Lewis and Brian Friedberg

Before the insurgence of the so-called 'Alt-Right' into contemporary political discussion, white supremacists have long used the internet as a means to organize and share information.[1] Early adopters of email and bulletin board technology – organizations such as the Aryan Nation and the Ku Klux Klan – saw great possibilities for using networked communication technology to circumvent social, physical and legal restrictions on the expression of racism and antisemitism. Sites like Aryan Liberty Net (1984) and Stormfront (1995) provided early platforms for the sharing of racist propaganda, novel means of organization and recruitment, and new tools to harass and intimidate vulnerable populations (Berlet 2008).[2] The increasing ubiquity of online communication has allowed white supremacist groups to grow and transform, preserving the movement's knowledge and tactics for decades.

More than a tool for communication, social media platforms are increasingly condemned for supporting the organization of a broad base of white supremacists. One key event, The Unite the Right Rally, held on August 2017 in Charlottesville, North Carolina, was organized by a broad coalition of white supremacists, many of whom were highly active online. This violent gathering led to the death of Heather Heyer and the injury of dozens of others. Much of the subsequent criticism lodged against social

---

[1] | According to the Associated Press Style Guide, references to the "Alt-Right" should always be in quotes. For more information, see: https://blog.ap.org/behind-the-news/writing-about-the-Alt-Right

[2] | Southern Poverty Law Center (2015): "Stormfront: A History", 25 March 2015 (https://www.splcenter.org/hatewatch/2015/03/25/stormfront-history).

media companies concerned the failure to enforce their own 'Terms of Service' contracts in the lead up to the rally. Corporations such as Google (including Youtube), Twitter, Facebook, Cloudflare, GoDaddy, AirBnB, Uber, Paypal, Discord, Patreon, and others reacted by 'no platforming' (i.e. refusing services) known white supremacists account holders.

The event revealed a fissure across platform companies' terms of service and their willingness to enforce them. Platform companies showed a commitment to ethical use by banning far-right and extremist accounts, which was debated in the media as a form of censorship. In this case, the actions by internet companies prompted a significant change in far-right organizing: the Alt-Right suddenly needed the support infrastructure of an 'Alt-Tech' movement. One of the organizers of the Charlottesville rally, Tim Gionet (aka Baked Alaska on social media) told the *LA Times*: "We're getting banned from using payment-processing services, so we have no other choice. If that's the gamble they want to take, I guess they can, and we'll make our own infrastructure" (Pearce 2017). This question of *infrastructure* emerges for social movements in the face of particular obstacles, and Donovan (2018) argues that this infrastructural turn happens when a movement's very survival is threatened.

Therefore, while no-platforming efforts have raised public awareness of online hate speech and racist organizing, they have also necessitated the development of alternative platforms to prolong the life of the movement. We argue that these so-called 'Alt-Tech' platforms also serve as recruitment and organizing sites for the far right, allowing for direct communication and continued engagement. All of which begs the question: what shifts in the sociotechnical organization of networked communication have enabled extremist communities to flourish? We take up this question by exploring how alternative sociotechnical systems have developed after the violence in Charlottesville.

In computer science, parallel ports were an early hardware solution for connecting peripherals, allowing for multiple streams of data to flow simultaneously. The concept of parallel ports as a type of forking (i.e. changes in the organizational flow of information to allow for processing different streams of data) is embedded within the design of technical systems and the open source movement (Kelty 2008). It is also an important frame for understanding the maturation of networked social movements as they are both structured by and structuring their own technological infrastructure (Donovan 2018). By porting the social movement community from one platform to another, movement leaders are making decisions about what technological features are necessary to sustain the movement.

We use the figure of parallel ports here to analyze the development of alternative platforms. We ask: is the 'forking' of the Alt-Right's technological development driven by a need for stabilization? Or, is it the case that the alternative technology developed in the wake of Charlottesville is something fundamentally different? In this article, we describe the development of a social media platform called Gab to show how technology was used by the Alt-Right to align with other online movements. While there are points of affinity where these movements have overlapped, we describe how the design and widespread adoption of Gab, a small online social media platform, rose in prominence after the riot in Charlottesville. Gab sought to bridge these movements not only to expand its user base but also because technology is a movement unto itself. Technological change is often intertwined with social movements learning to use the technology and innovating at the margins of utility (Mattoni 2013; Donovan 2016). As such, mapping technological change and the adoption of new technologies by social movements is a critical site for understanding sociotechnical systems designs and their challenges.

TACTICAL INNOVATION ACROSS THE ALT-RIGHT AND ALT-TECH

Doug McAdam (1983) explains the process of social movements' development and decline through a theory of tactical innovation. In order to develop and to reach their goals, social movements must understand the broader political context in which they are positioned and devise tactics accordingly. Violent and disruptive tactics have a higher success rate than more institutionalized routes (Piven/Cloward 1991), but to achieve success these disruptive tactics must change often (McAdam 1983; Piven/Cloward 1991). The transformation of tactics either leads to legitimate power or the insurgents must develop new forms of disruptive protest (McAdam 1983).

In order to study social movements in this way, McAdam develops three concepts that emphasize the relationship between movements and counter-movements: tactical innovation, tactical adaptation, and tactical interaction. Tactical innovation refers to "the creativity of insurgents in devising new tactical forms," i.e. an initial action. Tactical adaptation is "the ability of opponents to neutralize these moves through effective tactical counter," i.e. the responding action. Tactical interaction is the process through which these actions are understood and offset, much like a chess match (McAdam 1983: 736).

But, how does a social movement choose its tactics and decide on a course of action? The political opportunity structure is key to understanding how a movement's chosen tactics are limited to the legitimate and illegitimate means available to meet a desired goal. Holly J. McCammon (2003) illustrates how political defeats, factionalism, and the limitation of particular resources led in some cases to tactical stasis and in other cases provided an impetus for tactical innovation. As well, a movement's organizational readiness, its ability to mobilize resources and communicate tactics, often shapes what tactics they have in their repertoire.

Kim Voss and Rachel Sherman (2000), Melissa J. Wilde (2004), and Marshall Ganz (2000) have called attention to tactical innovation as it relates to the biography of a movement's leaders. While some measure of charisma must always be present for leadership to be effective, successful leaders often have affiliations with other movements, coupled with strong alliances both inside and outside the movement, and the ability to innovate to reach their desired outcomes.

In the case of the Unite the Right rally, we see the field of political opportunities opened wide for white supremacists in the lead up to and following Trump's 2016 election. Not only was the national media receptive to their messaging and dedicated a large amount of resources to covering their movement, but Jeff Sessions became the Attorney General, whose agenda was highly focused on other racialized issues, such as tracking the gang MS-13 across borders and labelling Black Lives Matter as 'Black Identity Extremists.' Within Charlottesville itself, the political gains of the Black Lives Matter movement included renaming Lee Park as Justice Park and removing the large statue of Robert E. Lee.

The Alt-Right, led by Richard Spencer and other charismatic figures popular on social media, chose Lee Park to stage the Unite the Right rally to protest the removal of the statue. This would also draw in counter-protesters who wanted to protect their earlier wins. Here, Spencer's choice to rally in Charlottesville was a tactical innovation that sought to produce a confrontation with local activists in order to gain media attention. In May 2017, prior to the Unite the Right rally in August, Spencer and others held a torch-lit protest in the same park. This protest got significant media coverage, despite the event itself being rather low-energy with only a few dozen people in attendance. By organizing events Spencer brought in new recruits and created alliances with new groups, mainly militias, who wanted to share the media attention.

Online recruitment for the Unite the Right rally depended largely on sharing digital fliers and memes. Spencer enrolled speakers from several other white supremacist organizations who raised funds so their members could attend. The mass rally was the most significant call to action across the US white supremacist movement in years. The organization of the event relied heavily on the belief that for the movement to grow and continue to influence politics, members had to show up in person. While communication about the event online occurred on every prominent social media platform, certain sites were key conduits of information, such as 8chan, discord chats, altright.com, and the Daily Stormer (a white nationalist message board) along with podcasts such as the Daily Shoah, Alt-Right Radio, and Youtube channels by Baked Alaska and others. The event itself was organized to bolster the leadership of several charismatic figures. The goal was to rebrand the image of the white nationalist movement as one with a youthful and rebellious vision. If they were too timid to face potential violence or could not afford to travel, others were asked to participate online.

The simultaneous use of multiple platform companies' products coupled with lesser known communication tools as their movement's infrastructure ensured that if one line of communication were shut down the event could still carry on. Online video streams from far-right public protests are often closely followed in discussion threads as they happen, so it was not surprising that when a major act of violence occurred in Charlottesville, online participants jumped at the opportunity to impact the course of events by manipulating media narratives in an attempt to get journalists to blame their political opponents.

For movements with their roots on the internet, it is imperative that tactical innovation occurs in real time, where offline events feed into online dialogues that shape a movement's followers' ability to communicate with one another. That is to say, infrastructure is integral to the socio-technical design of a movement like the Alt-Right. While charismatic leaders are instrumental in providing ideological frames and being spokespeople to the media, day-to-day participation in networked social movements is largely monotonous. With few possibilities to meet in public without opposition, the Alt-Right has relied on creating an abundance of online media, forums, and opportunities for engagement that require internet infrastructure for the survival of their movement. As platforms began to remove far-right accounts and content, the Alt-Right adopted a developer's mindset and fashioned solutions out of existing code and resources. In the next section, we describe these steps taken by the Alt-Right to align with an Alt-Tech community in the wake of no platforming after Charlottesville.

TACTICAL INNOVATION AS A RESPONSE TO 'NO PLATFORMING'

The Unite the Right rally was a horrifically violent event. In the lead up to it, much of the online discussion revolved around open-carry permits, where some posted pictures of themselves posing with homemade weapons, handguns, and rifles. In some online forums and chat services, the coming event was described as a 'civil war' and 'battle with Antifa'. For those counter-organizing in Charlottesville, residents repeatedly attended City Council meetings asking for the permit to be revoked because there was going to be violence.

Emboldened by previous symbolic victories of harassment campaigns such as Gamergate (Losh 2017) and far-right intervention in the 2016 presidential election (Daniels 2018), leaders of the Alt-Right and other white nationalist groups openly promoted Unite the Right on public forums, anonymous imageboards, social media and Youtube. Gamergate was a large-scale online coalition of anonymous trolls, right wing pundits and social reactionaries who united to attack prominent women in the video game industry in 2014. For the Alt-Right, coordinated amplification of the call for many far-right factions to coalesce under a single banner would not have been possible without strategic use of public-facing media and simultaneous backchannel coordination and communication. The tactics for coordination owe much to Gamergate, relying on similar social and technical networks for organization and amplification (Losh 2017; Massanari 2015).

After the violence of Charlottesville, many platforms that took lighter approaches to content moderation were forced to confront the growing threat of large-scale white supremacist organizing on their platforms. Symbolic targets, such as removing blue check marks on Twitter and the removal of Facebook pages, were chosen to give the impression that platforms were both willing and able to respond to this threat. Some, like Spencer, called for platforms to be regulated like other public utilities in the USA, where net neutrality applies to speeds afforded by internet service providers but not the content itself. In the USA, platforms are allowed to choke/censor/moderate content in the interest of the online community, which is key to market retention. In other countries, such as Germany, racist content is restricted by tighter government regulations, placing legal burden of removal on social media platforms and hosting sites. There are, however, easy technological circumvention techniques that allow for access, such as the use of the TOR browser or VPNs that mask location.

Others, in response, called for alternative platforms to arise and fill the communication and amplification void left by large-scale banning, or for right-wing operatives to double-down on pre-existing platforms with lax approaches to censorship or mission statements aligned with free-speech absolutism. This was a critical shift in the far-right's ability to stay organized as platform companies reacted to their violence. By shifting the focus from Alt-Right to Alt-Tech, a new wave of organizing continued online while offline events faltered or were completely overwhelmed by counter-protesters (Neuman 2017). One such influential platform, Gab, found its niche in the fall of 2017. While there were many other platforms competing for attention and users at this time – Voat, Bitchute, and Minds – Gab stood out as one that adopted a public stance on the issues of free speech, technological design, and white nationalism. We focused our study on the public communications of Gab founder, Andrew Torba, and analyzed the design of Gab to illustrate how the platform capitalized on this crisis within the far-right movement to simultaneously populate their platform and provide infrastructure to the floundering social movement.

During an interview with far-right media personality Alex Jones, Andrew Torba, founder of Gab.ai, encouraged the claim that, "This is a war we need to fight on Facebook, Google, Twitter everywhere – we gotta drive people to Gab.ai, to Infowars.com to Drudge Report."[3] Gab is a small social media platform that combines elements of Twitter, Reddit and Face-

---

3 | Source: https://www.youtube.com/watch?v=BmiXxPNy6NO, 5:15.

book (Sovryn 2017). Launched in 2016, Gab saw a rise in users in late 2017, after a summer of far-right public actions across the US. Designed to supplement or replace the regular social media habits of its users, Gab's designers consolidated the features of larger platform services for a user base vocally dissatisfied with other social media services.

In the summer and fall of 2017, Gab positioned itself to take on users abandoning Twitter as a fork in three overlapping movements: the free speech movement, the open technology movement, and the Alt-Right. In the US, freedom of speech as a public value is commonly invoked as a defense of vile and vicious speech. This is how liberal and progressive groups, such as the American Civil Liberties Union, got caught up defending the rights of neo-Nazis in Charlottesville (Goldstein 2017). Instead of exclusively pushing far-right propaganda, Gab saw itself as a defender of vile speech and movement infrastructure; both a place for organizing and technological development. By asking not only for users to join, but also technologists, free speech fundamentalists, and far right provocateurs, Torba's Gab was bringing together different factions of online movements across parallel ports.

THE POLITICAL IDEOLOGY DRIVING ALT-TECH

Two days before the Unite the Right rally, Gab announced the 'Alt-Tech Alliance.' They wrote:

"The Free Speech Tech Alliance is a passionate group of brave engineers, product managers, investors and others who are tired of the status quo in the technology industry. We are the defenders of free speech, individual liberty, and truth."[4]

However, on August 17, 2017 after the fallout from Charlottesville, Gab was removed from the Apple play store because, as Apple told *Ars Technica*:

"In order to be on the Play Store, social networking apps need to demonstrate a sufficient level of moderation, including for content that encourages violence and

---

4 | Gab (2017): "Announcing the Free Speech Tech Alliance", 10 August 2017 (https://medium.com/@getongab/announcing-the-alt-tech-alliance-18bebe8 9c60a).

advocates hate against groups of people. This is a long-standing rule and clearly stated in our developer policies. Developers always have the opportunity to appeal a suspension and may have their apps reinstated if they've addressed the policy violations and are compliant with our Developer Program Policies" (quoted in Lee 2017).

Torba used this decision as an opportunity to raise capital using a crowd campaign and redoubled his efforts at recruitment (Kircher 2017).

In press and marketing campaigns for his platform, Torba pushes the bounds of platform accountability by calling out other social media platforms for censorship. Taking a stance of American-centric free speech absolutism, Torba and staff refuse to monitor or moderate hateful content, despite Gab's community guidelines strongly advising international users to adhere to their particular nation's speech laws.[5] These policies create a haven for users banned from Youtube, Twitter, and Facebook. A lifelong conservative dissatisfied with his previous experiences in Silicon Valley startups, Torba has publicly embraced the controversy and began circulating white nationalist talking points in an attempt to draw in new users (Brustein 2017; Hess 2016).[6] On Gab, Twitter, Youtube and Medium, Torba frequently aligns himself with conservative and far-right causes. Immediately following Charlottesville, Gab became an important hub for the far right, where they coordinated trolling brigades to attack journalists and others on Twitter. In a Medium post entitled *We Are At War For A Free And Open Internet*, Torba walked back his claims about his platform's positions on free speech and hate speech while publicly defending his decision to remove a notorious neo-nazi hacker, Weev, for violation of their domain registrar's terms of service.[7] Asia Registry, the domain registry for Gab, threatened to take the site offline if they did not remove antisemitic

---

5 | For more information on Gab's Community Guidelines, see https://gab.ai/about/guidelines.

6 | Gab (2018): "EXPOSED: Anti-White 'Hate Speech' on Twitter By CNN, Buzzfeed, NYT, and LA Times Reporters", Medium (blog), 4 August 2018 (https://medium.com/@getongab/exposed-anti-white-hate-speech-on-twitter-by-cnn-buzzfeed-nyt-and-la-times-reporters-fa72327e5010).

7 | Gab (2017): "We Are At War For A Free And Open Internet", 4 September 2017 (https://medium.com/@getongab/we-are-at-war-for-a-free-and-open-internet-426629fba4bf).

posts by Weev (Hayden 2017). In an effort to reclaim their reputation, a new 'censor-proof social media protocol' IPO was launched to expand investment opportunities in the Gab 'family' of projects, and to keep Gab in the tech press.[8]

Gab's marketing, as a centralized platform for the far right, relies on the fear of social isolation coupled with a willingness to involve the platform's services in political debate. In 2017, emboldened by large-scale rallies in California, Tennessee, and Virginia, far-right groups escalated their ongoing attacks against both the mainstream media and racialized groups using targeted harassment on platforms. Known white supremacists operated openly on Twitter, with only the most violent content subject to removal. In response to public pressure and critical reporting on the continual harassment and spreading of extremist propaganda, Twitter issued an updated Hateful Content policy on December 18, 2017. Aimed at curbing hate speech and harassment, the policy would more aggressively ban users for violent and egregious behavior observed both on and off the platform. Twitter's announcement regarding tighter control of hate speech on their platform was preemptively decried as a form of 'censorship' amongst far-right communities. For several weeks leading up to Twitter's Terms of Service update, conservative and far-right networks employed the hashtag #TwitterPurge.

Gab has experienced difficulties raising funds as they are both unwilling and incapable of supporting or acquiring advertisers. Alt-Tech platforms, like Gab, are limited in their ability to interact with financial and advertising systems available to larger established platforms, like Twitter. On other platforms, advertisers threaten and withdraw support when it is discovered their marketing materials are paired with content promoting hate (Solon 2017). The influence of advertisers on a platform's standards for monetization and hosting limits bad actors who seek a means of amplifying their messages. Alongside the inability to secure advertising revenue, Gab's mobile app has been continually rejected from the Apple and Google mobile stores, limiting their audience. There are no third party applications that can work with Gab's architecture, which is limited by a

---

8 | For more information on fundraising see: https://www.startengine.com/gab-select.

private and reportedly fragile API.[9] We now turn to discussing the technological features of Gab to illustrate how the ability to consolidate so many
of the features popular on other platforms, like Twitter, Youtube, Facebook, and Reddit, shows the promise of such tactical innovation to provide
a all-in-one social media experience, but ultimately that the public uptake
of a technology depends largely on the charisma of leadership and the
values of its community of users.

THE TECHNOLOGICAL INFRASTRUCTURE
SUPPORTING ALT-TECH

Gab became a central hub for the Alt-Right movement following the Unite
the Right rally as Torba positioned his technology as the only unmoderated space online. Since then, Gab has continued to develop social
movement community, integrating new features as Twitter, Facebook,
and Youtube's Terms of Service pose problems for infrastructural stability. Keeping with their goal of being a one-stop community platform, Gab
offers users an experience designed to recreate Twitter, Facebook, and
Reddit in a 'censorship-free' environment – it mimics many functions of
its main rival Twitter, the social connectivity of Facebook, and the news
aggregation and voting system of Reddit. These are not merely inferences;
Gab's creators and community posit the platform as a viable alternative
for users unsatisfied (or permanently banned) from these major social
media sites.[10] Gab is therefore a prime example of how the greater Alt-
Tech space integrates and modifies the pre-existing models of interaction
their user base has come to expect from their social media experiences
elsewhere. Here, Gab is not one platform among many, but is a hub that
brings together many nodes – including white supremacist, misogynist,
and 'free speech' communities – under the banner of Alt-Tech.

   While largely replicating and consolidating features found elsewhere,
Gab has a few unique tools or early innovations. Gab includes the ability to

---

9 | For more information on Gab's API: https://dev.to/welcome/the-day-i-broke-
gabai

10 | Gab (2017): "Announcing the Free Speech Tech Alliance", 10 August 2017
(https://medium.com/@getongab/announcing-the-alt-tech-alliance-18beb
e89c60a).

filter keywords and followers, predating Twitter's ability to remove certain terms entirely from a feed, as well as muting individual users who may be engaged in harassment. However, Gab does not feature a block system on ideological grounds. The introduction of 'Pro memberships' expands dedicated users' power to control their experience, as well as introducing features to incentivize creators to use Gab as their primary broadcast platform.

Moreover, international news of white nationalists being banned from hosting services or detained while travelling has bolstered use of Gab in countries outside the US. As a result, Gab provides a place for discussion and coordination of translocal ideologies called 'networked nationalisms', "a belief that national borders are strengthened by the international cooperation of far-right politicians and 'Identitarian' movements to preserve the white race and culture" (Donovan et al. 2018). While 'strong borders' are often invoked by white nationalists in order to establish ties between Europe and the USA, the use of online platforms has digitized this rhetoric in the form of popular memes. These memes, such as the 'no more brother wars' series, propagate on Gab and help other users to identify with each other as a form of solidarity.

Alt-Tech Alliance. By DeviantArt user SwyTheQ.[11]

---

11 | Source: https://www.deviantart.com/swytheq/art/8-14-2017-The-Alt-Tech-Alliance-is-Coming-698733718.

While being begrudgingly accepted by right-wing pundits, journalists, and content creators, Gab has yet to find its 'cool' among younger
users. Gab's logo itself is a transparent appropriation of Pepe, a cartoon
frog meme associated with the culture of the image board 4chan, the Alt-
Right and the online campaign for Donald Trump. Breitbart and Infowars
writers have amplified hostile attitudes to major tech firms in their reporting, helping to bolster Gab's reputation. Resultingly, Gab has become
an echo chamber for the most disgusting content offered online, where
antisemitism, misogyny, anti-LGBTQ, and racist epithets circulate expo-
nentially. While technologically Gab can be glitchy and unstable, it has
integrated some of the most popular features offered by other social media
platforms. However, few journalists comment on the innovative incorporation of technological features because Torba's public expressions of his
political ideology overshadows every discussion of its design.

CONCLUSION

Our analysis shows that technology is not politically neutral. Instead, the
leadership of the platform company, alongside the profile of the user base
and the content they circulate have a significant impact on how platforms
are perceived by the public. Gab provides a limit-case for analyzing how
the Alt-Tech movement continues to be wedded to the values espoused by
the developers. Instead of assessing the technology on the qualities of its
design, its designers' politics are built in and can alienate potential new
users. By cloning features common to larger platforms and consolidating them into a single user experience, Gab's platform is both political
and infrastructural. In *The Politics of Platforms*, Tarleton Gillespie writes
that platforms, "like the television networks and trade publishers before
them, [...] are increasingly facing questions about their responsibilities:
to their users, to key constituencies who depend on the public discourse
they host, and to broader notions of the public interest" (Gillespie 2010:
348). He goes on: "Unlike Hollywood and the television networks, who
could be painted as the big bad industries, online content seems an open
world, where anyone can post, anything can be said" (ibid.: 353). The day
has come where Youtube, Twitter, Facebook, Reddit, and Google have now
become media giants, like Hollywood. As such, the social reckoning for
platform corporations requires attention to key communities, audiences,

and public interests. Alt-Tech platforms, like Gab, now serve as a warning that without moderation policies, users will share noxious content, which becomes a liability for indexing quality and for promoting the platform's features. Moreover, all communities have rules, both online and off. Responsibility lies not only in the design, but in the enforcement of a platform's Terms of Service, much like a code of conduct.

And so, we return to our main question: is technological development within the Alt-Right driven by a need for stabilization? The answer here is: sometimes. While movement leaders, like Richard Spencer and Tim Gionet (Baked Alaska), understand why Gab is important for organizing a social movement community online, they also recognize the need for staying on more established platforms, like Youtube and Twitter. Both called for new regulation to make net neutrality a feature of platforms that allow for unmoderated sharing of user generated content. Critically, while Gab would stabilize the internal life of the movement, it would not be ideal for reaching out to new audiences, recruiting new members, and capturing media attention; all of which are central for prolonging the life of movements (Donovan 2018). For networked social movements, having a presence on all available platforms ensures stability when counter-movements tactically adapt and create obstacles, like in the event of 'no platforming.'

Is it the case that the alternative technology developed in the wake of the violence in Charlottesville is something fundamentally innovative? While we identified that Gab both clones and consolidates features from other platforms, it does not significantly change how online movements connect, collaborate, or organize. In fact, the engagement on this small platform has become so vitriolic that it may do more to destroy the alliances across these movements than to build them. While Torba's public proclamations heralded the platform as the only place online where speech goes unmoderated, he had to remove some racist posts because online infrastructure does not stand outside of the information ecosystem. Pressure to change one's platform can come from the public, journalists, or from other infrastructure companies. No single user or platform can act in isolation given the architecture of the internet. That is to say, while platforms may be organized as parallel ports, which can function independently of one another, they must be plugged into other internet services such as service providers, domain registrars, and cloud services. As a result, the terms of service for companies that are deep in the stack may become the ultimate arbiters of what content gets to stay online.

In conclusion, because hundreds of movements coexist online and use internet infrastructure to recruit and get organized, the charisma of movement leaders and the political values of the movement will determine how their social movement community tactically innovates both online and offline. The violence in Charlottesville both gained the Alt-Right widespread media attention, but also propelled online companies to 'no platform' white nationalists. The use of violence by social movements often has similar effects, whereby movements that resort to violence often become heavily surveilled by formal authorities, such as the police. However, in this case, sanctions came from platform companies who were implicated in the communication and coordination of the Alt-Right, which suggests that technology makers are a movement unto themselves. As such, the burgeoning Alt-Tech movement as well as the online free speech movement will have to choose their political alliances more carefully if they are to succeed in recruiting and retaining members that do not also support far right perspectives. Platforms, as sociotechnical infrastructure, will adapt to new forms and norms of conduct, but the values that support design must also support a diversity of tactics and users.

REFERENCES

Berlet, Chip (2008): "When Hate Went Online", 7 April (http://www.researchforprogress.us/topic/34691/when-hate-went-online/)

Brustein, Joshua (2017): "How a Silicon Valley Striver Became the Alt-Right's Tech Hero", 29 August 2017 (https://www.bloomberg.com/news/articles/2017-10-09/how-a-silicon-valley-striver-became-the-Alt-Right-s-tech-hero).

Daniels, Jessie (2018): "The Algorithmic Rise of the 'Alt-Right.'" In: Contexts 17/1, pp. 60–65.

Donovan, Joan (2018): "After the #Keyword: Eliciting, Sustaining, and Coordinating Participation Across the Occupy Movement." In: Social Media + Society 4/1, pp. 1–12.

Donovan, Joan (2016): "'Can You Hear Me Now?' Phreaking the Party Line from Operators to Occupy." In: Information, Communication & Society 19/5, pp. 601–617.

Donovan, Joan/Lewis, Rebecca/Friedberg, Brian (2018): "Networked Nationalisms", 11 July 2018 (https://medium.com/@MediaManipulation/networked-nationalisms-2983deae5620).

Ganz, Marshall (2000): "Resources and Resourcefulness: Strategic Capacity in the Unionization of California Agriculture, 1959–1966." In: American Journal of Sociology 105/4, pp. 1003–1062.

Gillespie, Tarleton (2010): "The Politics of 'Platforms'." In: New Media & Society 12/3, pp. 347–364.

Goldstein, Joseph (2017): "After Backing Alt-Right in Charlottesville, A.C.L.U. Wrestles With Its Role." In: The New York Times, 17 August 2017 (https://www.nytimes.com/2017/08/17/nyregion/aclu-free-speech-rights-charlottesville-skokie-rally.html).

Hayden, Michael (2017): "Nazis on Gab Social Network Show There is no Such Thing as a Free Speech Internet", 22 September 2017 (https://www.newsweek.com/nazis-free-speech-hate-crime-jews-social-media-gab-weev-66861).

Hess, Amanda (2016): "The Far Right Has a New Digital Safe Space", 30 November 2016 (https://www.nytimes.com/2016/11/30/arts/the-far-right-has-a-new-digital-safe-space.html).

Kelty, Christopher M. (2008): Two Bits: The Cultural Significance of Free Software, Durham: Duke University Press.

Kircher, Madison M. (2017): "Alt-Right-Friendly Social Network Gab Raises $1 Million", 17 August 2017 (http://nymag.com/selectall/2017/08/Alt-Right-gab-raises-usd1-million.html).

Lee, Timothy B. (2017): "Google Explains why it Banned the App for Gab, a Right-Wing Twitter Rival", 18 August 2017 (https://arstechnica.com/tech-policy/2017/08/gab-the-right-wing-twitter-rival-just-got-its-app-banned-by-google/).

Losh, Elizabeth (2017): "All Your Base Are Belong to Us: Gamergate and Infrastructures of Online Violence", 28 April 2017 (https://culanth.org/fieldsights/1116-all-your-base-are-belong-to-us-gamergate-and-infrastructures-of-online-violence).

Massanari, Adrienne (2015): "#Gamergate and The Fappening: How Reddit's Algorithm, Governance, and Culture Support Toxic Technocultures." In: New Media & Society 19/3, pp. 329–346.

Mattoni, Alice (2013): "Technology and Social Movements." In: Snow, David/Della Porta, Donatella/Klandermans, Bart/McAdam, Doug (eds.): The Wiley-Blackwell Encyclopedia of Social and Political Movements.

McAdam, Doug (1983): "Tactical Innovation and the Pace of Insurgency." In: American Sociological Review 48/6, pp. 735–754.

McCammon, Holly J (2003): "'Out of the Parlors and into the Streets': The Changing Tactical Repertoire of the U.S. Women' Suffrage Movements'." In: Social Forces 81/3, pp. 787–818.

Neuman, Scott (2017). "Boston Right-Wing 'Free Speech' Rally Dwarfed by Counterprotesters", 19 August 2017 (https://www.npr.org/sections /thetwo-way/2017/08/19/544684355/bostons-free-speech-rally-orga nizers-deny-links-to-white-nationalists).

Pearce, Matt (2017): "Squeezed out by Silicon Valley, the Far Right is Creating its Own Corporate World", 8 November 2017 (http://www.latimes. com/nation/la-na-Alt-Right-money-20170811-story.html).

Piven, Frances F./Cloward, Richard A. (1991): "Collective Protest: A Critique of Resource Mobilization Theory." In: International Journal of Politics, Culture, and Society 4/4, pp. 435–458.

Solon, Olivia (2017): "Google's Bad Week: Youtube Loses Millions as Advertising Row Reaches US", 25 March 2017 (https://www.theguar dian.com/technology/2017/mar/25/google-youtube-advertising-ex tremist-content-att-verizon).

Sovryn, Stone (2017): "Gab: A Cultural Primer", 18 December 2017 (https:// medium.com/@stonesovryn/gab-a-cultural-primer-cefa5637f203).

Voss, Kim/Sherman, Rachel (2000): "Breaking the Iron Law of Oligarchy: Union Revitalization in the American Labor Movement." In: American Journal of Sociology 106/2, pp. 303–349.

Wilde, Melissa J. (2004): "How Culture Mattered at Vatican II: Collegiality Trumps Authority in the Council's Social Movement Organizations." In: American Sociological Review 69/4, pp. 576–602.

Creating a New Normal

The Mainstreaming of Far-Right Ideas Through Online
and Offline Action in Hungary

Philipp Karl

On 1 February 2011, hundreds of people demonstrated peacefully against the appointment of a known antisemite as the new Director of the Új Színház theater in Budapest. Roughly one hundred far-right counter protestors in paramilitary uniforms from a successor organization of the Hungarian Guard staged a counter protest, trying to attack the antifascist demonstrators. Four months later, on 7 July, Jobbik organized a protest march from the MSZP headquarters to the Fidesz headquarters with the support of various other far-right groups, marching triumphantly over Budapest's World Heritage Site, the boulevard Andrássy út. Only one lone counter demonstrator showed up. The contrasting turnouts of counter-activists at these two events indicate lots of things, not least the far-right's ability to mobilize grounded action in Hungary. The far right heavily advertised these events on the internet and used documentation of their strong showing at both as propaganda afterwards online.

This paper aims to analyze how Jobbik, as Hungary's main opposition party, mainstreamed far-right ideas through a combination of online and offline action. As a variety of terms are used in academic and general media discourses to describe political families with specific sets of characteristics, the notion of 'the mainstream' is analytically difficult to define and understand, as demonstrated by Aristotle Kallis (Kallis 2015). He observes that 'mainstream' and 'extremism' are mutually-dependent relational terms, as is the case with the left-right-dichotomy that presupposes an inherent center (Bobbio 1997). Using a Gramscian approach, Bert Cammaerts has most recently examined discursive strategies that the far right employed in the Netherlands and Belgium to mainstream its discourse (Cammaerts 2018). He described how a successful war of position, through provocations by far-right leaders, led to media coverage which amplified their message and helped to normalize their ideas. In Hungary the far-right discourse is not only normalized but actually institutionalized, by fences, laws, a new constitution and various other legal practices. Therefore, in the context of this chapter, the process of mainstreaming is understood as getting people to sympathize with a set of ideas so as to mobilize them to act accordingly, in order to institutionalize those ideas through legal or other actions. To put it more bluntly: mainstreaming is the attempt to define what is normal and, at the same time, to make or frame the meaning of events, actions, structures, and institutions at the level of popular political discourse. Every mainstreaming process necessarily involves an attempt to construct a new reality, a new normal. Since mainstreaming processes take place in dynamic and contentious settings, they do not necessarily have to succeed to become influential.

Grounded on ideas developed by Sidney Tarrow and Manuel Castells, I would argue that political mobilization processes (and mainstreaming is the final result of such a mobilization process) have a better chance of being successful when accompanied by interdependent and self-referential online and offline action. Tarrow identified the power of networks and organizations, as well as the power of frames, emotions and collective identities as two of the main "powers in [a] movement" that transform singular claims into actions (Tarrow 2011). Castells examined contemporary revolutionary events and new social movements and concluded that those movements were networked in multiple forms offline and online, they became movements through the appropriation of urban spaces, were highly self-reflective and aimed to change the values of society (Castells 2012). In this vein, this essay details how Jobbik used the internet and social media in synch with offline actions such as its May festivals to turn ethnonationalist obsessions into the new normal in Hungary.

SPREADING IDEAS AND MAKING MEANING: JOBBIK AS AVANT-GARDE ON FACEBOOK AND TWITTER

The internet, and particularly social networking platforms, offer alternative ways to circumvent more established media forums such as newspapers, television and radio, enabling communication with audiences without the interference of external editors. For example, Castells demonstrated how the internet and social networking sites such as Twitter helped to bypass censorship and the traditional media during the Tunisian uprisings in 2011 (Castells 2012). The potential audiences accessible via these new channels are also larger and more diverse. Crucially, too, they can be interacted with and analyzed at the same time. Barack Obama's election campaigns in 2008 and 2012 were considered ground-breaking in terms of how they used the internet to connect and reinforce support and supporters. But even before that, the Hungarian far right created an online network of websites and the earliest forms of social networking sites in conjunction with the street protests of 2006, which erupted when it became public knowledge that Ferenc Gyurscány, the then socialist Prime Minister, had willingly lied about the national economy. Not only were Jobbik instrumental to this online-offline action, they were also the earliest political party to become regular users of Twitter and Facebook in Hungary. New means of communication can facilitate social change when used appropriately. Therefore it is historically typical for social movements in general, and in some cases particularly for the far right, to become early adopters of new technologies (for example the use of cinema and mass propaganda by Nazi Germany). Referring to the new social movements he observed, Castells says:

"Historically, social movements have been dependent on the existence of specific communication mechanisms [...]. In our time, multimodal, digital networks of horizontal communication are the fastest and most autonomous, interactive, reprogrammable and self-expanding means of communication in history" (Castells 2012: 15).

Whether short messages, videos, clips, gifs or images, Jobbik has come to use everything at its disposal and has been hugely successful in doing so. For example, between June 2013 and June 2014 Jobbik had 142 individual Facebook posts that were either liked or shared by over 1000 users, while the other two major Hungarian parties lagged behind: Fidesz had 140 and MSZP 112. These statistics may now sound small, but for comparison Marine Le Pen's French Front National had merely ten. During the same period, Jobbik posted 67 short videos, 27 event advertisements, and 42 graphs. Fidesz shared 7 videos, 58 event advertisements, 54 graphs and 16 articles from their web page. MSZP posted 23 videos, 23 event advertisements, 49 graphs, and 11 articles from their web page (Karl 2016). To highlight the differences more precisely, one can take a closer look at the posts from 15 March 2014, which is the Hungarian national bank holiday. The differences between the three party's posts are telling. All three used photos, but while Jobbik posted joyful images from the midst of their annual festival, Fidesz posted photos of the renovation of the city square in front of the parliament building and MSZP posted a collage of pictures taken during speeches. In other words, Jobbik conveyed togetherness and included its Facebook users in the event through the lens of a photographer, while Fidesz depicted one governmental achievement and the MSZP post had the character of an official press release.

Jobbik's communication and online strategy is built around five pillars: interconnectedness with other far-right actors at the national level; international ties to parties, groups and associations; interactivity with its online audience; multi-mediality; and cross-mediality. At the national level, Jobbik is constantly interconnected through likes, links, shares and retweets with other far-right actors, be they groups, associations, brands or music bands. This network helps to spread messages across different spheres and so reach wider audiences – not exclusively the political or media spheres, but simultaneously the music, sports, clothing and even food spheres. At the international level, Jobbik's connections to Spanish, French and Italian far-right groups have been mutually supportive, with the communities sharing knowledge about best practice concerning online communication methods and modern styles of formulating political ideas. Via these connections we now know that Hungarian far-right practices have had an international impact. For example, in 2015, the German NPD showed a Facebook banner on its official page thanking Hungary for building the fence at their southern border. While such an act might seem superficial, it is still quite extraordinary.

Alongside these (inter-)national connections, interactivity is another pillar of Jobbik's communication strategy online. The official party accounts occasionally share and post contents from non-party-affiliated sources, and motivates its followers to actively share, retweet and engage through likes and follows. Such strategies have been rare for far-right parties who predominantly just share their own content. Those more traditional parties have a clear top-down approach to the management of social media channels, while Jobbik has a relatively bottom-up approach and interacts with its followers.

Jobbik's social media appearances are neither streamlined nor kept distinct from each other. When content on Youtube, Facebook or Twitter 'works' or 'goes viral' it is shared across the party's other platforms as well. While this is the essence of social network marketing, other political parties have been much slower at using cross-mediality to boost their online performance. This cross-medial approach goes hand-in-hand with multi-mediality. Be it videos, graphs, memes, articles or photos, different kinds of content are tailored by Jobbik to attract different audience types. And while other parties post long videos, Jobbik rarely posts videos that last more than 30 seconds, offering lots of quick content that only require limited bandwidth or small data transfers to access, and short attention spans to consume.

LIKING, LINKING AND APPROPRIATING: A STRATEGIC APPROACH

Those pillars made Jobbik's use of social networking sites efficient and successful. At a time when major parties in Hungary and elsewhere were just starting to form a strategic approach to social networking sites, Jobbik already had more than 300,000 followers on Facebook. Of course, it is not known how many of these users were actually fake profiles but their follower numbers grew at a steady rate from mid-2013. By June 2018, the party had already reached half a million followers, which is a remarkable proportion of the potential audience given that Hungary has only 10 million inhabitants and roughly five million Facebook users.

Donald Trump's successful election campaign is the most famous example of how repetition and echo-chambers can blur messages with facts. His enormous number of Twitter followers made him and his candidacy relevant and set him apart in the first place when vying for the Republican nomination. Although much less famous, Jobbik has also proven itself adept at reinforcing its messages in the simplest forms, beginning with its name. Jobbik is an abbreviation and play-on-words that stands, on the one hand, for 'more on the right' (*job* means right in Hungarian) and, on the other hand, for 'better' (*jobb* means better in Hungarian). The idea that Jobbik is the better right-wing alternative in Hungary is reinforced everytime its name is repeated. In fact, Jobbik had (and maybe still has) a special task force dedicated to communications on Facebook and Twitter with the goal of making the party appear more likable, young, family-oriented, modern and tech-affine. One telling example was the background image used on the official Facebook page in 2016 of then vice-chairman Előd Novák:

Background image of Előd Novák's official Facebook page.

The picture shows him, his wife (at the time the youngest female member of parliament) and their three kids. The background colors are warm and there is no obvious reference to Jobbik. The slogan on the left means "Hungarian family, Hungarian future". The flowery, ornamental symbols around the slogan, as well as those on the family's t-shirts, are derived from Hungarian folklore. The family of foxes in the background refer to a popular childrens' television series from the communist era called *Vuk*. The appropriation of images and symbols, as well as their synthesized repetition online, are hallmarks of Jobbik's strategy.

Interconnectivity online through links and banners was a major trait of both Jobbik and the Hungarian far right even before the growing influence of social media platforms. Yet on Facebook and Twitter those connections are made visible through likes and follows. Jobbik's official party account maintained a relatively neutral status, but its affiliate regional and youth groups' accounts were evidently connected with paramilitary groups, bands, labels, clothing brands and other organizations of the radical right network. Media sites that belonged to Jobbik, including its Youtube channel, were linked to that network even more strongly, retweeting or sharing content.

Those different platforms are used in slightly altered, reflexive ways. Jobbik's strategy on social networking sites is less concerned with substance – elaborate arguments, fact-based discourse or demonstrations of their goals (for that purpose they had the party manifesto) – but more with style and emotionality. Quite often they actively encourage users to share or retweet, which is a simple but highly efficient method to gain more likes and followers and so reach a wider audience. Real life events such as marches or festivals are advertised through social media. Afterwards, photos and videos from those events are shared with their followers again, creating a loop or connection beyond the temporary offline action.

GETTING TO THE NEW NORMAL THROUGH OFFLINE ACTION: BETWEEN STREET PROTESTS AND HAPPENINGS

Spreading ideas online is highly effective and helps to mainstream them, but online discourse needs to be transferred to the offline sphere for it to become part of everyone's lives. In other words, the threshold for a simple click is quite low but when the sheer number of clicks eventually transfer to votes, participation at events or to steer the topics of everyday discussions then the mainstreaming process has reached a new phase. An essential factor in Jobbik's success has been its use of a diverse set of offline activities that strengthened, defined and ultimately transformed the public image of the party. When it was founded in 2003, Jobbik was known because of its paramilitary sister organizations, such as the Hungarian Guard, and for the public swearing-ins it held at the very central Heroes Square in Budapest. Such ritualistic action created publicity and helped to make Jobbik's presence in Hungarian politics a topic in itself. Meanwhile, the party's symbiotic relationship with nationalist music helped to mainstream its frames and world view to non-political audiences. Jobbik's annual May festivals are central to this. At those festivals, which are open to the general public, not only do nationalistic bands play, co-developing new audiences with Jobbik, but a variety of family games are organized and – since it is officially an event organized by a political party – political speeches are held.

This appears to be in stark contrast to the Hungarian Guard and its various successor organizations who formed the public image of Jobbik and helped to popularize the party's original goal: to dominate the political discourse concerning the Roma minority. Then, the party was widely known for martial events and its connection to paramilitary and vigilante groups – thereby appearing to be at the fringes of the political spectrum. While militaristic, authoritarian and Romaphobic forms of offline action dominated the party's public image, they were secondary to building a new extreme discourse around the party's core ideological concern: nationalism and nativism. Therefore, commemorations and the fostering of an image as 'the' national party that defines what is Hungarian and what it is not were integral to developing and maintaining Jobbik's appeal. In many post-Soviet states, as well as many post-Yugoslav states, nationalism has been crucial for the formation of the 'new' state. Jobbik tried to spread a 'positive' message focused on nationalist ideals for the present and future while depicting the other parties – Fidesz and MSZP primarily – as traitors to the nation, corrupt and belonging to the past. While Jobbik wanted to ideologically define 'the national', Fidesz re-appropriated Jobbik's idea of national interest by using its ideas and concrete propositions as the basis for policies, thus pushing Jobbik's ideas from the fringes in to a mainstream reality.

In order to do that, especially in a way that speaks to young tech-savvy people and families, a key technique has been to create a kind of nationalist cool or nationalist spirit that transcends politics and becomes part of everyday life, permeating other spheres of society beyond the political. May festivals provide a good example of exactly how. From 2004 until 2018 the annual Jobbik May festival, dubbed *Nemzeti Majális* (Nationalist May festival), has been the most important far-right event organized by Jobbik each year. Taking place at the Óbudai Sziget in the Danube in Northern Budapest, the festival lasted three days in its peak and featured the leading bands in Hungary's *Nemzeti Rock* (nationalist rock) scene. The bands that played most often at the event represent the two different ideological branches of the far right in Hungary: the former ultra-band, Romantikus Erőszak is a prime example of the more violence-prone, minority-hostile, authoritarian-xenophobic branch; while the soft-rock band, Ismerős Arcok exemplifies the romantic-nationalist branch (Karl 2016). Many of the bands present at the venue are quite popular, closer to the mainstream than the fringes, yet fringe bands were always present as well.

In 2018, the May festival tradition has momentarily come to a pause, officially due to a lack of finance but more probably due to the internal party splits that became apparent because of Vona's resignation and the ongoing successor battle between the party's more moderate faction and its extremist faction. Prior to this, the public adverts for the festival sometimes resembled music festival promotions rather than party political adverts. The picture underneath shows the official advert for Jobbik's May festival in 2016. No party affiliation is mentioned. Apart from the word *nemzeti* (nationalist) and the right-wing Árpád-flag alongside the Hungarian flag on the right edge, it looks more like a mainstream festival than a far-right event: from the font, to the colours, to the plants and trees, it looks young, family friendly and well produced.

Official advert for Jobbik's Nemzeti Majális 2016.

The May festivals helped to attract young people and families to a party once known as militarist and authoritarian, using a blend of music, games and food. It evoked a kind of radical right flower power, a Woodstock-like feeling on the surface. At the event, antisemitic literature, chauvinistic shirts, nationalistic beer and paramilitary outfits (and memberships to the Hungarian Guard's successor organizations) were promoted and sold. Youth culture and subculture, as well as traditionalist and conservative values, were mixed together to appeal to as many people as possible.

First and foremost, the May festivals are political music events. But at the same time they showcase, highlight and define Jobbik's understanding of Hungarian identity. As events aimed at appealing to families, they can be analyzed in a broader context as a means of blurring the boundaries between traditional conservative and far-right values. For example, Jobbik's election manifesto of 2010 defined what types or model of 'the family' Jobbik wants to promote, devising its recipe around the ultimate nationalistic goal of the 'survival of the nation':

"Jobbik's goal is to slow, then halt, then gradually reverse the rate of population decline, through the use of a coherent family and social policy; so that the nation grows. To achieve this will first and foremost require the promotion and protection of the institution of the family, particularly from attacks by a liberalism whose objective is to put the family unit on an equal footing with every conceivable alternative living arrangement or deviant lifestyle."[1]

At the core, far-right parties see the family as the smallest unit of the nation, in particular mothers as they can give birth to new generations (Mudde 2007). However, many of the contemporary and recently formed far-right parties hold a supposedly 'modern traditional' view of women. Jobbik provided a perfect example of this view in its treatment of the aforementioned Dóra Dúro, wife of Előd Novák and mother of their three children, supporting her to gain election to the parliament in 2010, when she became the youngest MP at the age of 23.

FRACTURES AND COUNTERACTIONS

For a decade Jobbik mastered a strong and close relationship with Hungary's far-right subculture, but the more moderate and professional the party became the more it was estranged from that subculture which had made the party visible in the first place. Tarrow described this competition between radicalization and institutionalization as inherent for cycles of contention within political groups (Tarrow 2011). Whether this will trigger the downfall of the party in Jobbik's case remains an open question at the time of writing. So far, the party's leadership has shown creativity and

---

1 | Jobbik (2010): Radical Change. A Guide to Jobbik's Parliamentary Electoral Manifesto for National Self-Determination and Social Justice, (https://www.job bik.com/sites/default/files/Jobbik-RADICALCHANGE2010.pdf).

good communication skills with a variety of tools, and might be able to adapt once more to the ever-changing biosphere of the Hungarian political system. With respect to Fidesz and Orbán's policies in recent years, Jobbik's influence cannot be overestimated. The party created an environment in which radical right ideas flourished among large parts of the society and became acceptable across the political spectrum. Their 'nationalist chic' is currently the new normal in Hungary. In any case, it is an important example of how civil society, the media and other political parties should *not* deal with radical right parties – mainstreaming their ideas to compete for their supporters is never the best option. The institutionalized changes altering the constitution, the country's legal framework, its media system and educational landscape will have a lasting effect. The far right will dominate for the coming years in part because they have built a broad social base and continue to enforce their vision on the next generation through illiberal school curricula. Liberal Hungary will come back when it is ready to form a strong inter-party alliance and when it has finally learned its lesson from the disastrous socialist-liberal collaborations that collapsed in 2006.

In Hungary as well as in other countries it is crucial to contradict those that seek to define nationality through an ethnic lens. Put differently, an inclusive and pluralist vision of citizenship should be advocated as a multi- and inter-generational project. In the short term, different measures might help. First, far-right demonstrations or events in the public space need to be countered in those spaces otherwise those demonstrating are allowed to define what 'the public's' pressing concerns are. Second, virtual spaces need to be used for organizational as well as for attentional purposes. Since many traditional media outlets in Hungary provide a very narrow image of the political and social reality, as well as of what it means to be a Hungarian, social networking sites need to be used as counter-channels to contradict those narratives and discourses. Paradoxically, the history of both Fidesz and Jobbik provide an example of how this process might get started. Both parties were initially formed as student organizations. That might be how we begin to challenge the new normal.

REFERENCES

Bobbio, Norberto (1997 [1994]): Left and Right: The Significance of a Political Distinction, Chicago: University of Chicago Press.

Cammaerts, Bart (2018): "The Mainstreaming of Extreme Right-Wing Populism in the Low Countries: What is to be Done?" In: Communication, Culture and Critique 11/1, pp. 7–20.

Castells, Manuel (2012): Networks of Outrage and Hope. Social Movements in the Internet Age, Cambridge: Polity.

Kallis, Aristotle (2015): "When Fascism Became Mainstream: The Challenge of Extremism in Times of Crisis." In: Fascism 4/1, pp. 1–24.

Karl, Philipp (2016): Die Etablierung Jobbiks in Ungarn nach 2010. Zwischen Bewegung und Partei des Internetzeitalters, Dissertation, Andrássy University Budapest.

Mudde, Cas (2007): Populist Radical Right Parties in Europe, Cambridge: Cambridge University Press.

Tarrow, Sidney George (2011): Power in Movement. Social Movements, Collective Action, and Politics, Cambridge: Cambridge University Press.

Between Anti-Feminism and Ethnicized Sexism

Far-Right Gender Politics in Germany

Lynn Berg

In March 2018, more than 4,000 right-wing protesters demonstrated in Kandel, a small town in Rhineland-Palatinate, Germany. Their motivation was the death of 15 year-old Mia, who had been killed in December 2017 by her ex-boyfriend Abdul in a drugstore in Kandel. Mobilized under the slogan 'Kandel is everywhere' (*Kandel ist überall*) via Facebook, Youtube and Twitter, the murder was made into a political symbol of the supposedly flawed migration and refugee policy of the German government, since the perpetrator had fled from Afghanistan to Germany. The call was answered by a broad spectrum of right-wing actors, including neo-Nazis, the Identitarian Movement, far-right extremist hooligans as well as members of the National Democratic Party of Germany (NPD) and the Alternative for Germany (AfD) party, making '*Kandel ist überall*' a symbol of far-right resistance. By referring to the violated safety of girls and women, and the lack of protection for these groups, hatred and exclusion against migrants and fugitives is rationalized: "We mothers did not have children to have them defiled and slaughtered by the Merkel guests", was shouted over loudspeakers at the demonstration. The initiative also continues to mobilize online by using sexualized violence against women to justify far-right positions. Under the title 'Merkel's stumbling stones' (*Merkels Stolpersteine*), a picture of brass plates with names of murdered girls (such as Mia's) appears on the many online platforms of the initiative. They look like the stumbling stones used to memorialize the victims of Nazi purges, thus symbolically equating the crimes.

The *Kandel Manifesto* resembles a classic catalogue of far-right demands: Border closure for all types of immigration to Germany, deportation of "illegal immigrants", assimilation and *jus sanguinis* (the principle of descent for the acquisition of German citizenship). In pink letters they demand "Germany first" and the abolition of mosques, a ban on the full veil, the reintroduction of compulsory military service and information on "insurmountable cultural differences" between Europeans and non-Western migrants[1].

Online banner by the initiative Kandel is everywhere writing "Merkel's stumbling stones".[2]

Murders, sexualized violence, feminicide, women's rights and equality are no longer issues here. It is not surprising that these topics have no place in far-right discourse, since they advocate anti-feminist politics and practices. It is not the first time that the racist narrative of the violent migrant man who attacks 'German girls' has proved to be an enormous motivator for mobilization. It also shows how gender issues are absolutely central for racist and authoritarian demands and right-wing mobilizations. The AfD is a key group here because it has been the strongest opposition in the Bundestag since 2017 and is represented in almost all state parliaments. As the parliamentary arm of a far-right culture war, it represents anti-feminist positions by, on the one hand, opposing equality policies, gender studies, feminists and same-sex marriage, and on the other hand, supporting normative 'traditional' gender roles and concepts of family. At the same time, it emphasizes, as it did at the demonstration in Kandel, the rights of women and minorities – gender equality as part of 'German val-

---

1 | (Kandel ist Überall (2018): "Das Manifest von Kandel", (https://kandel-ist-ue berall.de/startseite/wp-content/uploads/2018/03/ manifest-von-kandel.pdf).
2 | Source: https://kandel-ist-ueberall.de/startseite/wp-content/uploads/2018/07/stolpersteine_titel_2.jpg.

ue culture' – and presents itself as protector of women against sexualized violence and for their sexual self-determination. It is thus representative of a new way of making politics with gender. The AfD will be used as an example in this chapter to show what far-right gender politics currently looks like and what functions it fulfils for them. In doing so I will ask: Which topics and terms are occupied and how? Which political strategies, rhetoric, linguistic images and narratives are used? How are anti-feminist positions combined with an emphasis on women's rights? What impact on public and political debate can be observed? What could gender-sensitive counter-strategies look like?

Threat Scenario Gender: Reproduction, Family and Far-Right Gender Hierarchy

"Hungary wants to abolish gender studies! Let's do the same: Cut funding for unscientific branches of research!". "Welcome culture for newborns and unborn babies" was posted on Facebook on Christmas Eve. The AfD-Bavaria demanded on Twitter: "Bavaria gender-free! No to gender mainstreaming and early sexualixation". According to the AfD, the goal of gender education is "to systematically 'correct' the classical understanding of the roles of men and women through state-sponsored re-education programs in kindergartens and schools."[3] The chairman of the AfD-Thuringia, Björn Höcke demanded at a demonstration: "We must rediscover our masculinity. Because only if we rediscover our masculinity do we become manly. And only if we become manly do we become fortified, and we must become fortified, dear friends!" (Lehmann 2018). On the occasion of World Women's Day 2018, the structural disadvantage of women in society was compared in the Bundestag with a "yeti" that everyone was talking about but that nobody had ever seen.[4]

Online campaigns, political speeches, party and election programs intertwine here to express the same content in different ways. Jasmin Siri

---

3 | AfD Basic Program from 2016, p. 55.
4 | Speech by AfD Member of Parliament Nicole Höchst on the occasion of World Women's Day 2018 in the Bundestag (https://www.bundestag.de/mediathek?videoid=7205644#url=L21lZGlhdGhla292ZXJJsYXk/dmlkZW9pZD03MjA1N jQ0&mod=mediathek).

(2016) describes how AfD party and election programs are worded much more liberally than campaigns and speeches by its politicians. It becomes clear that the more directly the contents are addressed to the citizens, the clearer and more radically they are worded, as Höcke's speech illustrates. Through social media they can directly address their sympathizers and it allows them to position themselves as the voice of 'the people' in a staged proximity to 'their own people' and their concerns (Reisigl 2012: 154). Gender politics in the AfD consists largely of anti-gender politics, i.e. mainly politics that oppose emancipative contents, actions and institutions. These anti-gender politics are defined in opposition to an imagined gender ideology, the goal of this gender ideology is defined as:

"Gender ideology marginalizes natural differences between the sexes and questions gender identity. It wants to abolish the classical family as a life model and role model. Thus it is in clear contradiction to the Basic Law which protects (classically understood) marriage and family as a state-supporting institute, because only this can produce the people of the state as supporters of sovereignty. Gender ideology contradicts the scientific findings of biology and developmental psychology as well as the daily life experience of many generations."[5]

AfD thus constructs a specific threat scenario on multiple levels:

1. The 'traditional family', as a heterosexual marriage with children, is attacked and abolished by a gender ideology that is present in all areas of life (work, school, science).
2. Gender ideology contradicts people's perception of gender and sex and endangers the natural development of gender and sexuality in children.
3. The 'traditional family' ensures the continued existence of the 'pure people', which is precisely what is threatened by the existence of gender ideology.
4. The governing parties promote the instruments of gender ideology and thus the abolition of 'their own people'.

On the basis of this threat scenario, the AfD can do two things: On the one hand, justify its anti-politics; on the other hand, legitimize its own

---

5 | AfD Basic Program from 2016, p. 40.

gender and family ideologies as national biopolitical policies, centred around the heterosexual family to save the 'pure people.' This 'rescue' involves an increase in the birth rate of the 'native population' and a new abortion register, legal changes to the abortion law and pregnancy-conflict counselling in the interest of 'life protection'. Strategically, key terms would become additionally 'protected': Just as *marriage* is granted exclusively to heterosexual couples, the term *family* is only accorded to those unions that follow the model of a heterosexual marriage with children.

Rhetorically, right-wing populist gender and family policies are described as protective (e.g. of the 'traditional family'), ending discrimination (e.g. of full-time mothers), supportive and facilitating (e.g. of women's freedom of choice for motherhood) (Siri 2016). Anti-gender-politics and the goals of oppressive gender ideology are also combined with an aggressive rhetoric of annihilation (Berg 2016). Strategically, a combination of defamation, emotionalization and annihilation goals are used to re-define terms and policies that relate to gender issues. At the same time, these re-definitions are contrasted with supposed common sense constructs – pseudo-general knowledge about heterosexual binaries being natural. All politics in support of gender equality appear, on these terms, as if imposed from above on people against their will, a far cry from their reality as a political instrument that is intended to protect people from various forms of discrimination. In the AfD's online campaigns a variety of staging strategies are also used to legitimize heteronormative ideas as natural. People from an educational elite, mostly men with professorships or doctoral degrees, act as educators, teaching concepts such as gender or gender mainstreaming (Berg 2016: 94). Another staging strategy is to have female party members appear as key witnesses. As a member of a discriminated group – as women, mothers or female politicians – they deny that there is discrimination and oppose countermeasures (ibid.: 95). In all of these ways and more, far-right gender and family politics focus strongly on the regulation of women and female bodies.

The AfD constructs a line of conflict between the 'pure people,' on the one hand, and gender ideology and the other parties, on the other. Ultimately, the AfD positions itself in this field of conflict on the side of the 'people', as a fighter for the survival of the German people and for their supposedly natural understanding of gender and sexuality, ideally represented by the normative family. This is where online media and speeches are particularly effective, as this narrative is especially suitable for addressing sympathizers directly. The lost ideal of masculinity campaigned for by Björn Höcke can be positioned here, as can the idealization of the mother role of female party members and the sexist posters of younger AfD members. The family politics of the AfD ultimately has two functions: First, an ethnicist concept of 'the people' is conveyed through the family. Second, the family, consisting of mother, father and several children, is constructed as a leading figure in order to realize a naturally and hierarchically structured society (Bebnowski 2015: 7–8).

GENDER POLITICS IN THE CONTEXT OF MIGRATION AND BELONGING

In recent years, far-right gender politics has increasingly shifted to a different thematic focus. Issues of gender and women's rights are linked to the topics of migration and Islam. Especially after the sexual assaults on New Year's Eve 2015/16 in Cologne, old right-wing narratives have been re-activated in order to position their own topics in the public debate. Various online media platforms such as Twitter, Facebook and Youtube have been used to push these topics into the political and public discourses with two central narratives. In leading this push, the AfD has demonstrated a sophisticated awareness of how to combine online tools with its offline political practices in a way that is publicly effective.

The first narrative is practically omnipresent in contemporary European public discourse. The AfD and its members publish posters on Facebook at very short intervals with messages such as, "Brutal group rape: 8 migrants attack 13-year-old" and "Sexual offences on trains & at train stations 'Everyday life in Merkel-Germany': the proportion of non-German perpetrators rises to nearly 60%". These are illustrated with photos of victims of violence, or dark silhouettes with or without weapons, in public spaces. While the posters and contributions were formulated less directly in 2015 (Berg 2016), today no room for interpretation is left by either the language or images. Now a more direct scenario of violence and fear is named: people who are being labelled as migrant or non-German as perpetrators, and 'German' women as victims. The constant repetition of these old narratives on the AfD's social media channels is followed by interviews and talk show appearances by individual politicians supposedly legitimizing the scare claim.

One example of an effective combination of media campaigning and parliamentary political work is the AfD's representation of the case of the murdered and raped 14-year-old student Susanna from Mainz. The alleged perpetrator, Ali was described as a 21-year-old refugee who had fled from Iraq to Germany. Member of Parliament Thomas Seitz brought the case to the Bundestag. In a speech that was meant to be about debates on the Rules of Procedure in the house, he instead brought up the death of the schoolgirl and then remained demonstratively silent. The presiding vice president of the *Bundestag* Claudia Roth then asked him to speak to the debate, as otherwise she would expel him from the desk, which she did. A short time later there was a video on Twitter entitled "Minute of Silence for Susanna: Revealing Reaction of the Other Parties", which led the narrative for the broad media coverage that followed.

The narrative is always the same. The violent offender is marked as foreign, immigrant, misogynist and often Muslim, and as someone who has sexually abused and/or killed a girl or woman who is marked as 'German' or 'ours'. The other parties are positioned on the side of the perpetrators while the AfD presents itself like lawyers on behalf of the victims. The rhetorical strategy behind this is to establish the attributes Muslim, immigrant, misogynistic and violent as synonymous with one another. Furthermore, the acts of violence are presented as evidence to mark a general threat group, to homogenize it and to create a constant threat situation. Translated, it would mean that all migrant or migrant-labelled men are violent and hostile to women, and from them emanates a new permanent threat to 'our women' and 'our society'. They are thus marked as not belonging and alien to 'our society' and are made into the antagonistic evil 'other'.

The second narrative is directly connected to this and concerns women wearing headscarves, burka or niquab: "The equal rights of women and men guaranteed by the Basic Law as well as the free development of personality are contradicted by the headscarf as a religious-political sign of the subordination of Muslim women to men."[6] A full veil stands for conscious demarcation as well as for "a rejection of our enlightened-democratic values and our image of humankind."[7] AfD faction leader Alice

---

6 | Ibid., p.40.

7 | AfD proposal in the Bundestag to ban full veiling in public spaces from February 21, 2018: (http://dip21.bundestag.de/dip21/btd/19/008/1900829.pdf).

Weidel said in a speech in the Bundestag: "Burkas, girls in headscarves and financially supported knifemen and other good-for-nothings will not ensure our prosperity, economic growth and above all the welfare state."[8] On Facebook, the full veil is frequently used as a symbolic image as soon as the word 'Islamization' appears, for example in the headline "Covering Swimwear for Everyone! An Islamization is not happening?" First, a homogeneous group is constructed, which includes all women with headscarves, niquab or burka. They are labelled as oppressed, not integrated, a financial burden on society and symbolic of Islam, which has been marked as threatening. As such they stand for an antagonistic and incompatible culture and become symbolic of everything that a supposedly German society and culture is not: backward, violent, anti-women, discriminatory, Muslim. As Leila Hadj-Abdou has explained, this narrative portrays an inequality between the supposedly emancipated and free women of "one's own people" in contrast with oppressed Muslim women, a portrayal that serves to obscure the inequality between men and women within "one's own society" (2010: 118).

There are two gender-specific threat images that are intended to jointly create a threat scenario for the safety of 'our society' or 'our people', which simultaneously creates two opposing gendered groups. First, a misogynist, oppressive and violent group is labelled as Muslim and immigrant and is thus characterized as foreign, non-affiliated and threatening. They form the negative image for a supposedly free, gender-equal, emancipated, liberal, 'our German' society, and at the same time are presented as a threat to it. Birgit Sauer calls this "ethnomasochism", an idea of 'suffering' caused by the patriarchy of the 'others' (2017: 12). These narratives are both racist and sexist, since they divert sexism and sexualized violence into a cultural and personal problem of an othered group of men, while also using ascription and homogenization to characterize this group as inferior and dangerous based on a constructed culture of values. Ruth Wodak calls this combination of homogenization, dichotomous confrontation and characteristic ascription "neo-colonial sexism" (2015: 160). Second, yet simultaneously, the externalization of misogyny, sexual violence and discrimination against "the others" allows the self-declared natives to

---

8 | Speech by Alice Weidel in the Bundestag from May 16, 2018 (https://www.bundes tag.de/mediathek?videoid=7227207#url=L21IZGlhdGhla292ZXJssYXk/dmlkZW 9pZD03MjI3MjA3&mod=mediathek).

legitimize the complete exclusion of this foreign group. Demands for national exclusion and the deportation of a group that is under general suspicion can thus be rallied behind an alleged need to protect 'our women'
and their rights to freedom, 'our values' and 'our culture,' along with the
promise of restoring a peaceful society. Koray Yilmaz-Günay has shown
how such strategies of argument are arranged around claims about civil
rights and liberties: "The reference to the freedom of individual women
(and today also: homosexuals) robs a patriarchal analysis of its contexts
[...] in order to conceal systematic inequality and to bring disadvantaged
groups into opposition to one another" (2013: 118).

THE FAR-RIGHT CLAIM TO HEGEMONY IN GENDER POLITICS

Far-right gender politics make it possible to establish a social structure of
inequality and standardization. Not only are exclusion and belonging established through a misconstrual of gender, but these divisions also create
a privileging and hierarchization within 'the people'. Birgit Sauer points
out that the far-right notion of natural gender inequality generates a general idea of inequality within a people, which subsequently legitimizes a
social subordination and superiority of some over the rest (2017: 13). By
excluding gender inequality, attributing it to a group of 'others' on the one
hand and constructing gender politics as a misguided and threatening
gender ideology on the other, the AfD can convey its idea of gender or
gender justice as the only right one for the people and as coming from the
people.

Behind this the AfD conceals its own concepts of inequality standardization and privileging. They claim sovereignty over the interpretation of
what the right idea of gender and gender justice should be. They try to
control the definitions of gender, family, marriage and sexuality, as well as
the family and gender politics that are subsequently constructed. It is a balancing act between a pseudo-emancipatory coating that appears to protect
women's rights or puts female MPs at the forefront of gender issues, and
anti-feminist positions that make women the object of national population
politics. However, this balancing act allows space for the ambiguities and
contents of a broad right-wing spectrum and at the same time enables the
AfD to connect to the center of society.

This anti-feminist position in combination with ethnicized sexism is shared in Europe and North America by many far right actors. The increased appearance of women as allies in the far right seems initially a welcome development, since they give movements and parties a 'softer' image, are considered less dangerous in mainstream discourse and thus cushion right-wing extremist content (Armstrong 2018). At the same time, they conflict with the notions of male supremacy within these groups, and are therefore only accepted if they advocate far-right content and do not develop emancipatory demands within the groups or publicly speak out against their assigned roles. The Anti-Defamation League (2018) published an analysis of the link between misogyny and white supremacy, showing how the other side of gender politics makes a special alliance possible. Male supremacy is, in this case, closely linked to the fear of white men losing their privileges. The fear of this loss unites classic far-right groups with women-hating men's rights groups in opposition to feminism and emancipatory gender roles. Similar to Sauer's argument, the notion of natural gender inequality and the inferiority of women is a gateway to an ideological notion of the natural inequality among people, who white men are supposed to lead. Politics with gender works in many ways and on different levels; it is not a German phenomenon but one that is represented internationally.

CONCLUSION

The AfD is only one of many anti-feminist actors in both Germany and Europe. Within Germany, the AfD can provide parliamentary backing for right-wing radical protest campaigns like *Kandel ist überall* where a wide range of far-right activists come together. They follow precisely the racist narratives about women's rights, sexualized violence and migration that have been described above, and combine online campaigns with street protests and public events as part of an online and offline strategy. In addition to women's rights and gender justice, the concept of feminism is here also reinterpreted in a racist and culturalizing way. Nevertheless, the terms, interpretations, narratives, language and images used are also reproduced in mainstream media and debates, and become represented and shared by actors in non-right contexts. The public debate about New Year's Eve 2015/2016 in Cologne is exemplary of this broad-spectrum alignment.

The increasing ethnicization of sexism we are witnessing now was also observed in earlier times (Jäger 2000). All of which shows that far-right politics offers a connecting space for these agendas, both in terms of its anti-feminism and familialism and in terms of the entanglement of sexism and racism, in particular anti-Muslim racism.

The aggressively conducted far-right culture war, with its new and old strategies and networks, presents democratic societies with a range of challenges. We must confront it online and offline and effectively counter the increasing normalization of far-right terms in and for public debates. Devaluation, discrimination, homogenization and hatred cannot be an 'opinion' in a democratic debate. It is necessary to disagree as an individual, group, organization or association with these terms for debate, and to debate their naturalization of misleading definitions of key terms. But first, we need to develop and share a common knowledge of far-right narratives and methods. Gender politics must become a more visible and significant aspect of our political battles. The acculturation of racist images linked to gender must be deconstructed, dismantling both the image of the 'oppressed woman wearing headscarves' as well as the 'migrant perpetrator of violence.' Narratives must be dealt with analytically. Ascription, homogenization and generalization must be identified and challenged. There needs to be a broad social debate about language and power. The aim may be to linguistically uncover far-right self-descriptions and terms, and to identify them for what they really are. The demand to construct appropriate meanings for key terms such as 'women's rights' and 'feminism' should not be handed over to the far right and their interpretations. Instead, we still need intersectional perspectives that can enable us to conceptualize the links between racial and gender inequality as well as the racist appropriation of both. This means, for example, that sexualized violence cannot be addressed and politicized only if the perpetrators can be othered. Sexism must continue to be identified as a structural problem and not a personal and cultural problem of a particular group of men. Resistance requires alliances, exchange and solidarity. Anti-racist positions and initiatives should not be positioned against feminist or queer content and groups. Both are affected by right-wing devaluations and attacks and can strengthen rather than divide each other. It is precisely in this way that effective and positive images of open, democratic coexistence within society can be created.

References

Anti-Defamation-League (2018): "When Women are the Enemy: The Intersection of Misogyny and white Supremacy", (https://www.adl.org/resources/reports/when-women-are-the-enemy-the-intersection-of-misogyny-and-white-supremacy#introduction).

Armstrong, Megan (2018): "Gender, Identity, and the Radical Right", 8 August (https://www.radicalrightanalysis.com/2018/08/08/gender-iden tity-and-the-radical-right/).

Bebnowski, David (2015): Die Alternative für Deutschland. Aufstieg und Gesellschaftliche Repräsentanz einer Rechten Populistischen Partei, Wiesbaden: Springer.

Berg, Lynn (2016): Bedrohung durch die 'Genderideologie'. Geschlecht und Familie in der Politik der 'Alternative für Deutschland' im Kontext eines Deutschen Rechtspopulismus, Unpublished Master Thesis, Goethe-University Frankfurt am Main.

Hadj-Abdou, Leila (2010): "Anti-Migrationspolitik im Namen der Geschlechtergleichheit. Das Paradox des 'Feministischen Rechtspopulismus.'" In: Femina Politica 2, pp. 117–119.

Jäger, Margarete (2000): "Ethnisierung von Sexismus im Einwanderungsdiskurs. Analyse einer Diskursverschränkung", (http://www.diss-duisburg.de/Internetbibliothek/Artikel/Ethnisierung_von_Sexis mus.htm).

Lehmann, Armin (2018): "Wie Wir Heldenhafter Werden Können", 3 June 2018 (https://www.tagesspiegel.de/politik/sehnsucht-nach-maennlich keit-wie-wir-heldenhafter-werden-koennen/22636620.html).

Reisigl, Martin (2012): "Zur Kommunikativen Dimension des Rechtspopulismus." In: Pelinka, Anton/Haller, Birgitt (eds.): Populismus. Herausforderung oder Gefahr für die Demokratie? Wien: New Acadmic Press, pp. 140–162.

Sauer, Birgit (2017): "Gesellschaftstheoretische Überlegungen zum Europäischen Rechtspopulismus. Zum Erklärungspotenzial der Kategorie Geschlecht." In: Politische Vierteljahresschrift 58/1, pp.1–20.

Siri, Jasmin (2016): "Geschlechterpolitische Positionen der Partei Alternative für Deutschland." In: Häusler, Alexander (eds.), Die Alternative für Deutschland. Programmatik, Entwicklung und Politische Verortung, Wiesbaden: Springer, pp. 69–80.

Wodak, Ruth (2015): The Politics of Fear. What Right-Wing Populist Discources Mean, Los Angeles: Sage.

Yilmaz-Günay, Koray (2013): "Sexuelle Selbstbestimmung als Topos im Antimuslimischen Rassismus." In: Bathke, Peter/Hoffstadt, Anke (eds.), Die Neuen Rechten in Europa: Zwischen Neoliberalismus und Rassismus, Köln: Papyrossa, pp. 255–268.

The Far Right Across Borders

Networks and Issues of (Trans)National Cooperation in Western Europe on Twitter

Caterina Froio and Bharath Ganesh[1]

Historically, far-right activism[2] has had a transnational dimension.[3] More recently, across Europe, various far-right organizations including the Identitarians and also the more established Italian Ligue have come together to promote continental campaigns targeting European borders and refugees. In an increasingly globalized world, information and communications technology plays a prominent role in fostering communication exchanges between far-right organizations across borders (Burris et al. 2000). More precisely, hashtags like #DefendEurope, #StopMigrantsAlpes or #chiudiamoiporti (let's lock the harbors) underline the importance of Twitter in contemporary right-wing activism. Low costs and the opportunity to produce and rapidly spread user-generated content online should ease international cooperation between like-minded groups, especially those that do not enjoy similar opportunities in other parts of the public (offline) sphere. This chapter analyzes transnational exchanges between audiences of far-right organizations on Twitter, comparing parties and social movements across the borders of nation states.

---

1 | This chapter draws upon material from Froio/Ganesh (2018).

2 | The chapter uses the umbrella concept of far right to refer both to extreme and radical right populist organizations sharing nativism, authoritarianism and populism (Mudde 2007: 15-30) and encompassing political parties and social movement organizations.

3 | For a discussion on the history of far-right transnationalism see Albanese/ Hierro 2016; Macklin 2013; Mammone 2015; Zuquete 2015.

Defining the transnational aspect of far-right activism is not an easy task. Social movements literature distinguishes between transnational issues, targets, and mobilization (Rucht 1999; Schain et al. 2002). We qualify far-right activism as transnational when organizations from more than one country place similar discursive emphasis on particular issues. In our understanding, focusing on common issues (such as immigration or European integration) is a preliminary step in the construction of the necessary interpretative frames, i.e. interpretations of social reality elaborated by the leaders of organizations who orient activists' actions (Snow/Benford 1988; Castelli Gattinara 2017). In doing so, we do not claim that common issue attention is disconnected from other dimensions of transnationalization or more important than the others. We simply argue that focusing on similar issues provides a fertile ground for other forms of mobilization and organizational cooperation across national contexts.

While existing studies dealing with progressive movements show that Twitter facilitates transnational mobilization and frames (Castells 2012; Gerbaudo 2012), to the best of our knowledge no systematic study exists that accounts for the way in which Twitter might ease the construction of a transnational discourse between parties and movements on the far right. Here, we focus on retweets across country borders, which we understand as signs of transnational discourses (more on this below). To do so in an evidence-based way, this chapter relies on a dataset collated by us (Froio/Ganesh 2018) on the activities and audiences of far-right Twitter users in France, Germany, Italy, and the United Kingdom.

Data and Methods

Although established and less established far-right organizations of the sort we studied are active in the four countries, the configuration of the far-right spectrum in each differs. While France and Italy host two of the most electorally successful and long-lived radical right populist parties (the Front National and the Ligue respectively), in Germany and the United Kingdom the far right has experienced only modest electoral performances so far (for instance, the National Front then British National Party in the UK) and the success they have enjoyed has mainly been achieved recently (like the Alternative for Germany). Less established far- right organizations like movements and other loose groups are particularly active in Italy and France, where political opportunity structures for the far right have been shown to be more open than in Germany and the UK.[4]

To begin with, based on official reports and secondary literature by scholars and watchdog organizations, we built an initial purposive sample, identifying the most important far-right actors (e.g. established and non-established organizations, as well as individuals related to them) that are active in the four countries and that use Twitter. Subsequently, we built a network graph of Twitter users that retweeted one of our selected far-right accounts more than five times. Retweeting is a function on the platform that allows a user to share another's Tweet with their own followers. While there are debates about whether retweeting constitutes support for a cause or a statement, it is the best available metric for identifying users that seek to engage with far-right discourse by embedding themselves in a particular discursive context (Murthy 2012a; Boyd, et al. 2010). Many who seek to disrupt a far-right group on Twitter might follow its account, but retweeting such content and sharing it with their own set of followers suggests that a user is using their political agency to broadcast an idea or statement (Bruns/Stieglitz 2012; Williams/Burnap 2016: 215; Murthy 2012b: 7). Thus, the retweet resonates with the user retweeting it and that they have a desire for the message to reach other users of the platform (Halavais 2014). Retweets, then, allow us to explore the resonance of the messages of a given user.

Finally, we analyzed the content of retweets that remained within the national community and retweets that did not to identify the types of content that are most likely to garner transnational audiences. Because our data spans far-right content from 2016 and 2017, we are able to go beyond specific issues and analyze discourse trends over time rather than those that centre around specific events.[5]

---

4 | For a discussion of this trend, see Castelli Gattinara/Pirro (2018).
5 | For further methodological details please refer to Froio/Ganesh (2018).

RESULTS

How transnational is the far right on Twitter? Figure 1 shows how complex the far-right network is, including accounts belonging to far-right parties (like the party Forza Nuova), social movements (UKPegida), grassroots groups (Riposte Laïque), and far-right leaders (Marine Le Pen Officiel). The far-right network includes 6,454 nodes representing unique Twitter users. Each edge in the graph represents a retweet. There were 2,398 unique tweets authored by the named nodes which were retweeted 55,983 times in total. Of these retweets, only 1,617 retweets were identified as transnational (in term of content).

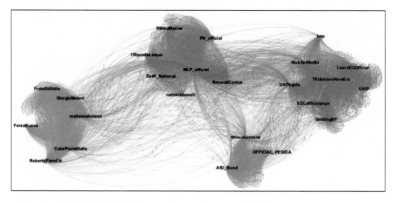

Figure 1: Far-right retweets network, 2016 and 2017. From left to right: Italy, France, Germany, UK (Froio/Ganesh 2018).

To begin the investigation, we explored whether the network could be partitioned into communities that represented each of the countries sampled, in different colors in Figure 1. Using a community detection algorithm (Blondel et al. 2008), four communities emerged corresponding to each of the four countries from which we had gathered samples. Nodes that have edges between one or more communities – and were consequently located between clusters in the graph – are identified as transnational retweeters. The results appear in Table 1.

Type of retweet	Initiator				Total
	Party		Movement		
National	1099	45.83%	1299	54.17%	2398
Transnational	411	51.83%	382	48.17%	793
Total	1510	47.32%	1681	52.68%	3191

National and transnational far-right retweets by parties and movements
Source: Froio/Ganesh 2018

The results show that most retweets stayed within country borders and so were intranationally connected. Thus, far-right transnationalization, at least as it regards its audiences' willingness to retweet, is a relatively rare phenomenon and accounts for less than 3% of activity in the filtered network. There are 2,398 unique tweets, of which 793 were retweeted by a user belonging to a different national community. A small majority of the tweets are authored by accounts of individuals belonging to far-right social movements or the official accounts of movements themselves.

We then shifted to examine the issues that are more likely to garner attention and retweets from transnational audiences. To address this question, we qualitatively analyzed the content of the tweets to identify the interpretative frames accompanying transnational issue focus between parties and movements. In other words, we are interested in understanding which arguments are chosen by political actors to justify their positions and mobilize activists and supporters transnationally. Of all issues, it seems tweets that reflect anti-immigration and economic discourses are more likely to gain traction beyond the national context.

To begin with, the importance attributed to immigration in transnational retweets is hardly surprising and it mirrors broader offline tendencies. In his seminal 2007 study, Cas Mudde suggested that nativism – i.e. xenophobic nationalism – is indeed a core ideological feature of the far right, despite the heterogeneity that characterizes this side of the political spectrum. More precisely, it is an ideology that wants congruence between the state (a political unit) and nation (a cultural unit). Nativists want a state for every nation and one nation for every state. They perceive all non-natives (people or ideas) as threatening (2007: 18–20). Still, by analyzing the content of tweets in this category, it appears that, at least in our sample, nativism is driven far more by Islamophobia than by other forms of xenophobic and exclusionary nationalism. Although other minorities are mentioned (such as Roma people in Italy) or vaguely referred to as "asylum seekers", Muslims are targeted most vehemently. They are described by two main interpretative frames, positioning Muslims as a cultural threat to the West or as security threats.

To portray Muslims as a threat in cultural terms, tweets emphasize a classic fear of cultural invasion and replacement. The transnational form of such a discourse is well illustrated in a tweet from UKPegida, ideologically related to its sister organization Pegida in Germany. The tweet includes a video of an allegedly Muslim preacher shouting about an Islamic takeover in a city square. UKPegida posted the video with the following text: "Islamic cleric in Germany warns Germans at a city square: Sharia Law is coming. 'Yr [your] daughters will marry Muslims.'" Reminiscent of Huntington's theory of the Clash of Civilizations and by civilizationist understandings of national identities (Brubaker 2017), in this worldview the 'West' is portrayed as vulnerable to the invading Muslims and their purported plan to institute Islamic law in Europe. Islam is described as being homogeneous, inherently fundamentalist, and as a "religion cum ideology" (Mudde 2007: 84). This frame incorporates liberal and civic characteristics of national identity such as women's rights, animal well-being and halal slaughter, and LGBTQ rights to paradoxically present the far-right actors as the only 'authentic' defenders of the nation's reputation for tolerance (Froio 2018; Halikiopoulou et al. 2013). In March 2017, referring to a morning radio broadcast, Marine Le Pen provides an example of such a frame, quoting herself in a tweet: "I defend women's rights in the face of fundamentalist Islam. I am, by the way, the only candidate to speak about this problem."

Such stereotypes are well documented in literature on far-right discourse (Virchow 2016; Berntzen/Weisskircher 2016). What our findings add is that Islamophobia and anti-Muslim claims are more frequent in transnational rather than in national retweets. Given the well documented links between anti-Muslim ideologues in the US and Europe (Bail 2015), we demonstrate that Islamophobia is a cornerstone of the production of transnational far-right social movements and parties. Beyond culture-based prejudices, tweets often relate Muslims to domestic security threats, most notably terrorism, but also frame them as criminals and violent sexual deviants. One tweet from UKPegida referred to migrants as "rapefugees" with photographs of a march in 2016 that protested "migrant sex attacks". While 'Muslims' are not mentioned specifically in the tweet, the implication is clear from Pegida's counter-jihad stance that this is specifically a 'Muslim' problem. In response to an article about prominent British celebrities signing an open letter calling for migrant children to be rescued from the Calais 'jungle', the British National Party reiterated this discourse more explicitly: "How many jihadi rapists will these hypocrites be welcoming into their homes...I bet a £ to a penny it will be none." This is characteristic of the ways in which Islamophobia is at the core of far-right animosity toward migrants, as when they ask why it is that British police do not prosecute the 'Muslims' who they idenitify as 'jihadi rapists'. The allegation that rape, molestation, and crime are natural, inherent tendencies for Muslims is repeated frequently in far-right discourse (Awan 2016; Tell MAMA 2014; Tufail/Poynting 2016).

A third emphasis of the transnational tweets is put on the economy. The economy has traditionally been part of far-right discourses, however it does not constitute an ideological priority for these actors. As illustrated by Mudde (2007: 119–137), over time far-right parties do not hold a coherent position on the dominant state-market axis even if these organizations may differ somewhat with respect to their economic program (Betz 1994; Betz/Johnson 2004; Kitschelt/McGann 1997). In the same way, third-way ideologies associated with programs that reject both the free market and the state economy are common among far-right movements but not shared by all of them (Albanese/Hierro 2016). In the tweets, we find a major interpretative frame through which the economy features at the core of far-right transnational concerns: economic nativism. Just as it happens offline, also online such organizations use their economic programs in a nativist way, assuming that the economy is not a goal in itself but only a means at the service of the interests of the (native) nation. In accord with this framework, in the tweets, economic procedures concerning budgets, labor and industrial development should serve only the economic interest of the country. This economic nativist rhetoric is particularly evident in a tweet referring to a speech from Marine Le Pen calling for economic protection of the nation's sovereignty after the eurocrisis, stressing that the French want to decide their own economic fate rather than face anything imposed by foreign pressure. This interpretation is particularly the case for organizations coming from the so-called tradition of the Social Right (Destra Sociale) in Italy and France, like the party Fratelli d'Italia and the

Front National, as well as the less established extreme-right groups, like CasaPound Italia and Egalitè et Reconciliation.

On the matter of economic nativism, our results confirm previous findings about far-right transnationalism offline (Macklin 2013) and online (Caiani/Kröll 2015). What our data adds is that, compared to the national level, at the transnational level the economy is described more and more in nativist political terms rather than merely economic ones. In other words, if there is a form of economic discourse that is likely to favor the construction of a transnational far-right discourse, it is less about the state-market dichotomy *tout court* than about a political and nativist interpretation of this economic cleavage. This in turn might ultimately lead to incoherent economic positions that are sufficiently free-market to appeal to petty bourgeois supporters while simultaneously arguing to increase welfare spending to avoid alienating support by the working-class.

In sum, our discourse analysis reveals that two main interpretative frames operate as unifying factors for the far right in Western Europe: the idea of a 'civilizational conflict' that targets Muslims, which has cultural and security dimensions, and nativist economics, which is associated with the state and/or market-based protection of the economic interests of the native population by those in power.

Finally, it is important to highlight that in our dataset the category of 'Electoral Politics' does not receive much attention in transnational retweets. This category includes general references – with no policy content – to domestic political opponents, and electoral debates. Although this is a rather crude measure for 'populism', it appears that anti-establishment tweets are less frequent than anti-Muslim ones. While populist tendencies might be prevalent in the national discourses of these groups, their development of international audiences depends on their politicization of Islamophobic feelings.

So WHAT?

This chapter has explored a dimension of far-right politics that is surprisingly neglected in an otherwise rich literature: the transnational efforts of parties, movements, and organizations on Twitter. We considered four Western European democracies to examine how these audiences share information, map salient issues and explore interpretative frames that favour transnational exchanges despite differences in the configurations of the far-right spectrums in each of those countries. To do so we used Twitter data.

We illustrated that while the internet may provide the far right with better opportunities for exchanges (Davey/Ebner 2017), far-right transnationalism on Twitter is moderate at best, and it depends on issue focus. Our network analysis has shown that the number of cross-border retweets is particularly limited, suggesting that far-right Twitter activity remains mostly intranational.

As for issue focus, the qualitative content analysis shows that the issue emphasized in any tweet plays a key role in whether it gets shared transnationally or not. We found that tweets that reflect two issues have the greatest likelihood of becoming transnational: anti-immigration and the economy. More than immigration in general, it is an opposition to Islam and Muslim minorities, based on arguments referring to cultural difference and security, that garners cross-border attention for far-right social media content. As far-right anti-Muslim prejudices are well-established in previous research, our results add that Islamophobia seems to be the transnational glue of these networks, bringing together extremely heterogeneous organizations operating in different political systems.

For future analyses, it might be worth re-evaluating the relative importance of nativism and populism on the far right and their combination at the transnational level at least. Given the resonance of Islamophobic tropes in these discourses, reference to such organizations as simply 'populist' might obscure the nativist and specifically anti-Muslim beliefs that underlie their ideologies and that may fuel their anti-establishment critiques. In addition, the description of the economy in nativist (rather than just economic) terms is also favoured in transnational exchanges on Twitter. At that level, the economy is politicized by describing economic programs as catalyzers of the interests of native people. Here again anti-migrant nativist arguments prevail over economic ones, or (at least) encompass them. Hence, more than the state-market dichotomy in general, the far right speaks about protectionism or neoliberalism to preserve the nation's economic interests, at least in our sample. New studies may use our data to investigate how economic issues are framed in more detail, also in relation with European integration, and may hopefully disentangle similarities and differences between left and right organizations.

Although interesting for specialists on far-right politics and the internet, these results are likely to be affected by at least three major shortcomings of our research. First, our 'minimal' definition of transnationalism focused exclusively on common issue emphasis across state borders. Future contributions might expand it to account simultaneously for other dimensions of transnational activism by the far right, such as targeting and mobilization. This major emphasis on issue focus, organizational types and analyzing interpretative frames to explain far-right transnationalism pushed us to downplay other important factors connected with the ideological differences and divisions between extreme and radical right populist organizations. Second, this chapter does not consider that there may be obstacles to far-right transnationalism online, such as language differences and attempts by governments and tech companies to counter extreme content. Finally, any future contributions which include more countries may integrate our inferences with others to account (more accurately) for political opportunity structures both online and offline. These and other related research questions that arise from our work could further benefit from comparisons with other social media platforms (e.g., Facebook or Youtube) and in-depth studies of users' profiles.

Despite these limitations, what we have shown is the limited transnational potential of the far right on Twitter. At least in Western Europe, the idea of a 'dark international' is far from reality, even when considering social media, which are commonly described as 'perfect' habitats for radicalization. The ideological and organizational heterogeneity that characterizes this side of the political spectrum appears to be too big to be overcome, even virtually. Indeed, only two issues appear to be able to build transnational audiences: opposition to Muslims and opposition to 'anti-native' economic programs. Transnational counteraction should probably invest energy in creating counter-narratives to these specific issues, issues that the far-right's discourses demonstrate an increasingly hegemonic stance regarding.

REFERENCES

Albanese, Matteo/Hierro, Pablo del (2016): Transnational Fascism in the Twentieth Century: Spain, Italy and the Global Neo-Fascist Network, London: Bloomsbury Publishing.

Awan, Imran (2016): "Islamophobia on Social Media: A Qualitative Analysis of the Facebook's Walls of Hate." In: International Journal of Cyber Criminology 10/1, pp. 1–20.

Bail, Christopher (2015): Terrified: How Anti-Muslim Fringe Organizations Became Mainstream, Princeton and Oxford: Princeton University Press.

Berntzen, Lars E./Weisskircher, Manès (2016): "Anti-Islamic PEGIDA Beyond Germany: Explaining Differences in Mobilisation." In: Journal of Intercultural Studies 37/6, pp. 556–573.

Betz, Hans-Georg (1994): Radical Right-Wing Populism in Western Europe, New York: St. Martins Press.

Betz, Hans-Georg/Johnson, Carol (2004): "Against the Current – Stemming the Tide: The Nostalgic Ideology of the Contemporary Radical Populist Right." In: Journal of Political Ideologies 9/3, pp. 311–327.

Boyd, Danah/Golder, Scott/Lotan. Gilad (2010): "Tweet, Tweet, Retweet: Conversational Aspects of Retweeting on Twitter", 6 January 2010 (https://www.danah.org/papers/TweetTweetRetweet.pdf).

Bruns, Axel/Stieglitz, Stefan (2012): "Quantitative Approaches to Comparing Communication Patterns on Twitter." In: Journal of Technology in Human Services 30/3–4, pp. 160–185.

Brubaker, Roger (2017): "Between Nationalism and Civilizationism: The European Populist Moment in Comparative Perspective." In: Ethnic and Racial Studies 40/8, pp. 1191–1226.

Burris, Val/Smith, Emery/Strahm, Ann (2000): "White Supremacist Networks on the Internet." In: Sociological Focus 33/2, pp. 215–235.

Caiani, Manuela/Kröll, Patricia (2015): "The Transnationalization of the Extreme Right and the Use of the Internet." In: International Journal of Comparative and Applied Criminal Justice 39/4, pp. 331–351.

Castelli Gattinara, Pietro (2017): "Framing Exclusion in the Public Sphere: Far-Right Mobilisation and the Debate on Charlie Hebdo in Italy." In: South European Society and Politics 22/3, pp. 345–364.

Castelli Gattinara, Pietro/Pirro, Andrea L. P. (2018): "The Far Right as Social Movement." In: European Societies.

Castells, Manuel (2012): Networks of Outrage and Hope: Social Movements in the Internet Age, Cambridge: Polity Press.

Davey, Jacob/Ebner, Julia (2017): "The Fringe Insurgency. Connectivity, Convergence and Mainstreaming of the Extreme Right", Institute for Strategic Dialogue (http://www.isdglobal.org/wp-content/uploads/2017/10/The-Fringe-Insurgency-221017.pdf).

Froio, Caterina (2018): "Race, Religion or Culture? Framing Islam between Racism and Neo-Racism in the Online Network of the French Far Right." In: Perspectives on Politics 16/3, pp. 696–709.

Froio, Caterina/Ganesh, Bharath (2018): "The Transnationalisation of Far Right Discourse on Twitter." In: European Societies, pp. 1–27.

Gerbaudo, Paolo (2012): Tweets and the Streets: Social Media and Contemporary Activism, Pluto Press.

Halavais, Alexander (2014): "Structure of Twitter: Social and Technical." In: Weller, Katrin/ Bruns, Axel/Burgess, Jean/Mahrt, Merja/ Puschmann, Cornelius (eds), Twitter and Society, New York: Peter Lang, pp. 29–42.

Halikiopoulou, Daphne/Mock, Steven/Vasilopoulou, Sofia (2013): "The Civic Zeitgeist: Nationalism and Liberal Values in the European Radical Right." In: Nations and Nationalism 19/1, pp. 107–127.

Kitschelt, Herbert/McGann, Anthony J. (1997): The Radical Right in Western Europe: A Comparative Analysis, Ann Harbor: Michigan University Press.

Macklin, Graham (2013): "Transnational Networking on the Far Right: The Case of Britain and Germany." In: West European Politics 36/1, pp. 176–198.

Mammone, Andrea (2015): Transnational Neofascism in France and Italy, Cambridge: Cambridge University Press.

Mudde, Cas (2007): Populist Radical Right Parties in Europe, Cambridge and New York: Cambridge University Press.

Murthy, Dhiraj (2012a): "Towards a Sociological Understanding of Social Media: Theorizing Twitter." In: Sociology 46/6, pp. 1059–1073.

Murthy, Dhiraj (2012b): Twitter: Social Communication in the Twitter Age, Cambridge: Polity.

Rucht, Dieter (1999): "The Transnationalization of Social Movements: Trends, Causes, Problems." In: Della Porta, Donatella/Kriesi, Hanspeter/Rucht, Dieter (eds.), Social Movements in a Globalizing World, Basingstoke: Palgrave, pp. 206–222.

Schain, Martin/Zolberg, Aristide/Hossay, Patrick (2002): Shadows Over Europe: The Development and Impact of the Extreme Right in Western Europe, New York: Palgrave.

Snow, David L./Benford, Robert D. (1988): "Ideology, Frame Resonance, and Participant Mobilization." In: Klandermans, Bert/Kriesi, Hanspeter/Tarrow, Sidney (eds.), From Structure to Action: Social Movement Participation Across Cultures, Greenwich: JAI Press, pp. 197–217.

Tell MAMA (2014): "Facebook Report: Rotherham, Hate and the Far Right Online", 1 March 2017 (http://tellmamauk.org/wp-content/uploads/2014/09/ Rotherham.pdf).

Tufail, Waqas/Poynting, Scott (2016): "Muslim and Dangerous: "Grooming" and the Politics of Racialisation." In: Pratt, Douglas/Woodlock, Rachel (eds.), Fear of Muslims? Boundaries of Religious Freedom: Regulating Religion in Diverse Societies, Wiesbaden: Springer, pp. 79–92.

Virchow, Fabian (2016): "PEGIDA: Understanding the Emergence and Essence of Nativist Protest in Dresden." In: Journal of Intercultural Studies 37/6, pp. 541–555.

Williams, Matthew L./Burnap, Pete (2016): "Cyberhate on Social Media in the Aftermath of Woolwich: A Case Study in Computational Criminology and Big Data." In: The British Journal of Criminology 56/2, pp. 211–238.

Zuquete, José Pedro (2015): "The New Frontlines of Right-Wing Nationalism." In: Journal of Political Ideologies 20/1, pp. 69–85.

Zine Publishing and the Polish Far Right

Kaja Marczewska

The rise of the far right in Poland during the last decade has been chilling. The 60,000-strong controversial Independence Day march in Warsaw in 2017 – called "a beautiful sight" by Mariusz Błaszczak, the Interior Minister (Chrzczonowicz 2017), and "a great march of patriots" by one of the state-owned TV stations[1] – was the subject of extensive coverage in the Western media. The march was not an isolated incident but a culmination of the far right's growing strength Poland today. Incidents such as setting fire to a flat occupied by a Chechen family in 2013 in Białystok, the stoning of a Yemeni doctor and his son in Toruń in 2016, and the violent assault of a black female passenger by two ticket inspectors on a bus in Bydgoszcz in 2017 are increasingly becoming an everyday occurrence in the country. A Polish NGO, the Centre for Monitoring Racism and Xenophobic Behavior, reports that as many as 100 racist incidents are logged by the organization daily (Dulkowski 2017).

In this context, diverse forms of publishing and circulating information serve as an important tool for promoting far-right ideology. For example, Blood and Honour, an international far-right network very active in Poland, regularly releases online lists, the so-called 'redwatch' lists, of individuals identified as future targets for attacks. In 2017, Młodzież Wszechpolska (All-Polish Youth) – a prominent far-right youth organization – circulated a collection of fabricated death certificates for a number of Polish city mayors, whose future demise would be apocryphally based on their continued support of 'liberalism, multiculturalism, and stupidity', i.e. the mayors' readiness to offer support for refugees. Online plat-

---

1 | Wiadomości TVP (2017): "Szkalują patriotów, gardzą Polakami", 13 November 2017 (http://wiadomosci.tvp.pl/34794068/szkaluja-patriotow-gardza-polakami).

forms and periodicals focusing on far-right content are also increasingly popular. For example, Nacjonalista.pl, Poland's most prominent far-right online publication, enjoys 270,000 clicks and 100,000 individual page visitors per month and *Szczerbieniec*, a radical nationalist monthly, is published in 4000–5000 copies per issue. Narodowe Odrodzenie Polski (NOP/National Rebirth of Poland), an ultranationalist political party, runs a successful online bookstore selling far-right books, music, and periodicals.

While, predictably, publishing online is the most common form of far-right communication today, in Poland an unusual phenomenon of far-right zine publishing constitutes an important and an increasingly prolific sphere of activity. A report published in 2012 by the Polish Ministry of the Interior identified zines as one of the tactics that most contribute to the threat posed by far-right organizations in Poland.[2] Zines were listed in the report alongside music concerts, marches and demonstrations, as well as maintenance of internet forums and websites as means of far-right community building. This chapter explores the parallel resurgence of far-right nationalism and DIY forms of publishing since the change of the political system in Poland in 1989. It draws on these recent histories of Polish radical nationalism and self-publishing to explore the ways in which zine culture has been co-opted by the far right today. It focuses in particular on the use of print as a tool of organizing and consolidating groups already strongly embedded in far-right circles to suggest that the very limitations of zines as a media form make them an important and useful safe space for radicalization and far-right community enlargement.

ZINES AND UNDERGROUND PUBLISHING IN POLAND

Zines are a unique form of publishing. They are handmade, self-published, non-commercial, small-run periodicals, usually photocopied, characterized by a cut-and-paste aesthetic and amateur feel. They tend to be distributed through independent networks, often bartered rather than sold. Stephen Duncombe (2008) traces zines back to the 1930s North American

---

2 | Ministerstwo Spraw Wewnętrznych (2012): "Raport o Stanie Bezpieczenstwa w Polsce w 2011", (https://mil.link/instytut/wp-content/uploads/2012/09/Raport _o_stanie_bezpieczenstwa_w_Polsce_w_2011_roku.pdf).

fanzines, self-published at the time by the science fiction community, but they are best known as a product of the 1970s' punk scene. Evocative of its DIY ethos and defiance of the commercial and mainstream media, zines helped to perform that community's commitment to radical, often anarchist politics. The punk heritage heavily informs the approach to cultural production represented in zines: zine publishing not only works outside of the market, it actively opposes its logic, working against the corporate media and the culture of late capitalism. As such, it is also implicitly associated with predominantly left-wing politics. Zines tend to explore subjects as wide ranging as environmental justice, body image, the housing crisis, and queer sex, alongside everyday interests approached from points of view that interest readerships with unusual tastes, often covering topics unacceptable or of little concern to mainstream publications. Although many zines are not focused on politics per se, the great majority explicitly support political agendas that show allegiances with, and active support for, the working class, the marginalized, and the disenfranchised.

The formation of a popular and widespread far-right zine culture in Poland seems antithetical to strategies of zine publishing. But in this unusual appropriation of the form, the phenomenon is perhaps symptomatic of the broader history of zines in the Polish context. This history differs quite significantly from the familiar narratives of their USA and UK-based equivalents. Until 1989, a strict censorship regime was in place in Poland, which made publishing independently almost impossible. Offset printing, a relatively cheap method widely available in the West by the 1980s, was, before the fall of communism, only available in Poland to state-supported organizations and so beyond reach for most groups interested in the cultural underground. At the time when corner Xerox shops were emerging on an unprecedented scale in the USA – a phenomenon that exerted huge impact on surrounding zine communities (Eichhorn 2016) – the few Xerox machines available to the general public in Poland from late 1980s onwards were also controlled heavily by the state censorship apparatus. Although officially all publications in print runs of up to 100 copies were not subject to censorship – a legislation loophole readily exploited by early Polish zinesters – independent publishers attempting to copy their work were often refused the service by copy shop owners.

In spite of – or perhaps precisely because of – the limited and highly controlled access to cheap reproduction technologies, a rich underground publishing culture emerged in Poland at the time. The underground itself, however, developed into two distinct strands. Publishing in the communist People's Republic of Poland was organized into the so-called first, second, and third circulations. The first circulation included all publications that were approved by the authorities and supported the political status quo, and the second and third circulation was constituted by the opposition and spheres of independent publishing (Dunin-Wąsowich/ Varga 1995; Sławiński 2000; Pęczak 1988). The second circulation, which emerged in the 1970s, included publishing activities most typically associated with the political opposition at the time but also illegally worked to 'supplement' the first circulation by publishing and distributing banned books including works by George Orwell and Milan Kundera as well as Polish oppositional authors, such as Tadeusz Konwicki (Doucette 2018). Although actively resisted by the censorship apparatus, it was well established by the 1980s, operating widely known publishing houses and sophisticated, semi-official distribution networks.

Unlike second circulation publishing, third circulation was decentralized, self-organized, and relied on strategies of self-publishing that gave rise to what could be described as a Polish zine culture. As a publishing movement, third circulation formed at least in part in response to the activities of second circulation. It was associated with alternative movements, punk – somewhat belatedly arriving in Poland in the early 1980s – and publishing that was not focused on exploring political topics (although, similarly to zines more broadly, it was always politically motivated). The publishing communities associated with third circulation did not support the government and its politics, but they did not look favorably at the second circulation either, which they saw as the new establishment (Dunin-Wąsowich/Varga 1995: 228).

For both second and third circulation, however, publishing outside of the mainstream was a necessity rather than a choice. The political system and then the introduction of Marshall Law in 1981 in particular, which strengthened censorship and imposed further limitations on personal freedoms, were a natural context for zine publishing to develop, even if the system they opposed was radically different from the environment that gave rise to zines in the first place. A gradual relaxing of the political system in the years leading up to 1989 meant that increasingly small print run self-publishing was becoming a possibility in Poland. This transformation subsequently led to an explosion of independent publishing in the 1990s.

ZINES AND THE POLISH FAR RIGHT

In 2001, an anthology of Polish zines was published – the first comprehensive attempt at addressing this form of publishing in the Polish context.[3] The anthology included information about 1,000 underground publications created after 1989. In the introduction, Dariusz Ciosmak, its editor, foregrounds his focus on publications addressing questions of anarchism, antifascism, music, ecology, and animal rights, i.e. topics typically associated with zine publishing. Ciosmak also explicitly stresses his lack of interest in, and intentional exclusion of, zines produced by the far right (2001: 3). This declaration and the absence of far-right zines in the anthology is perhaps the most telling statement on the complex makeup of the contemporary Polish zine scene. It is an acknowledgement of the unusual but active presence of these far-right publications in the country's underground publishing circles.

Zines have been a communication method used by the Polish far right for some time now. Their appropriation of the zine form can be attributed to two parallel histories: the transformation of the public sphere, including the print and publishing sectors, in the early years of transition from dictatorship to democracy, and transformations of the far right in Poland during the same period. The fall of communism and the change in the political system meant, among other things, the opening of borders, the introduction of the free market, the end of censorship, and the reintroduction to Poland of civil liberties, including freedom of speech and freedom of organization.

The consequences of these dramatic changes were many. A new influx of media from the West meant new forms of access to all sorts of publications, both mainstream and underground. In this new political reality, the Polish underground, as it operated before 1989, lost its purpose and ceased to exist, with books distributed by second circulation now entering the mainstream and many third circulation publications transforming into official though independent publishers. New access to technology and print (paper could now be purchased legally, materials reproduced in unlimited and uncensored copies) also lead to an enthusiastic explosion

---

3 | The title of this compilation is a misnomer. The publication is a lexicon of short entries about zines rather than an anthology. It remains, however, a useful and most comprehensive source of information about zines in Poland to date.

of new forms of independent publishing at the time. Kajtoch estimates that by 1995, 1800 new publications were created (2006: 55–56). But as the new official, independent publishing culture was forming, so was a new underground. In the 1990s, there was a legal zine scene in Poland – i.e. publications which were registered and allocated an ISBN number, transforming from zines into small, independent magazines – and an illegal one – i.e. publications operating as zines, without ISBN registration and so, according to then new Polish legislation, in breach of the trade laws (Flont 2018: 159). The new underground, however, unlike its censored equivalent pre-1989, was allowed to operate freely and the limitations of trade laws were not exercised with respect to very small publishers. This state of affairs opened space for a rich and diverse zine scene in 1990s Poland.

The systemic transformations in the early 1990s also led to an almost instantaneous proliferation of new subcultural activities and youth organizations, including far-right groups, who were almost entirely stifled before 1989 but who grew in strength rapidly at the time. Marta Polaczek (2006) explains that immediately after the fall of communism, it was the political left that was the focus of widespread attention. Fears of post-communist left-wing organizations growing in strength again meant that little to no attention was paid to the activities of the quickly expanding far right. In the 1990s, the focus of far-right organizations was on creating a pan-Slavic program, driven by pagan and racist ideologies. A commitment to an ethnically-Polish, white community that heavily informed this far-right revival was a consequence of the long history of Polish nationalism, with its roots in 123 years of partitions,[4] the restoration of the independent Polish state in 1918, and the establishment, as a result of the events of World War II with its territorial changes and forced migration, of an ethnically homogenous Polish state in 1945. This revival of far-right organizations after the transition was geared in the early years towards establishing new organizational structures and expanding and strengthening their community of supporters. The appropriation of zine publishing was part of this program.

---

4 | Three annexations of Polish territory in the 18th century by Habsburg Austria, Prussia and Russia which resulted in the elimination of sovereign Poland and Lithuania (at the time the Polish-Lithuanian Commonwealth) for 123 years.

The turn to zines was a directly oppositional response to liberal left-wing activities and publications, both those continuing the work of third circulation titles and the rapidly proliferating new ones. The expansion of diverse forms of self-publishing at the time served as an important means of accessing the younger population at a crucial moment in the country's socio-cultural development. To the re-emerging far right, this was a key priority. For them, zine publishing in the early 1990s was a means of partaking in this new subcultural environment. The logic of this approach was simple: left-wing, progressive and liberal groups had zines, and so right-wing communities had to have zines too.

The publications of far-right groups discussed here have been referred to as zines by their creators since the early 1990s. Like their left-wing equivalents, these developed from third circulation publications and were disseminated without an ISBN number (second circulation far-right publishing also existed before 1989, including, for example, *Jestem Polakiem* [I am a Pole], a magazine published by NOP since 1983, transformed in 1992 into an official, registered magazine). But, typically, the far-right zines of the transition period lacked the collage, cut-and-paste aesthetics or zines' characteristic DIY feel. Their makers took little interest in the broader aesthetics and politics of the form itself. For reasons described above, the character of the zine was only tentatively appropriated by far-right communities to promote and consolidate, somewhat under the radar, their ideology. *White Storm*, for example, a skinhead zine created in the early 1990s, was produced on a desktop computer. Its pages were set using a relatively large font and its text was spaced out to make it easily legible (unlike a typical zine, often messy and difficult to decipher due to its layout and design). In its design and feel *White Storm* was akin to an amateur independent magazine, but due to its unregistered status and the models of distribution it relied on, it operated as a zine. Its aesthetic was explicitly and unambiguously a manifestation of a far-right sensibility. The pages of *White Storm* included ornamental margins into which the Othala rune was incorporated, a symbol used by Nazis, as a reference to Aryan heritage. This use of Nazi symbolism on pages of far-right zines was frequent, as was the incorporation of numerical codes applied to communicate far-right messages (e.g. 18 for Hitler, 88 for 'Heil Hitler' as well as David Lane's *88 Precepts*), symbols all easily identified by the community these zines were aimed at, and identifying them almost instantaneously as radical publications. This approach remains prominent in far-right zines today, which maintain a similar aesthetic and rely on the same forms of symbolic communication.

Since the 2011 parliamentary elections there has been a continuous movement of far-right ideology in Poland from the margins into the mainstream. Tomasz Słupik (2009) associates this recent re-emergence of right-wing radicals in Eastern Europe more broadly with what he describes as post-transformation trauma. Poland's aspirations since 1990 have been heavily influenced by a vision of an idealized Western order that the country was hoping to adopt. But this vision has proven to be an impossible dream and has only been realized in part. The far right today often draws on this disappointment, to accuse the EU, liberalism, and refugees of what they see as major failures in the process of systemic change. This perception of post-1989 transformations has been an important trigger for the turn towards the right in Polish politics during the last decade. Inevitably, an increasingly widespread support for right-wing ideology legitimizes the activities of radical groups, including radical publishers. But the content that might have, ten years ago, only been published via zines or dedicated online forums, has today entered our everyday discourses. Thrust into this context, the underground character of zines also changes. These publications are now *not* a tool of propaganda and a means of communicating messages otherwise invisible in the mainstream, but *rather* a form of community building and inter-group association. Whereas far-right zines in the early 1990s served as one of the tools employed to re-introduce the far right in the public imagination, today they serve an altogether different purpose. Utilized first and foremost as an internal communication method, these zines are designed to maintain an already established network.

This focus on community, which was prominent in a different sense for underground, sub- and counter-cultural groups before, is today central to the general aim of mainstreaming the extreme ideologies in which Polish far-right zines play a part. The approach is typical for zines more broadly, which are, Chris Atton explains, "primarily concerned with the object of their attention" (2001: 54) and as a result often serve as a means of building and maintaining an alternative community. According to Atton, a zine "is dialogical in intent and offers itself as a token for social relation" (2001: 55). Today, Polish far-right zines are less a space for reading and writing and more a tool for community formation. Their capacity to connect is important not only as a tool for networking; it is also a tool for establishing the agency of community members. It demonstrates a simple model of making and sharing in which they can actively participate by self-publishing. Such actor-participants have the capacity to co-create the culture of far-right nationalism by engaging in this form of publishing, not just as readers but also as publishers.

What emerges, then, from the pages of these zines, is a sense of collective and highly homogenous identity and a sense of a community that speaks in a unified voice. Characteristic distinctions between different far-right groups are almost entirely obscured on the pages of their zines and as a result neo-Nazi, Pagan, and skinhead zines, for example, tend to be strikingly similar both in their design and content. This approach is a direct outcome of the role zines play within far-right communities. It also speaks to the ways in which far-right supporters tend to create their identity, as individuals and communities, always constructed in opposition to any form of diversity and difference. However, its manifestations in the Polish context are unusual insofar as contemporary Poland is one of the most ethnically homogenous European countries, and ethnic minorities as well as immigrant communities are almost non-existent.[5] As Daniel Płatek suggests, this ethnic homogeneity means that the Polish far-right's attitude grows out of historical resentment (e.g. antisemitism, anti-German sentiments) and is not formed in a direct response to the makeup of contemporary Polish society (2015: 4). As a result, Płatek argues, the Polish far right today relies on creating an 'enemy' for itself, fabricating a target of hate that is almost always absent from its immediate environment. The Polish far-right's approach, then, is deeply rooted in an understanding of a traditional national identity, defined through Catholicism, Polish language and Polish ethnicity, and a commitment to traditional values, including familial bonds and religion. Central to the contemporary far right in Poland, is a certain historical nostalgia for the interwar nationalist programs and an idealized vision of a patriotic Poland that once was.

---

5 | Both a recent Polish census and a 2017 Eurostat survey suggest that only 0,2 of Poland's residents are of a nationality other than Polish. In this ninth most highly populated country in Europe of over 38m people, there are estimated 30,000 Muslims, 30,000 Asians, and ca. 5,000 people of African descent, making Poland one of the least diverse countries in the world. James D. Fearon's (2003) diversity study places Poland among the bottom 10 out of 160 studied countries in the world with respect of diversity.

The homogeneity that far-right zines are characterized by and seek to promote is counter to what could be described as the radical differencing of traditional zine communities, which, as a phenomenon, are committed to a project of creating spaces for a great diversity of voices to be heard. This tension in the way the zine form is used by the far right is a direct result of its appropriation, one that is inherently antithetical to the ideological project that informed the emergence of the zine phenomenon in the first place. The imagined and fabricated context for an exclusionist, racist, nationalist cause makes publications such as the far-right zines so much more important to mainstream politics than traditional zines. In their appropriated, unified voice they become a space where a common or consistent 'enemy' can easily be constructed, a space that makes it possible to create imaginary communities made up of those enemies against whom the right-wing groups can position themselves. In the context of the Polish far right, the role of publication is central to making the community a community in the first place.

THE INVISIBLE COMMUNITY

Unlike publishing formats that are easily accessible online by a range of readers, regardless of their political views, access to these zines is limited to those who are already 'in the know' due to their small print runs and dependence on direct distribution. Whereas 'traditional' contemporary zines, which in their celebration of print, the zine fair, and the independent niche bookshop, also embrace the digital sphere as a tool of circulation and a means of reaching communities far beyond their local networks, contemporary far-right zines remain somewhat outside of digital distribution channels.[6] Their visibility online is limited and any means of accessing and sourcing copies of current or past issues are often ambiguous or obscured. These small publications are sometimes mentioned on portals such as Nacjonlista.pl., referred to earlier, but access to them is unambiguously reserved to far-right supporters who already participate in

---

6 | There are, of course, exceptions, and a sub-phenomenon of far-right e-zines also exists in Poland. Published and distributed exclusively online, these publications however, are rare and a not representative of the broader far-right zine phenomenon today.

far-right networks. They are often made available during football match-es, right-wing marches, and dedicated far-right gatherings. This relative invisibility to any general public is a conscious choice made by the far-right zine publishers and not a failure on their part. It is an important manifestation of the role the medium itself plays among the communities it speaks to.

This is not to say that right-wing zine communities are invisible online. A lot of contemporary far-right zines develop out of or are published along-side a website or a forum. The football fan zine, *Droga Legionisty*, supported by a prominent online platform is a good example. But the content pub-lished in zines tends to be unique to their pages and is rarely made avail-able via online channels. This turn to self-publishing in print in the context of the far-right's active online presence is key to developing a characteristic aesthetic and discourse; it allows for an unfiltered conversation about ideas that would be considered controversial at best in the mainstream. The lim-ited nature of zine circulation, then, creates a space for the use of more extreme ideas, language, and imagery, unconstrained by the norms and standards that still dictate the mainstream's boundaries, even if the Polish mainstream, especially when it comes to publicly owned media, is heavily controlled and manipulated by today's right-wing government.

Open declarations of antisemitism, the promotion of racism as a cen-tral value, and a commitment to white supremacy are common on the pages of far-right zines. While the same ideals and beliefs are central to on-line communications by far-right groups, their expressions tend to differ. What is published online and made widely accessible, like the Blood and Honour lists mentioned above, is often a provocation, a trigger for greater visibility on a wider scale, inside and outside of right-wing circles. The turn to zines among the far right serves the opposite role. This distinction between the use of print and digital as far-right spaces of communication is particularly interesting as it reverses the logic of publishing today. The seemingly unfiltered digital sphere becomes, for these groups, the space of relative (self)censorship; whereas publishing in print, in small print runs, and outside of mainstream circulation, serves as a space to manifest open and unconstrained expressions of the ideology they support. This move away from the digital is devoid of the kind of retro-nostalgia that often characterizes contemporary zine publishing. Nor does it appear to be informed by the new commitment to 'making' so central to the zine communities. Rather, the materiality of the form, and its characteristic amateur status, is primarily utilitarian in far-right contexts. It offers a means of communicating somewhat under the radar within the growing far-right community, and it carries connotation of a struggle against the repression of free speech or radical ideas. Hidden in plain sight, far-right zines are a powerful tool exactly because of their limited reach. Their proliferation is one manifestation of a community growing in strength, yet their constrained, underground circulation makes any form of response to them significantly more difficult.

While independent media and organizations report an alarming rise of far-right activity in Poland, the most recent report on national security published by the Ministry of the Interior in 2017 (i.e. after the election of the current, conservative government) under the directorship of Mariusz Błaszczak describes the activities of the far right as limited and broadly unthreatening.[7] A new risk, according to the report, is posed by the "radical left-wing pro-Islamists". However, this apparent left-wing radicalism, i.e. the activities of groups who support refugees and oppose the anti-immigration sentiment of the current government, is not flagged up in the report as a threat in and of itself. It is instead identified as a problem because of its potential to provoke the anti-refugee far right, the same far right that the report claims not to be a problem; the same far right for whom Poland is fast becoming a new international cradle.

REFERENCES

Atton, Chris (2001): Alternative Media, London: Sage.

Chszczonowicz, Magdalena (2017): "Błaszczak: Wszyscy Mogli Manifestować, Było 'Bezpiecznie' i 'Pięknie'. Zapomniał o Manifestantach Wynoszonych do 'Suk', Znieważanych, Poturbowanych", 11 November 2017 (https://oko.press/blaszczak-wszyscy-mogli-manifestowac-bezpiecznie-pieknie-zapomnial-o-kontrmanifestantach-wynoszonych-suk-zniewazanych-poturbowanych/).

Ciosmak, Dariusz (2001): Antologia Zinow 1989-2001, Kielce: Wydawnictwo Liberation.

---

7 | Ministerstwo Spraw Wewnętrznych (2017): "Raport o Stanie Bezpieczenstwa w Polsce w 2016", (https://bip.mswia.gov.pl/bip/raport-o-stanie-bezpie/18405, Raport-o-stanie-bezpieczenstwa.html).

Doucette, Siobahn (2018): Books are Weapons: The Polish Opposition Press and the Overthrow of Communism, Pittsburgh: University of Pittsburgh.

Dulkowski, Konrad (2017): "Nawet sto Ataków na Obcokrajowców Dziennie – Tak w PolsceKkwitnie Ksenofobia", 29 June 2017 (https://www.polityka.pl/tygodnikpolityka/spoleczenstwo/1710550,1,nawet-sto-atakow-na obcokrajowcow-dziennie--tak-w-polsce-kwitnie-ksenofobia.read).

Duncombe, Stephen (2008): Notes from the Underground: Zines and the Politics of Alternative Culture, Cleveland: Microcosm Publishing.

Dunin-Wąsowicz, Paweł/Varga, Krzysztof (1995): "Trzeci Obieg." In: Dunin-Wąsowicz, Paweł, Varga, Krzysztof, Parnas Bis – Słownik Literatury Polskiej Urodzonej po 1960 Roku, Warsaw: Lampa i Iskra Boża, p. 228.

Eichhorn, Kate (2016): Adjusted Margins: Xerography, Art and Activism in the Late Twentieth Century, Cambridge: MIT Press.

Fearon. James D (2003): "Ethnic and Cultural Diversity by Country." In: Journal of Economic Growth 8/2, pp. 195–222.

Flont, Mateusz (2018): "(Anty)estetyka Wizualna Polskich Zinów. Część II: 'Obieg Alternatywny' w Latach 90". In: Wszołek Mariusz/Grech, Michał/Siemes, Anette (eds.), Badanie Komunikacji, Wrocław: Libron, pp. 155–175.

Kajtoch, Wojciech (2006): "Fanzin". In: Pisarek, Walery (ed.), Słownik Terminologii Medialnej, Kraków: Universitas, pp. 55–56.

Pęczak. Mirosław (1988): "Kilka Uwag o Trzech Obiegach." In: Więź 352/2, pp. 25–35.

Płatek, Daniel (2015): "Instutucjonalizacja Skrajnej Prawicy w Polsce", (https://pl.boell.org/sites/default/files/uploads/2015/12/polityka_ protestu_polska_platek_0.pdf).

Polaczek, Marta (2016): "Neofaszyzm w Polsce – Geneza, Characterystyka I Zagrozenia", 11 April 2016 (http://krytyka.org/neofaszyzm-w-polsce-geneza-charakterystyka-i-zagrozenia/).

Sławiński, Janusz (2000): "Trzeci Obieg." In: Głowiński, Michał, Sławiński, Janusz, Kostkiewiczowa, Teresa. (eds.), Słownik terminów literackich, Wrocław: Ossolineum, p. 593.

Słupik, Tomasz (2009): "Cztery fale modernizacji w Polsce." In: Barański, Marek (ed.), Modernizacja polityczna w teorii i praktyce, Katowice: Śląsk Wydawnictwo Naukowe, p. 319–327.

Unmasking

What Makes a Symbol Far Right?

Co-opted and Missed Meanings in Far-Right Iconography

Cynthia Miller-Idriss

"Many right-wing extremists don't understand their own T-shirts", a VICE-Germany headline proclaimed in March 2018 (Vorreyer 2018), summarizing research I had conducted with youth in and around far-right scenes about the meaning of far-right symbols, codes, and iconography (Miller-Idriss 2018). I had found that German young people do not always correctly interpret the messages in symbols on T-shirts marketed to and by the far-right – even when those codes are on brands that those same youths know are banned from their schools because of their far-right ideological connections.

As I was writing up the findings about the German case, across the Atlantic a cartoon character with no relationship whatsoever to the far right, Pepe the Frog, suddenly became co-opted by the emerging Alt-Right[1] – in part through a series of memes depicting Pepe with a Hitler-style mustache, in a KKK hood and robe, and wearing a Nazi uniform, among other caricatured links (Roy 2016). Within a year, the connection between Pepe the Frog and the US far right was so strong that Hillary Clinton

---

1 | The phrase Alt-Right is contested. Created by the modern US far right, it is criticized for the ways that it can soften or mask the extremist ideas of the varied groups that constitute it. Despite these concerns, the term carries a specific connotation to a unique development in the far-right scene in the US since 2015, which is distinct from older factions of the American far right such as the Ku Klux Klan and the Aryan Brotherhood. I have opted to deploy the term here but use single quotation marks around my first mention of the phrase to signal its contested nature.

denounced Pepe publicly, and the Anti-Defamation League added the cartoon character to their hate symbols database (Daniels 2018). These two examples reflect the complicated nature of far-right iconography and messaging in both offline and online spaces. Sometimes symbols are created and distributed with intentional messages that are not received as such – and other times, symbols with no deliberate messaging may be co-opted and marked as ideological in ways that were never intended. These developments challenge both our understanding of how far-right ideas spread and social scientists' understandings of symbology more generally. What happens to a symbol if its meaning is not understood, even by its own consumers? What happens when new meaning is assigned in ways that were never intended?

HOW DO SYMBOLS WORK?

Social scientists have long relied on the linguist Ferdinand de Saussure to help understand how symbols and signs work to construct and convey meaning. De Saussure's work in the field of linguistics separated signs into two parts: the concept (signified) and the sound-image (signifier). Crucially, de Saussure argued that the relationship between concept and image is arbitrary: there is no logical reason why the word 'sister', he explains, is linked to the concept of a sister. However, he argued that symbols were different in this regard:

"One characteristic of a symbol is that it is never wholly arbitrary; it is not empty, for there is the rudiment of a natural bond between the signifier and the signified. The symbol of justice, a pair of scales, could not be replaced by just any other symbol, such as a chariot" (de Saussure 2017[1966]: 120).

If de Saussure is right, then far-right symbols should be logically connected to, and understood as, far-right concepts or ideas. But in fact, as this essay will show, that is no longer clearly the case. The rapid evolution of symbols in online spaces offers a specific challenge to de Saussure's argument about symbols, while the 'missed messages' in coded clothing iconography raises additional questions about how symbols work and whether their power holds even when those who display them do not understand them.

ICONOGRAPHY AND THE FAR RIGHT

In the following sections, I outline three ways in which symbols and iconography are deployed in far-right clothing and products: brands created by or for far-right consumers, in products deliberately laced with far-right symbols and codes; brands, logos, images and symbols that at their origins have no relationship to the far right, but become co-opted as far-right symbols; and brands and products which deliberately or accidentally deploy far-right symbols and codes, either through attempts to draw media attention, or through ignorance and coincidence. Each of these three cases also illustrates the ways in which online and offline iconographies interact with one another as images, memes, symbols and iconography circulate in both domains.

Madagascar T-shirts: Brands Marketing to the Far Right

The first category of iconography appears in brands created by or for the far right. This is a relatively recent European innovation – the first high-quality, commercial brand marketing products to far-right consumers was Thor Steinar, a German brand which burst onto the scene with a slick mail-order catalog in 2002, but quickly developed physical stores and a sophisticated online presence with a website offering international currency conversion and translation (Miller-Idriss 2018). Other brands rapidly followed in Thor Steinar's footsteps, marketing T-shirts, hoodies and other clothing products coded with messages and iconography that directly invoked or indirectly evoked the Nazi and colonial era, Norse mythology, the Christian crusades, and other contemporary and historical anti-immigrant and Islamophobic references.

Some of the references in these brands are quite arcane, drawing on historical allusions that are rarely understood by consumers or observers. For example, the brand Erik & Sons sells a T-shirt depicting a passenger ship with the phrase "Sweet Home Madagascar". Madagascar was discussed as an original Nazi 'final solution' – an island to which European Jews could be deported – before concentration camp gas chambers were constructed (Herf 2006: 146–47; Miller-Idriss 2018: 62). But when I showed an image of this T-shirt to 51 students as part of a series of far-right symbols and images during interviews in 2013-14, only three of them understood the historical reference. Four respondents understood a similarly obscure historical reference in a T-shirt depicting the 'Expedition Tibet', which refers to the National Socialists' *Schutzstaffel* (SS) expeditions to Tibet that were part of the broader *Ahnenerbe* (ancestral heritage) movement to research the Indo-Germanic roots of the Aryan 'race' (Reitzenstein 2014). But even then, one of those students' responses was an educated guess about the Nazi origins of this code, based on other contextual clues in the image, including the old German script and the use of the word 'expedition' – rather than a response that indicated understanding of the meaning behind the 'Expedition Tibet' reference (Miller-Idriss 2018).

Pepe the Frog: Co-opted Symbols

The second category refers to brands and symbols that are appropriated from non-far-right contexts and infused with far-right messages and meanings. In some cases, it is simply some coincidental symbolic resonance of their logos that leads to assimilation by the far right. Thus the 'N' in New Balance sneakers signified 'neo-Nazi' for a generation of racist skinheads in Germany in the 1980s and 1990s, while the American military-style bomber jacket produced by Alpha Industries was co-opted in the same period because the Alpha Industries logo is similar in appearance to a civil badge used to denote the Nazi *Sturmabteilung* (SA). German neo-Nazis wear the sporty British brand Lonsdale because when displayed under a half-zipped bomber jacket, the letters NSDA are visible – the first four letters of the Nazi party's initials, NSDAP (Miller-Idriss 2018). Other symbols, images, or brands are favored because they are perceived as aligning with radical right ideologies in some way. In the US, a well-known far-right website named the pizza company Papa John's the "'official pizza' of the Alt-Right" due to the CEO's donations to the Trump campaign as well as statements and positions that many viewed as aligned with Alt-Right ideologies (Maza 2017).

But still other symbols have been appropriated with little explanation at all. The evolution of Pepe the Frog is a perfect example, and also illustrates how seamlessly online and offline iconographies are interacting with one another as a means through which symbols spread and evolve. Originally created by cartoonist Matt Furie for the comic *Boy's Life*, Pepe's original character was an affable if crass frog whose antics revolved around life with his three roommates and the pranks that characterized their everyday interactions. Furie originally produced the character in paper form, in zines that he printed himself at a local copy shop and distributed (Serwer 2016). Eventually, Pepe made his way to online spaces, and sometime in 2015, the nascent Alt-Right decided to "remake Pepe" as a "white nationalist icon" (Daniels 2018: 64). Memes began to circulate on sites like 4chan and Reddit that adapted Pepe the Frog in varied right-wing extremist ways – dressed as a Nazi, spouting racist and antisemitic vitriol, and in images accompanied by far-right figures (Serwer 2016).

Pepe's popularity with the far right was not only due to the iconographic representation of the frog with Nazi and far-right symbols but also because of the way the frog symbolized a kind of superior nonchalance toward others, helping to normalize hostile attitudes toward minorities and political opponents. Part of the growing use of memes as "emblematic representations of words and images" that act as "short-hand tools for political communication online" (Önnerfors 2018), the Pepe meme communicated both far-right ideological positions and a kind of anti-elite arrogance and condescension. By the time a meme of Pepe as Donald Trump was re-tweeted by the Trump campaign during the 2016 election (Sanders 2017), Pepe the Frog had become a clear symbol of the Alt-Right, not only through online memes but also through the use of the cartoon character in emojis, pins, patches and more. In the autumn of 2016, the Anti-Defamation League added the cartoon character to its online database of hate symbols.[2] Then things got even stranger, as *Washington City Paper* reporter Baynard Woods concisely explains:

"At the same time as the far-right elements on message boards began to adopt Pepe, they also began using the letters KEK instead of LOL to indicate online laughter. Then, when they noticed that there was an Egyptian god named Kek, which was depicted as a frog-headed man, these guys – and they are decidedly guys – had a mythology and a god. ...To go along with their new half-ironic religion, they created a purely digital (and imaginary) country called Kekistan and after the election they made Trump their God-Emperor. And they started getting flags made" (Woods 2017).

---

2 | Anti-Defamation League (2016): ADL Adds "Pepe the Frog" Meme, Used by Anti-Semites and Racists, to Online Hate Symbols Database, 27 September 2016 (https://www.adl.org/news/press-releases/adl-adds-pepe-the-frog-meme-used-by-anti-semites-and-racists-to-online-hate).

In this way, a "prank with a big attention payoff" (Daniels 2018: 64) – the appropriation of a cartoon character designed for a homemade magazine – evolved into a widely circulated series of far-right memes in online spaces, inspired a fantasy mythological far right 'nation', and led to the production of physical flags that began to appear at Alt-Right rallies in offline spaces (Neiwert 2017). In 2018, cartoonist Matt Furie, Pepe's creator, filed a lawsuit against the US right-wing media platform Infowars, charging copyright infringement (Sommerlad 2018), which is ongoing at the time of writing.

Pepe is an extraordinary case, but there are other examples where elements from the offline world are co-opted, infused with new meaning, and circulated online for and by the far right. The appropriation of the tiny Swedish industrial town of Finspång into a fantasy far-right 'execution meme' is one such case. Sometime in mid-2017, as Andreas Önnerfors (2018) explains, a far-right website posted a meme of two people dressed in protective clothing and gas masks entering through a doorway leading to a 'white reservation' named Finspång, described as a place established to protect the 'biological exceptionalism' of white Swedes. Subsequent images and text depicted a polluted, collapsed 'multi-cultural Sweden' outside the walls of Finspång, in contrast to the 'clean' and 'free' white reservation. In this future fantastical world, tribunals in Finspång will lead to executions of 'traitors of the people' in street-lamp hangings lining the roadways. The real town of Finspång was thus appropriated into a meme of a fictional place where national traitors would be executed under a future fascist regime. This evolved into a broader Finspång meme used to convey various far-right ideological positions and threats against groups and individuals through the phrase "See you in Finspång" alongside images of hangings, echoing German far-right extremists who use the phrase "See you in Walhalla", the mythical hall of the dead in Norse mythology. The meme moved out of niche far-right subcultures into more mainstream usage, as Önnerfors describes in greater depth, when it was deployed by the leaders of a right-wing alternative news site that reaches 8% of Swedish news readership (Önnerfors 2018). In this way, a real place rooted in the offline world became a fantastical place in online spaces and was infused with far-right meanings.

Deliberately or Cluelessly Offensive

The third category refers to brands which deploy far-right or related iconography either unintentionally or as part of a strategy to draw attention or be 'edgy'. The clearest example in this category is the so-called 'Nazi' logo adopted by the fashion label Boy London, whose trademark logo depicts the Imperial Eagle deployed in the Nazi eagle symbol, except instead of holding a wreath with a swastika in its talons, the eagle is holding the "O" in the word "BOY". As journalist Sandy Rashty reported in 2014, a representative from the brand rejected the association to Nazism, arguing that the logo was "inspired by the eagle of the Roman Empire as a sign of decadence and strength. Its aim is to empower people rather than oppress". Retailers pulled the brand off shelves anyway (Rashty 2014).

BOY London logo on a Sweatshirt. Photo by Ranim Helwani from Drensteinfurt, Germany.

The US store Urban Outfitters has repeatedly produced and then pulled offensive products from its shelves too, including some with far-right references, like a yellow T-shirt with a nearly-identical star to the six-pointed star badge that Jews were forced to wear under the Nazis (Chakelian 2012) and a gray-and-white striped tapestry with a pink triangle which was strikingly similar to the uniforms gay men were forced to wear in Nazi concentration camps (Sieczkowski 2015). Other offensive products included a blood-red-spattered Kent State university sweatshirt (in reference to the

1970 shooting of unarmed college students by the Ohio National Guard) (Ohlheiser 2014). In each case, the brand issued an apology, but the frequency of the incidents has led to speculation that the offense is an intentional public relations strategy (Haruch 2014; Wang 2014).

Online spaces are largely responsible for the ways in which public outrage builds in reaction to such products. Both the fast-food hamburger chain Wendy's and the Spanish clothing chain Zara have issued public apologies after customers shared social media images linking their logos or products to Pepe the Frog. Wendy's was celebrated by the Alt-Right after a company representative tweeted a meme of Pepe-as-Wendy on the company's social media account; the company's official response was to plead ignorance, noting that the employee who had sent the tweet was "unaware of the recent evolution of the Pepe meme's meaning" (Maza 2017). In 2017, Zara pulled a denim skirt with a patch depicting a Pepe-like cartoon from both its "real and virtual shelves" (Serwer 2016) after a customer tweeted an image of the skirt. Like Urban Outfitters, this wasn't Zara's first offense; the company had previously apologized for selling a shirt similar to a concentration camp prisoner's uniform and pulled a purse it had sold with embroidered swastikas on it (Raab 2014; Roy 2017).

DISCUSSION: MISSED MESSAGES OR MIXED MESSAGES?

What does the simultaneous circulation of three separate categories of far-right symbols in online and offline spaces – intentionally-coded, co-opted, and deliberately-or-coincidentally offensive – mean for the way we understand the meaning and messaging of far-right symbols? There are several lessons.

First, the supposedly non-arbitrary nature of symbols that de Saussure pointed to has been clearly disrupted in the case of far-right symbols. While this process may well have started before the digital age, it is clear that online platforms and communities through sites like 4chan and Reddit have accelerated it. In many cases, it is the rapid and 'viral' spread of online memes and messages that has shifted the linear relationship between symbol and meaning to one characterized by more random associations. There is no clear reason why Pepe the Frog or the Swedish town of Finspång should become far-right symbols, for example, and their rapid evolution as such defies explanation through traditional theories about how symbols work.

Second, these categories illustrate how the global nature of the internet itself has helped disrupt the logical or linear association between symbols and their intended meanings. On the one hand, online communities contribute to the rapid and global spread of far-right symbols, enabling icons and symbols from nationalist resistance movements from one particular geography to be claimed and appropriated by social and political movements in different locations, for example. As I have argued in greater depth elsewhere (Miller-Idriss 2018), the use of global codes and references is ubiquitous in far-right scenes and subcultures, and the very nature of online sharing has helped facilitate that usage. But online communities have also helped create completely new symbols that would be hard to imagine in the absence of online far-right culture. It is hard to imagine neo-Nazis raising a flag representing the fantasy nation of Kekistan – or embedding frogs on those flags – a decade ago. Online communities are primarily responsible for the rapid creation, evolution, appropriation, and circulation of far-right memes in the contemporary era, even when they later appear in offline spaces too.

The online nature of consumer goods laced with far-right messages has also affected the reception of messages. While previous iterations of commercialized goods – such as T-shirts and hoodies with far-right symbols or slogans – were sold on folding tables at concerts or in physical storefronts – most of today's commercial products marketed to far-right youth are sold through commercial websites and distributers. This reduces the likelihood of a conversation between consumer and salesperson, in which the meaning of particular symbols or messages might be discussed. Although some products are accompanied by website text that explains the meaning, this is not the case for all products, particularly those which rely on references to the Nazi era. These historical symbols and messages were not often understood by youths in my interviews (Miller-Idriss 2018).

Finally, it is also important to think about how online spaces might build online and offline community in new and different ways around consumer goods and symbols. Some brands marketing to far-right youths maintain their own Twitter feeds, Facebook and Tumblr pages, and Instagram accounts. Those pages then become a constantly-updating feed of posts from 'friends' and others who share information, update followers on new products, and issue announcements about political actions, events, rallies, and festivals that take place in offline spaces.

Counter-Practices and 'Styles' of Resistance

The same viral nature of online spaces that led to Pepe the Frog's rapid adaptation into a white nationalist icon also provides the means for the rapid development of public outrage and protest. Viral tweets of offensive products and symbols generate anger as consumers and observers share photos and videos on social media, often tagging brand representatives and CEOs in ways that force a more rapid response from companies than might have been the case through traditional media reporting. There have also been some viral efforts to combat the use of coded and co-opted symbols by the far right. For example, in 2016 the Alt-Right began using triple-parentheses 'echo' symbols around Jewish names online (aided by the use of an automated Chrome extension, which was removed by Google) – supposedly to signify the 'echo' or reverberating effect of Jewish people across generations. Both Jews and non-Jews aiming to show solidarity quickly began to claim the echo symbol directly, placing ((( ))) around their names on Twitter and other social media sites (Hern 2016), effectively taking the antisemitic purpose of the symbol away.

In Germany, a strong counter-protest culture has begun to deploy creative tactics to protest the far right in ways that co-opt or transform far- right symbols for the left. The de-radicalization group EXIT-Germany produced a 'trick' T-shirt in 2011, for example; the T-shirt had iconography which imitated typical far-right symbols and styles, and was distributed for free at a far-right concert. Once washed, however, the T-shirts revealed messaging and a telephone number to encourage people to seek help if they want to leave far-right extremism.[3] Elsewhere, an antifascist group called Endstation Rechts created a parody of the brand Thor Steinar with a stork mascot called 'Stork Heinar' – a play on the brand name – and sells umbrellas, T-shirts, accessories and more, all adorned with the stork logo (Miller-Idriss 2018: 191).

---

3 | BBC News (2011): "Trojan T-shirt targets German right-wing rock fans", 9 August 2011 (https://www.bbc.co.uk/news/world-europe-14465150).

More research is needed in order to paint a fuller picture of the ways in which counter-protesters and resisters to the far right deploy similar or different kinds of tactics around iconography and symbols. There are also important distinctions across symbols according to their relative permanent or ephemeral nature that merit further study. Symbols that require bodily modification, like tattoos or shaved heads, likely require deeper kinds of ideological commitments than symbols on T-shirts that can be taken on and taken off. Online memes are more ephemeral still and might even be shared anonymously, enabling the most experimental or playful engagements with far-right ideas in ways that could act as a gateway to later, stronger commitments. More empirical research and analysis is needed to disentangle variations in the utility of symbols in offline and online spaces for insider and outsider recognition, communication of far-right messages, and the degree of commitment they require to far-right ideas. What is clear, however, is that symbols and iconography move between online and offline spaces as they are deployed and co-opted by the far right in ways that deserve our close attention. Whether meanings are missed, co-opted, or cluelessly offensive, far-right symbols have rapidly evolved. The visual nature of online spaces might suggest that their use will only accelerate in the years to come.

REFERENCES

Chakelian, Anoosh (2012): "Urban Outfitters Under Fire over 'Holocaust T-Shirt'", 23 April 2012 (http://newsfeed.time.com/2012/04/23/urban-outfitters-under-fire-over-holocaust-t-shirt/#ixzz1to1q2p0N).

Daniels, Jessie (2018): The Algorithmic Rise of the 'Alt Right'. In: Contexts 17/1, pp. 60–65.

De Saussure, Ferdinand (2017) [1966]: "Arbitrary Social Values and the Linguistic Sign." In: Lemer, Charles (eds), Social Theory: The Multicultural, Global, and Classic Readings, Philadelphia: Westview Press, pp. 119–124.

Haruch, Steve (2014): "Is Courting Controversy an Urban Outfitters Strategy?", 16 December 2014 (https://www.npr.org/sections/codeswitch/2014/12/16/370329870/is-courting-controversy-an-urban-outfitters-strategy?t=1534549133280).

Herf, Jeffrey (2006): The Jewish Enemy: Nazi Propaganda During World War II and the Holocaust, Cambridge: The Belknap Press of Harvard University Press.

Hern, Alex (2016): "Antisemitism Watchdog Adds ((((Echo))) Symbol to Hate lLst after Jews Targeted", 7 June 2016 (https://www.theguardian.com/technology/2016/jun/07/us-antisemitism-anti-defamation-league-echo-hate-symbol-chrome).

Maza, Cristina (2017): "Why Neo-Nazis Love Papa John's Pizza- and Other 'Official' Alt-Right Companies", 10 November 2017 (https://www.newsweek.com/white-supremacists-nazis-Alt-Right-pizza-papa-johns-taylor-swift-wendys-brands-708722).

Miller-Idriss, Cynthia (2018): The Extreme Gone Mainstream: Commercialization and Far Right Youth Culture in Germany, Princeton: Princeton University Press.

Neiwert, David (2017): "What the Kek: Explaining the Alt-Right 'Deity' Behind their 'Meme Magic'", 8 May 2017 (https://www.splcenter.org/hatewatch/2017/05/08/what-kek-explaining-Alt-Right-deity-behind-their-meme-magic).

Ohlheiser, Abby (2014): "Urban Outfitters Apologizes for its Blood-Red-Stained Kent State Sweatshirt", 15 September 2014 (https://www.washingtonpost.com/news/morning-mix/wp/2014/09/15/urban-outfitters-red-stained-vintage-kent-state-sweatshirt-is-not-a-smart-look-this-fall/?nore direct=on&utm_term=.18ab68ac6fcb).

Önnerfors, Andreas (2018): "'Finspång' – An Execution Meme of the Swedish Radical Right Ignites the Political Discourse", 6 July 2018 (https://www.radicalrightanalysis.com/2018/07/06/finspang-an-execution-meme-of-the-swedish-radical-right-ignites-the-political-discourse/).

Raab, Lauren (2014): "Zara Apologizes, Stops Selling Shirt Likened to Holocaust Uniform", 27 August 2014 (www.latimes.com/fashion/.../la-ar-zara-sheriff-holocaust-shirt-20140827-story.html).

Rashty, Sandy (2014): "Boy London Fashion Brand Rejects Concern over 'Nazi' Logo", 5 March 2014 (https://www.thejc.com/news/uk-news/boy-london-fashion-brand-rejects-concern-over-nazi-logo-1.52822).

Reitzenstein, Julian (2014): Himmlers Forscher: Wehrwissenschaft und Medizinverbrechen im 'Ahnenerbe' der SS, Paderborn: Ferdinand Schöningh.

Roy, Jessica (2017): "Zara Pulls Denim Skirt after 'Pepe the Frog' Accusations", 19 April 2017 (www.latimes.com/business/la-fi-zara-skirt-pepe-frog-20170419-story.html).

Roy, Jessica (2016): "How 'Pepe the Frog' Went from Harmless to Hate Symbol", 11 October 2016 (www.latimes.com/politics/la-na-pol-pepe-the-frog-hate-symbol-20161011-snap-htmlstory.html).

Sanders, Sam (2017): "What Pepe the Frog's Death Can Teach us About the Internet", 11 May 2017 (https://www.npr.org/sections/alltechcon sidered/2017/05/11/527590762/what-pepe-the-frogs-death-can-teach-us-about-the-internet).

Serwer, Adam (2016): "It's Not Easy Being Meme", 13 September 2016 (https://www.theatlantic.com/politics/archive/2016/09/its-not-easy-being-green/499892/).

Sieczkowski, Cavan (2015): "Urban Outfitters Under Fire for Selling Tapestry Reminiscent of Uniforms Worn by Gay Nazi Prisoners", 2 October 2015 (https://www.huffingtonpost.com/2015/02/10/urban-outfit ters-tapestry-gay-prisoner-uniforms_n_6652934.html?guccounter=1).

Sommerlad, Joe (2018): "Pepe the Frog Creator Sues Infowars for Breach of Copyright", 7 March 2018 (https://www.independent.co.uk/life-style/ gadgets-and-tech/news/pepe-the-frog-infowars-copyright-lawsuit-Alt-Right-alex-jones-matt-furie-white-supremacists-neo-a8244001.html).

Vorreyer, Thomas (2018): "Viele Rechtsextreme verstehen ihre eigenen T-shirts nicht, sagt diese US-Soziologin", 28 February 2018 (https:// www.vice.com/de/article/59k4m5/viele-rechtsextreme-verstehen-ihre-eigenen-t-shirts-nicht-sagt-diese-us-soziologin).

Wang, Connie (2014): "Is Urban Outfitters Offending People on Purpose?", 16 December 2014 (https://www.refinery29.com/2014/12/79562/ur ban-outfitters-controversy).

Woods, Baynard (2017): "Where the Hell is Kekistan? How Pepe-posting Meme Warriors Responded to Real Violence of the Alt-Right", 27 September 2017 (www.citypaper.com%2Fnews%2Fdic%2Fbcp-092717-dic-kekistan-20170926-story.html&usg=AOvVaw18r9OndM5aquQvEkbs 8GOQ).

"Do You Want Meme War?"

Understanding the Visual Memes of the German Far Right

Lisa Bogerts and Maik Fielitz[1]

"People respond to images in a stronger way than to text. By using images, we can do excellent memetic warfare and bring our narratives to the people" (Generation D. 2017: 2).[2] Commenting on "the power of images", in 2017, German far-right activists widely circulated a "manual for media guerillas" that offered advice about how to effectively engage in online activism that would challenge the real world. Just a few months later, a far-right online activist under the pseudonym Nikolai Alexander initiated the project Reconquista Germanica (RG) and invited adherents to "reclaim" cyberspace. The Youtuber launched a mass project on the gaming forum Discord to invade the web with coordinated raids that would disseminate far-right propaganda. However, his ambitions went far beyond mere rhetoric: He assembled 'patriotic forces' to use RG as a place for convergence, attracting members and sympathizers of the far-right party Alternative for Germany (AfD), the German and Austrian sections of the Identitarian Movement and loosely organized neo-Nazis. He envisioned the largest far-right online network active in Germany, one willing to shake the pillars of liberal democracy and build a community that pushes far-right agendas. In just a few weeks, RG counted several thousand members who were ready to attack opponents, distort digital discourse and polarize online interactions. One of their central weapons: internet memes – graphics of visual and textual remixes shared and widely distributed in online spaces.

1 | Special thanks to Stephen Albrecht, Merle Strunk and Philip Wallmeier for their thoughts on this contribution.

2 | All German quotations were translated by the authors.

Just a lousy joke by some kids, one might think. How could a troll army without any real-world interaction seriously engage in collective action? Some years ago, these virtual communities were irrelevant for researchers on far-right extremism. Only recently has the online space entered the research agenda as a venue of antagonistic politics and "cultural wars" (Nagle 2017). For some time, the far right has explored the internet as a hub for mobilization, propaganda and cultural subversion (Caiani/Kröll 2015). With the general expansion of online communication into all spheres of life, the internet has become a natural medium and catalyst space for far-right propaganda, making digital space a central site for the current resurgence of far-right influence.

If far-right groups, just like other political actors, utilize cultural means to win the hearts and minds of potential adherents, we must go beyond purely cognitive accounts to also examine affective and aesthetic means. While ideology is often projected onto images, no doubt, political actors also employ images strategically in order to disseminate their ideology in more or less subtle ways and to persuade others to share or reject certain views and values (Sturken/Cartwright 2001: 21). Drawing on methodological tools from visual culture studies, this essay highlights the importance of taking visual memes seriously instead of reducing them to a merely illustrative role. Although, at first sight, memes seem to be humorous, sometimes silly and absurd – but in any case, harmless – everyday expressions of online cultural creativity, they can still convey hate messages, attract new supporters and give rise to bigotry. In fact, we can barely understand recent far-right cultures without taking into account the diverse messages that memes disseminate.

While there is plenty of reflection on the spread of memes in the broader digital world, this essay focuses on the strategic use of visual meme content by far-right entrepreneurs, asking: What visual language, narratives and strategies do RG memes employ to appeal a broad spectrum of potential supporters? Taking the case of RG, we want to expand the debate on far-right efforts to co-opt online cultures as a gateway to express different hate messages and mobilize supporters.

VISUAL CULTURE AND MEMES IN FAR-RIGHT MOVEMENTS

Emphasizing the political power of everyday images and popular culture, visual culture assumes that everyday images inform how we *see* the world, and thus literally shape our world*views* (Sturken/Cartwright 2001: 10). The world of entertainment, everyday images and popular culture are loaded with political interests and more or less subtle ideological assumptions (Hall 1993). Therefore, Fahlenbrach et al. argue that critical visual research must disclose key visual narratives of memes by both anonymous and visible activists as part of the public discourse (Fahlenbrach et al. 2014: 210).[3]

Engaging with visual online memes is a participatory practice of interjecting cultural information and normative narratives within ideological conflicts, which may "shape the mindsets and significant forms of behavior and action of a social group" (Knobel/Lankshear 2007: 199; see also Hristova 2014: 265; Nooney/Portwood-Stacer 2014: 248). Employing humor and rich intertextuality, online memes can be spread fast, anonymously and efficiently. Concerning the affective potential of humor and joy in social movements, an associate of the internet activist collective Anonymous claimed: "[...] boredom is counterrevolutionary. Political resistance needs to be fun, or no one will want to participate" (cited in Ferrada Stoehrel/Lindgren 2014: 252). Due to their participatory incitement, "memes appear to be democratic in their widespread use and mutation as they survive and grow through participation, while they remain structurally autocratic in their conservation of a key idea" (Hristova 2014: 266).

The possibility of conserving and disseminating key messages while displaying creativity 'from below' may render online memes an especially attractive medium for far-right entrepreneurs. Memes take to a digital level the New Right's effort to appropriate Antonio Gramsci's idea of the struggle over cultural hegemony – i.e. the production of consenting ideas in civil society – what they call meta-politics (Bar-On 2013). Along with the increasing significance of social media, the web may be considered a metapolitical terrain for the reshaping of public opinion. Likewise, far-right activists in Europe, as Nicole Doerr argues, strategically use "[...] visual or symbolic media provocation that speaks to multiple audiences"

---

3 | For research on memes from a visual culture perspective, see the 2014 special issue of the Journal of Visual Culture (Nooney/Portwood-Stacer 2014).

(Doerr 2017: 4). Reconquista Germany aimed to become a central actor in this battle over ideas and – overall – attention.

RECONQUISTA GERMANICA: JUST ANOTHER TROLL NETWORK?

Reconquista Germanica hit the headlines in the context of the German federal elections of 2017 by attempting to subvert online discourses, to intimidate supporters of democratic parties and to support the election of the AfD (Davey/Ebner 2017: 21). Formed in September 2017, RG can be described as a far-right network that organizes collective digital action against political opponents and pushes the agendas of far-right movements and parties in online space. Strongly inspired by the American Alt-Right, RG's interventions center around the common topics of ethno-nationalism, anti-Muslim racism, anti-Feminism and the rejection of immigration.

Using the online gaming platform Discord, far-right online activists converge to exchange on political beliefs and plan digital political actions. Before the deletion of their server in February 2018 by Discord, RG could assemble around 5000 members (Kampf 2018). However, metrics are hardly convincing in the digital world where even a few savvy activists can influence the discourse through fake accounts, bots and multiple identities (Kreißel et al. 2018). Usually there is no physical contact between the users. Every user acts under a pseudonym and is careful about sharing personal details.

Repeatedly, the group has described itself as a "satirical project that has no connection to the real world".[4] But this is not true. RG's aim is to provide a forum to "effectively connect and pool patriotic forces".[5] Unsurprisingly, we find a mosaic of the most important far-right parties and movements represented on the platform, such as the Identitarian Movement, the National Democratic Party of Germany (NPD) and the AfD. It is noteworthy

---

4 | Quotation retrieved from the welcoming text of the Reconquista Germanica Discord server discussed in the TV documentation "Lösch dich" (Delete yourself). See Anders, Rayk (2017): "Lösch Dich! So organisiert ist der Hate im Netz", 26 April 2018 (https://www.youtube.com/watch?v=zvKjfWSPl7s)
5 | Reconquista Germanica (2018): "Unsere Wunderwaffe im Kulturkampf", 17 June 2018 (https://www.bitchute.com/video/1ObHTNg73wOG/).

that RG endorses strong references to National Socialist ideology, the international far right and neo-Nazi community.[6] Hence, the appearance and language are strongly martial, misogynist and vulgar, while the organization follows a fixed hierarchy, centralized orders and military ranks. To climb up the ladder, one needs to prove commitment by joining organized raids when RG activists target social media platforms by attracting public attention through the seizure of hashtags or the massive spamming of the comment columns.

A VISUAL ANALYSIS OF FAR-RIGHT MEMES

In our empirical analysis we examined 110 publicly accessible images that had been uploaded to the RG meme gallery.[7] By using memes, RG focusses on a mélange of humor, misanthropy and political message. Accordingly, RG developed a meme factory in their internal forum that was open for users to copy and paste the content and spread their compositions on social media. The group even appointed a 'memelord' responsible for the dissemination of favorable memes, which shows how central memes are to their practice of online mobilization. On their official, publicly accessible website, RG provides a meme gallery that counts several hundred copy-paste images for visitors to freely use. While most are categorized around the preferential topics of the Alt-Right, such as *immigration*, *leftists*, *foreign politics* and the *media*, we find one category called *Reconquista* that strongly represents the self-understanding of the group.[8] For our empirical analysis, we have analyzed the different ways that content from this

---

6 | For instance, we took the title of this chapter from a meme in our database, that depicts the cartoon character Pepe the frog in Nazi uniform reminiscent to the infamous Sportpalast speech by Joseph Goebbels in 1943 invoking 'total war'. RG modified it into: "Do you want meme war?".

7 | While most of the images are so-called caption memes, the database also includes several GIFs (moving images). See http://reconquista-germanica.info/meme-galerie/reconquista/

8 | The content varies widely according to the categories and the much more aggressive imagery in categories, such as *immigration*, is likely to deliver interesting results as well. However, we decided not to reproduce these predominantly racist and violent images. It is noteworthy that *Reconquista* contains some of the most

category targets broader audiences and have deconstructed the aesthetic methods that are applied.

In order to identify common visual elements and narratives, we first conducted a visual content analysis (Bell 2004; Rose 2016) utilizing the software MAXQDA, and then examined the specific strategies of some representative images in more depth. By coding the images and counting the code frequencies, we shed light on which persons, objects, animals and symbols appear in the image files and how they are linked with each other. In another round of coding, taking into account the text elements as well, we identified nine key topics (*theme codes*) usually addressed by RG[9] as well as six stylistic and aesthetic features. The aesthetic styles include cartoons (used in 23 memes), 1980s vaporwave style (17), video game aesthetics (8) and hipsterish nature photography (5). Further, they often use historical image material (32) or refer to popular culture (24). In the following, with the help of representative image examples, we demonstrate how RG memes combine a variety of stylistic and aesthetic strategies and visual tools to appeal to multiple audiences, and still convey messages in line with their core ideological far-right beliefs. These memes represent "remixes" (Hartmann 2017) of the most frequently identified stylistic and aesthetic traits and are arranged according to RG members prime motive.[10]

---

professional images of the entire site. This shows how important it is for RG to generate some kind of group identification (through images and memes).

9 | Frequencies of key themes: Militarism (addressed in 58 images), nationalism (49), sympathy with National Socialism/fascism (27), ethnic and cultural supremacy (17), anti-system/anti-establishment (16), traditional values/nature and family (14), anti-leftism (13), patriarchic gender roles (11) and racism, Islamophobia and anti-Semitism (10). Additionally, we used the code "non-explicit/unclear" for images without a direct reference to any of these themes (17).

10 | Although, against the backdrop of our research question and the wider body of data, we provide only one of many possible interpretations, we are aware that image interpretation is highly subjective and varies according to the viewer's individual background and knowledge.

Cartoon Remixes

Numerous RG memes re-contextualize fictional characters from comics or cartoons and employ aesthetic styles associated with this media genre. Such references to popular culture include Pepe the frog (16), adopted from the US American Alt-Right (see Miller-Idriss in this volume), and figures from Japanese anime/manga culture, inter alia. A meme with the title *Captain Germanica* (figure 1)[11] depicts the Marvel superhero *Captain America*, who in 1941 was designed as a patriotic soldier with superhuman fighting abilities. Military uniforms (31) and male characters (51) are the two most frequent visual elements in our dataset. The heroic figure is here remixed with characteristics from the German context, such as the national flag (black-red-gold) (8) and the logo of the AfD (3), which consists of a red curving arrow

Figure 1: Cartoon remix. Text on the bullets: culture of guilt
("Schuldkult"), Islamism, liberalism, degeneration, communism and
political correctness.

---

11 | Source: http://reconquista-germanica.info/meme-galerie/reconquista/#!
http://reconquista-germanica.info/wp-content/uploads/2018/02/Captain-Ger
manica.jpg.

pointing towards the upper-right, symbolizing future and progress. Both the modification of "America" to "Germanica" (in old-German Fraktur script) and the RG logo on the shield leave no doubt that the group considers itself the defender (here: the shield) of the only political party (the AfD) it considers able to protect Germany against the 'threats' (the bullets) of liberalism, communism, Islamism and 'political correctness'. The bullet with *Schuldkult* (cult of guilt) indicates the common far-right rejection of acknowledging and memorializing Germany's guilt for the atrocities of the Nazi regime (Suermann 2016: 270). Borrowing the biological/medical term 'degeneration', the authors describe an alleged backward evolution of the human species, referring either to the political parliamentary system or to 'degenerated' gender roles in feminist or LGBTQI identities.

Tracing back the evolution of this meme, we see clearly that it was copied from a neo-Nazi meme creator. In this earlier version, there are swastikas instead of the German flag, the RG logo and the AfD logo, and another bullet is labelled with "jews".[12] No doubt, although the reversion of a popular and historical comic superhero may look humorous and creative at first sight, it reproduces far-right themes such as militarism, nationalism, and Islamophobia as well as anti-leftism and opposition to the political establishment.

Historical Remixes

As the *Captain America* example demonstrated, numerous memes make use of historical images with a focus on military battles, attributing them with a new meaning. In our dataset, such imagery includes WWII propaganda posters or black-and-white photos from the Nazi era (e.g., of heroic *Wehrmacht* soldiers or members of NS youth organizations) or paintings from art history (e.g., portraits of the German emperors Frederick the Great and Otto von Bismarck). Representing a historical version of militarism, swords (12) and knights (13) – mounted elite soldiers from the Late Middle-Age – are among the most frequent visual elements in the *Reconquista* meme gallery. The knight is a common role model in historical German iconography, providing a heroic figure of mystic identification with the Fatherland in a Christian nationalist mission (Krüger 2011: 98–100).

---

12 | https://www.deviantart.com/neetsfagging322297/art/Captain-America-Rebellion-poster-633861202.

More specifically, several memes depict knights with the Crusader's cross (a red cross on white grounds) (4), who defended the Mediterranean and the 'Holy Land' from Muslim rule in a series of religious wars.

Figure 2: Historical remix.

One of the memes (figure 2)[13] builds on a painting of the Battle of Montgisard (1177) by the artist Charles Philippe Larivière, in which King Baldwin IV defeated the Muslim sultan Saladin. A huge army of Crusaders descends from a castle, following two leaders with a sword and Christian crosses, while on the horizon, large clouds of smoke indicate an already ongoing battle. Combined with the dominant bold lettering *Reconquista Germanica* and the group's logo (49), this image illustrates one of RG's main narratives: reference to the so-called Reconquista (reconquest) of the Iberian Peninsula in the name of several Christian kingdoms between 722 and 1492. Many far-right groups, especially the Counter-Jihad network, play with this allegory and contemporize the crusade images to express anti-Muslim sentiments, claiming Islam to be incompatible with 'Christian' Europe. Claiming to 'defend Europe' against an alleged 'islamization of the occident' due to migration (Virchow 2016), RG aims to present itself as standing in the tradition of the Crusades and thus subtly reproduces Islamophobia. Understanding its activities as a contemporary crusade mis-

---

13 | Source: http://reconquista-germanica.info/meme-galerie/reconquista/ #!http://reconquista-germanica.info/wp-content/uploads/2018/03/reconquis ta3-1.png.

sion, it is no coincidence that RG's rune-like symbol[14] is a modification of the Greek letters Chi (χ) and Rho (ρ) of the Monogram of Christ, or that in other versions of the logo it also contains a sword. While historical 'sources' carry the authority of visual 'evidence' supporting their claims with a trans-historic legitimacy of a long tradition, the mix with more contemporaneous stylistic features gives the narrative a more 'youthful' appearance.

Vaporwave Remixes

Figure 3: Vaporwave Remix. Text: "The Future Belongs to Us."

In some of the memes, works from art history are combined with more contemporary aesthetic styles and a future-oriented narrative. For instance, Figure 3[15] mixes a famous painting with so-called vaporwave aesthetics

---

14 | Due to its similarity with the bluetooth logo, the German entertainer Jan Böhmermann mocked RG's symbol as indicating "a very bad bluetooth connection" when he launched his counter-campaign "Reconquista Internet" in April 2018 (https://www.youtube.com/watch?v=fAYjSLtz6wQ)

15 | Source: http://reconquista-germanica.info/meme-galerie/reconquista/ #!http://reconquista-germanica.info/wp-content/uploads/2018/02/Zukunft-geh%C3%B6rt-uns.jpg.

(see also figure 2). Many of RG's memes employ this retro style, which draws on technology, design, music, TV and video game culture from the 1980s by using neon colors (mainly pink and purple), chrome logo typography, blurred or pixelated images and grid optics.[16] These trendy visuals make historical references less 'old-fashioned' and more appealing to a younger audience and/or persons with an affinity to 80s popular culture. The artist of this recontextualized painting *Wanderer above the Sea of Fog* (ca. 1817), Caspar David Friedrich, is one of the most important painters of German Romanticism, who has been praised by the Nazis for his allegorical landscape paintings attributed with a nationalist message. Similar to his paintings, RG memes often depict romantic natural settings, such as sunsets or sunrises (8), with people seen from behind gazing towards the horizon (12). The composition of this image puts the viewer in the same perspective as the person depicted in the image, seeing – just like him – the Black Sun symbol (2) rising on the horizon. This occult Nazi symbol includes three swastikas superimposed upon each other and was inscribed in the SS headquarter *Wewelsburg*. It is often used as a substitute for swastikas, whose depiction is forbidden by German law. In the memes, *sympathy with National Socialism/fascism* is repeatedly expressed by such visual elements, *Wehrmacht* uniforms and the black-white-red flag of the German Empire (3), which was also used in the early days of Nazi government (1933–1935). The text "The future is ours" (Die Zukunft gehört uns) implies a 'we', promising the viewer that they to will become part of a strong and heroic community whose days are about to come.

---

16 | Arena (2016): The State of Vapor[Wave]: An Interview with Gran Turismo, 18 September (https://arena.com/article/the-state-of-vapor).

Nature Remixes

Figure 4: Nature Remix.

As another far-right theme, the memes frequently address *traditional values* regarding *nature and family*. These images commonly depict mountains (11), fields (2) and forests (10), focusing on landscape associated with Northern or Central Europe. In far-right imagery, nature represents "the majesty of the Fatherland" (Forchtner/Kølvraa 2017: 266), providing an idealized habitat for the German *Volksgemeinschaft*. Being the smallest cell of this supposedly genetic community, the ideal core family lives in harmony with nature, which is envisioned as being pure and safe from the decadent influences of urban spaces. One meme, for instance (figure 4),[17] depicts woodcutting as grounded, honest work in contrast to the money-grubbing workplaces of the cities. Notably, both the woman and the children of the 'natural family' are blonde and blue-eyed, symbolizing the

---

17 | Source: http://reconquista-germanica.info/meme-galerie/reconquista/
#!http://reconquista-germanica.info/wp-content/uploads/2018/02/15105222
71514.jpg.

'Aryan' prototype of an alleged Germanic heritage. This theme of *ethnic and cultural supremacy* is reinforced by the graphic element in the center of the collage. Symbolizing the reproduction of racial purity, the Othala rune is popular in neo-Nazi circles with blood-and-soil references. It was used by an SS mountain trooper unit in the Second World War and later referred to the neo-Nazi Viking Youth group that was banned in 1994.[18] It expresses a *völkisch* thinking, the idea that genetic heritage makes people "an organic unity, a true subject of history" (Forchtner/Kølvraa 2017: 255). While the beautiful woman in the upper-right wears a white, traditional dress, symbolizing purity, and seems to be responsible for the domestic realm, the man on the left upper-left side wears a contemporary military uniform, defending and protecting the idealized traditional lifestyle by using the latest means of ground warfare available. In terms of restrictive visual representations of *patriarchic gender roles*, the collage visually reproduces the binary opposition between active male (attributed with power and productive work) and passive female (attributed with beauty and reproductive work) (Mulvey 1999: 839), which John Berger famously described as "men act and women appear" (Berger 1972: 47).

However, it must be mentioned that not all of RG's memes employ misogynist stereotypes. Some also visualize women in strong fighting positions as well, probably to appeal to and integrate female supporters (Forchtner/Kølvraa 2017: 268). Regarding aesthetic style, the collage combines nature and family photography with the simplicity of modern graphic design, giving the meme an aura of what hipster culture idealizes as a nostalgic return to a simple and (self)sustainable lifestyle.

Conclusion

Throughout history, fascist mass movements have fascinated the people not only because of their charismatic leaders and policies, but also by their aestheticization of politics (Benjamin 2002). This wider cultural appeal is pursued by contemporary fascism as well (Miller-Idris 2018). Regarding the online imagery of the extreme right, Forchtner and Kølvraa argue that images serve as vehicles in the delivery of political identity (Forcht-

---

18 | Anti-Defamation League: "Othala Rune", (https://www.adl.org/education/references/hate-symbols/othala-rune).

ner/Kølvraa 2017: 262). Since the far right, too, has undergone a process of (post-)modernization, it must be regarded as closely intertwined with post-modern (youth) cultures who express themselves creatively and often ironically on social media. However, although the self-representation and the attraction of followers requires a more contemporary aesthetic than the formal uniformity associated with National Socialism, far-right online imagery manages to conserve ideological core values despite the tensions between references to symbolic heritage and an updated graphic style (Forchtner/Kølvraa 2017: 254).

While, at first sight, memes appear to be harmless instances of everyday visual culture and merely ironic, they still manage to convey key ideological narratives of hate and bigotry. Far-right media strategists are aware of the dual nature of memes and have turned ambivalence into a mode of contestation in the digital space. Memes have been central to a transformation of far-right visual cultures, making them attractive to wider circles and subcultures. Humor and satire are key to contemporizing hate messages and distorting public discourse (Schwarzenegger/Wagner 2018), but also to veiling the ideological roots of Nazi symbols and to circumvent censorship. As the *Handbook for Media Guerillas* claims: "An adversary who is laughing is already halfway on our side" (Generation D. 2017: 9). Moreover, in image-text combinations typical of memes, text elements (including titles, if any) are able to give images completely new meanings. In our dataset, most of the memes (82) are a combination of images and text elements, while several contain only images (24) and only a few (4) consist only of text. In the manner of postmodern aesthetic eclecticism, they link historical narratives with more contemporary styles, and thereby normalize militaristic, nationalist, völkisch and racist content. In other words, the content seems contemporary even though it is old.

Assuming that RG memes combine a variety of aesthetic styles, we argued that they appeal to multiple audiences far beyond those who unambiguously identify with neo-Nazi and other far-right symbolism. No doubt, this case study gives only a limited insight into the contradictory galaxy of internet memes produced and conveyed by the far right. Since we decoded only one of RG's many meme categories, we did not take into account more violent and provocative messages, which may also be found on the internal community server. While here we have here focused on the representations directed outwards to society at large (front stage), internal meme communication strategies (back stage) may be another promising field of research, even if the lines between both are increasingly blurred (see also Introduction in this book). By employing humorous ambiguity, 'hipsterish' aesthetics or references to popular culture, particularly cartoons and video games, this more subtle, not overtly political imagery may offer access points for undecided and not-yet politicized users to develop affinities with and support for far-right causes. Hence, we need to put more emphasis on the power of everyday images in order to understand the ways that the far right attracts supporters, especially if we hope to reverse their mainstreaming strategies.

REFERENCES

Bar-On, Tamir (2013): Rethinking the French New Right. Alternatives to Modernity, Abingdon: Routledge.

Bell, Philip (2004): "Content Analysis of Visual Images." In: van Leeuwen, Theo/Jewitt, Carey (eds.), The Handbook of Visual Analysis, London: Sage: pp. 10–34.

Benjamin, Walther (2002): "The Work of Art in the Age of Its Technological Reproduction." In: Eiland, Howard/Jennings, Michael (eds.), Selected Writings, Volume 3, Cambridge: Harvard University Press: pp. 101–134.

Berger, John (1972): Ways of Seeing, London: Penguin Books.

Caiani, Manuela/Kröll, Patricia (2015): "The Transnationalization of the Extreme Right and the Use of the Internet." In: International Journal of Comparative and Applied Criminal Justice 39/4, pp. 331–351.

Davey, Jacob/Ebner, Julia (2017): "The Fringe Insurgency. Connectivity, Convergence and Mainstreaming of the Extreme Right", Institute for Strategic Dialogue (http://www.isdglobal.org/wp-content/uploads/2017/10/The-Fringe-Insurgency-221017.pdf).

Doerr, Nicole (2017): "Bridging Language Barriers, Bonding against Immigrants: A Visual Case Study of Transnational Network Publics Created by Far-Right Activists in Europe." In: Discourse & Society 28/1, pp. 3–23.

Fahlenbrach, Kathrin/Ludes, Peter/Nöth, Winfried (2014): "Critical Visual Theory. Introduction." In: TripleC – Communication, Capitalism & Critique 12/1, pp. 202–213.

Ferrada Stoehrel, Rodrigo/Lindgren, Simon (2014): "For the Lulz: Anonymous, Aesthetics, and Affect." In: TripleC – Communication, Capitalism & Critique, 12/1, pp. 238–264.

Forchtner, Bernhard/Kølvraa, Christoffer (2017): "Extreme Right Images of Radical Authenticity: Multimodal Aesthetics of History, Nature, and Gender Roles in Social Media." In: European Journal of Cultural and Political Sociology 4/3, pp. 252–281.

Generation D. (2017): "Handbuch Für Medienguerillas: Teil I. Shitposting 1x1", (https://www.hogesatzbau.de/wp-content/uploads/2018/01/HANDBUCH-F%c3%9cR-MEDIENGUERILLAS.pdf).

Hall, Stuart (1993): "Encoding and Decoding in the Television Discourse." In: During, Simon (ed.), The Cultural Studies Reader London, New York: Routledge, pp. 90–103.

Hartmann, Flora (2017): Meme: Die Kunst des Remix. Bildsprache Politischer Netzkultur, Berlin: Amadeu-Antonio-Foundation.

Hristova, Stevka (2014): "Visual Memes as Neutralizers of Political Dissent." In: TripleC – Communication, Capitalism & Critique 12/1, pp. 265–276.

Kampf, Lena (2018): "Wie Rechte Internet-Trolle Versuchten, die Bundestagswahl zu Beeinflussen", 20 Februar 2018 (https://www.sueddeutsche.de/politik/manipulation-im-netz-wie-rechte-internet-trolle-versuchten-die-bundestagswahl-zu-beeinflussen-1.3875073).

Knobel, Michele/Lankshear, Colin (2007): "Online Memes, Affinities, and Cultural Production." In: Knobel, Michele/Lankshear, Colin (eds.), A New Literacies Sampler, New York: Peter Lang, pp. 199–228.

Kreißel, Philip/Ebner, Julia/Urban, Alexander/Guhl, Jakob (2018): "Hass auf Knopfdruck. Rechtsextreme Trollfabriken und das Ökosystem Koordinierter Hasskampagnen im Netz." Institute for Strategic Dialogue (https://www.isdglobal.org/wp-content/uploads/2018/07/ISD_Ich_Bin_Hier_2.pdf).

Krüger, Matthias (2011): "Nationale Leitbilder." In: Handbuch der Politischen Ikonographie. Vol. 2, München: C.H. Beck, pp. 95–102.

Miller-Idriss, Cynthia (2018): The Extreme Gone Mainstream. Commercialization and Far Right Youth Culture in Germany, Princeton: Princeton University Press

Mulvey, Laura (1999 [1975]): "Visual Pleasure and Narrative Cinema." In: Braudy, Leo/Cohen, Marshall (eds.), Film Theory and Criticism: Introductory Readings, New York: Oxford University Press, pp. 833–844.

Nagle, Angela (2017): Kill All Normies. The Online Culture Wars from Tumblr and 4chan to the Alt-Right and Trump, Winchester and Washington: Zero Books.

Nooney, Laine/Portwood-Stacer, Laura (2014): "One Does not Simply: An Introduction to the Special Issue on Internet Memes." In: Journal of Visual Culture 13/3, pp. 248–252.

Rose, Gillian (2016): Visual Methodologies. An Introduction to Researching with Visual Materials (4th ed.), London: Sage.

Schwarzenegger, Christian/Wagner, Anna (2018): "It's Funny Cause it's Hate: Political Satire as Right Wing Propaganda. A Study on Activism in Disguise", Unpublished Conference Paper at the 68th Annual Convention of the International Communication Association (ICA).

Sturken, Marita/Cartwright, Lisa (2001): Practices of Looking. An Introduction to Visual Culture, Oxford: Oxford University Press.

Suermann, Lenard (2016): "Schuld-Kult." In: Gießelmann, Bente/Richterich, Robin/Kerst, Benjamin/Suermann, Lenard/Virchow, Fabian (eds.), Handwörterbuch rechtsextremer Kampfbegriffe, Schwalbach/Taunus: Wochenschau Verlag, pp. 269–281.

Virchow, Fabian (2016): "PEGIDA. Understanding the Emergence and Essence of Nativist Protest in Dresden." In: Journal of Intercultural Studies 37/6, pp. 541–555.

The Murder of Keira

Misinformation and Hate Speech
as Far-Right Online Strategies

Alina Darmstadt, Mick Prinz and Oliver Saal

A young girl has been murdered in the German capital, Berlin. But before the police can launch their investigation, the German-speaking alternative right claims to have identified the perpetrator – or at least his origin: "On Wednesday, Keira has been slain in her bedroom. Everyone suspects that the perpetrator is not named 'Thorsten',"[1] posted a Twitter user going by the alias Walden. "We did not know such atrocities before the invasion of evil itself", tweeted another user.

The case of the 14-year-old Keira is eagerly absorbed in right-wing echo chambers. Sadly, it blends all too well into the scene's world-view, thanks to rumors that the murderer has a non-German background. All media outlets and influential actors of the alternative right contribute baseless speculations about the perpetrator's origin. They weave Keira's murder into a narrative by which Germany has turned into a hotbed of violent crime ever since the increased influx of refugees in 2015. Advocates who draw this picture see the country en route to civil war because of perceived 'mass immigration' and 'Islamization'.

Consulting social media on today's spectrum of political opinions, one quickly develops the impression that a majority of users support misogynous, racist, and anti-refugee sentiments. Such hateful positions are expressed aggressively, seeking to dominate and frame public debates. This poses a problem as online discussions are increasingly seen as a truthful

---

1 | Authors decided to not refer to websites, posts or tweets of the alternative right sphere with URLs, but do possess screenshots of every posting cited and will provide them for journalist or research purposes.

reflection of public opinion. In news reports, social media posts replace vox pop interviews with people on the street to represent what the public really thinks.

The German discussion about the deterioration of decency in online debates revolves around two phenomena: hateful comments and 'fake news'. Both aspects can be subsumed under the rubric of 'hate speech'. In terms of content, the debate is rather imprecise as it ignores one central aspect: both fake news and hateful comments are essential tools of a far-right media strategy. Hate speech, targeted misinformation, and strategic attacks on political opponents and minorities are employed to sow enmity and strengthen an antagonistic narrative.

The comments in the wake of Keira's murder shine a light on the argumentative and functional logic within far-right echo chambers (Amadeu Antonio Foundation 2017: 9; Brodnig 2016: 21–35). We analyze these chambers to demonstrate how rumors and false reports are used purposefully to strengthen right-wing narratives, but also because such case-studies can help those who want to oppose hateful speech, unfounded rumors and fake news. These phenomena cannot be marginalized as problems exclusive to the internet. Instead, they threaten minorities, erode social cohesion and thus pose a threat to democracy itself. The second part of this chapter highlights strategies to counter this treat, considering the reactions by the German state as well as providers of social networks, the remaining loopholes, and which promising counter strategies can help empower actors within civil society.

FAR-RIGHT POLITICS ONLINE

The importance of the internet and social media for organized right-wing currents can hardly be overstated. Ever since the dawn of the internet age, right-wing actors utilized the internet for networking, recruitment of new followers, strategic communication, and the propagation of their world view (Dinar/Heyken 2017: 41–42; Caiani/Parenti 2013). The triumph of social media since the 2000s coincided with a surge of ethno-nationalist *völkisch*, and radically derogatory ideas that have been and are being spread through these new channels.

Initially, such ideas lingered on the fringes of non-existence within social networks. Organized enmity primarily found its niches in closed and non-public groups or little-known websites. Here, hateful speech against entire populations could thrive without the public's notice. In 2015, this isolated sphere burst open in Germany due to the establishment of the anti-Muslim Pegida movement and the rise of the far-right party Alternative for Germany (AfD). According to Simone Rafael, the far-right spectrum has become significantly emboldened by the successes of the AfD and Pegida: "Racist, anti-refugee, and anti-Islam contents now occur undisguised on non-right-wing pages or are expressed vehemently in comments to stories by popular media outlets" (Rafael/Ritzmann 2018: 2). By and large, the discourse online has been gravitating to the right-wing and thus encouraged the normalization of hostile positions. "These positions have now become visible and a serious problem", continued Rafael.

For now, online hate speech has become a popular topic in Germany. The term itself comprises expressions that aim to deprecate and denigrate individuals because they are identified as part of a specific group. Hate speech stands in for several forms of group-focused enmity, such as antisemitism, racism, or hostility towards Sinti and Roma. (Zick et al. 2016: 33–41) Other than cyberbullying or personal insults, hate speech always seeks to denigrate characteristics that are ascribed to a certain group (Committee of Ministers 2016: 77). Victims of this form of online abuse are bereft of the capacity to lead a self-determined life, as hate speech is fueled by an ideology of inequality, directed against the democratic principle that all people are created equal.

We decided to use the term *Alternative Right* to describe the variety of contemporary far-right groups and ideologies which try to convince others that the 'identity of the German people' is threatened by multiculturalism. The concept has been criticized – with some justice – as being euphemistic. Still it seemed more appropriate to us than speaking only of the *New Right*: While both phenomena share an ideology that emphasizes cultural and racial homogeneity in one country, the heavy use of social media is characteristic for the 'Alternative Right' – as the 'Keira case' highlights. (Amadeu Antonio Foundation 2017: 2; Nagle 2017)

The 'Keira Case' and Its Hijacking by the Alternative Right

On 7 March 2018 a girl was killed at home in the Berlin district Hohenschönhausen. Several stab wounds injured the 14-year-old severely. Paramedics tried to save her life but could not help. A day later, Berlin's Police

Department issued a press release about the horrible event: The homicide division had begun investigations but details on the sequence of events or potential suspects were not publicized.[2]

Shortly after the press release, the first posts on Facebook and Twitter using the hashtags #keira and #keiraberlin started to appear. Alternative right actors did not need verified information on events or perpetrators to instrumentalize Keira's tragic death for their own political agenda. "20 stab wounds! The culprit was definitively not German!" wrote one user on Twitter. Another suggested: "It is Merkel's fault, even in the unlikely case that the culprit is *biodeutsch*. Because: We did not know such atrocities before the invasion of evil itself". This last tweet is remarkable in several aspects. Its argument provides the justification for improper speculations: Even if their allegations are false, they claim to still be entitled to identify migrants as "evil itself". The existence of such violent crimes before the summer of 2015 is being ignored despite the facts. The expression *bio-deutsch*, which roughly translates to 'biologically German', contains a cultural essentialism, according to which only those can be German that have a certain number of Germanic ancestors. Its opposite would be 'passport Germans' (*Passdeutsche*), who are German citizens, but 'only' according to their papers and can therefore be singled out as migrants by 'biological' Germans. Exclusion based on origin becomes ineluctable. And last but not least: Angela Merkel is eventually responsible for the whole disaster. Not only individual users of social media proliferate such interpretations and the corresponding posts. They only retweet and share points made by certain actors – right-wing extremists, far-right populist groups, parties, media – who stir up fear and hate.

On 11 March, two days after the first press release, Berlin police announced that they had arrested a suspect who was being interrogated by homicide detectives. No additional information was published, which only kindled further speculations: "The skanky PR department of @polizeiberlin refuses to name the cultural origin of the suspect in the case of #Keira who was butchered with a knife", wrote attorney Maximilian Krah on Twitter. Krah is a member of the AfD and a popular speaker for the party. Gunnar Lindemann, an AfD state representative in the Berlin parliament, addressed the local police's Twitter account directly: "Why

---

2 | Berlin.de (2018): *"Tatverdächtiger ist geständig"*, 11 March 2018 (https://www.berlin.de/polizei/polizeimeldungen/pressemitteilung.682619.php).

are no details made public? E.g. the perpetrator's origin? Is something being played down?".

In its response the police department simply referred to the press code. The German Press Council (Deutscher Presserat) states in its guidelines for reasonable reporting on crimes that generally neither ethnic nor religious affiliation should be reported. The rule was designed to avoid "discriminating generalizations of individual acts of wrongdoing".[3] Lindemann received support from Julian Reichelt, editor-in-chief of BILD, a tabloid with the highest circulation in Germany. According to him, the press code does not apply to a police Twitter account, tweeting: "We'd like to have the regular information on the perpetrator. Thank you!". By this time, speculations on the culprit had been circulating within the alternative-right echo chambers for two days. The leading far-right magazine *Compact* wrote that the rumors were justified since the police declined further comments.

Toxic Narratives

On the blog PI-News one could read already on 9 March: "'Mia – Maria – Keira' and hundreds of other injured, raped, and sacrificed German girls: Merkel and her system lackeys [*Systemlinge*] joined in the murders." The website's name stands for 'politically incorrect news'. It is one of the most-read right-wing populist and anti-Islam blogs in Germany. By listing three girl's names, Keira's murder was connected to two other victims of recent violent crimes. For the murder of the student Maria L., an Afghan refugee was sentenced to life in prison in Freiburg in 2016. Fifteen-year-old Mia from Kandel in Rhineland-Palitinate was stabbed to death in December 2017. The suspect is her ex-boyfriend, also a refugee from Afghanistan.

Characteristic for far-right echo chambers, several narratives have been interwoven in the short statement on PI-News. The three female names serve as an insider reference to the blog's readership that creates assumed connections between refugees, Islam, and violence. It is further suggested that the increase in asylum seekers correlates with a dramatic rise in violent crimes, especially against women: An external threat is

---

3 | Presserat: *"Richtlinie 12 - Diskriminierungen"*, (http://www.presserat.de/pressekodex/pressekodex/#panel-ziffer_12____diskriminierungen); Schade (2017).

infiltrating and destabilizing the country. Another sweeping insinuation posits that all arriving Muslim men are murderers and rapists (Amadeu Antonio Foundation 2016a: 4–7). Politicians, collectively signified in the original quote with 'Merkel', facilitate this development by not regulating immigration and even encouraging it. By doing so, they are opening doors to the 'Islamization' of Germany. *Systemlinge* are all those who are arbitrarily identified as part of 'the establishment'. Generally, this includes all parties – except for the AfD – journalists of the 'lying press', and 'do-gooders' (*Gutmenschen*).

Narratives help to explain the world as they establish sensible connections between isolated events. They provide a wider frame of interpretation that structures personal opinions. Narratives stir up emotions and can help to motivate and mobilize. Thus, they are valuable tools for sowing fear and hatred – cornerstone emotions that help exclude whole groups of people. One way to trigger such emotions is to repeatedly postulate correlations and causalities that do not exist. Utilized in this manner, narratives become toxic to society. As the Alternative Right constantly preaches the bleak dystopian vision of the demise of Germany and its people, the groups create an artificial need to take action (Amadeu Antonio Foundation 2017: 9).

This is the playbook that far-right populist AfD party followed in the case of Keira. Since its foundation in 2013 as an anti-Euro platform, the party has seen a meteoric rise as it continually drifts towards the far-right fringes. It masterfully taps into the hysteria raging in alternative-right echo chambers. On 31 May 2018 the party's national Twitter account reached 118,000 followers and amassed more than 400,000 likes on Facebook.

On the morning of 12th March, the party published a graphic illustration via both social media accounts showing a blood-splattered wall as a background and a stylized knife in the front, accompanied with an all-caps warning: "KNIFE EPIDEMIC RAMPANT!". The posts' text listed eleven crimes that involved knives, counted during the previous week. It claimed that Turks, Kurds, Chechens, Afghans, Eritreans, Gambians, and Syrians had committed all attacks. Keira's case had also been listed, accompanied with the rhetorical question: "Is this still Central Europe?" Factually, only five of the eleven crimes fit the party's suggested pattern (Vorreyer 2018). Despite its false allegations, the post was shared almost 3,000 times on Facebook.

Such statements distort the discussion on criminality and ethnic belonging. With its wrongful accusations and non-existent connections the party caters to narratives of Germany's decline, threatened from both outside (read: refugees) and inside (read: rotten establishment). The 'logical' conclusions are implied and do not need to be spelled out: taking action against refugees and their supporters, backing up the AfD's restrictive refugee and immigration policies.

Targeted Misinformation

On the eve of 11 March, the Berlin police informed the public that the perpetrator had been arrested in his parents' apartment and confessed to the crime. According to the press release it was a 15-year-old student from the victim's circle of acquaintances.[4] And yet again the speculation machine went into overdrive.

Lutz Bachmann is one of the initiators of the right-wing populist Pegida marches (Amadeu Antonio Foundation 2016b: 4). On 12 March, Bachmann posted a picture of a 15-year-old boy on both his Twitter and Facebook accounts, slandering him in the process. Bachmann wrote: "The murder of Keira [...] Now it seems to be official: The beast from Caucasus [here Bachmann uses the young man's name], a Chechen Muslim, and former refugee". The post provided a hyperlink to the youth's Facebook page. The images that Bachmann used were snapshots taken from the juvenile's profile. This type of collection and publication of personally identifiable information is called doxing and, in this case, there is a particularly deceitful quality to it: Bachmann's online vigilantism targeted the wrong person on purpose. The youth in question had no connection to Keira. He merely shared the first name and the initial of his last name with the real perpetrator.

The term 'fake news' has been in broad circulation since Donald Trump was elected as President of the United States. Trump himself has titled all media that reported critically on him as fake news, accusing those outlets of deliberately drawing an unfavorable image of his presidency. In the run-up to the German elections in September 2017, many commentators feared that false reporting could impact and sway voters.

---

4 | Berlin.de (2018): *"Tatverdächtiger ist geständig"*, 11 March 2018 (https://www.berlin.de/polizei/polizeimeldungen/pressemitteilung.682619.php).

Researchers from the Stiftung Neue Verantwortung (SNV), a think tank at the intersection of technology and society, investigated the reach of and ways through which fake news was proliferated. The authors concluded: "'Fake news' are targeted, false or at least deceptive information, designated to harm someone (individuals, organizations, or groups)" (Sängerlaub et al. 2018: 11). The willful intention behind the information is essential. Intentionality is what differentiates fake news from sloppily researched reporting ("poor journalism") or glossy headlines online that captivate readers' interest to generate clicks but deviate from the article's contents – a scheme known as 'click-baiting'.

As the SNV's study suggests, the fake news in Germany have been predominantly spread by right-wing populists or right-wing extremists. Their use of the concept to discredit established media constitutes "a double perversion of truth" criticized by the authors. "While they berate established media as fake news and lying press (*Lügenpresse*) they do not put truthfulness front and center. Only the type of media content that supports one's own world-view is regarded as legitimate – the rest is 'fake news'" (ibid; Brodnig 2017: 28–38).

In order to protect himself from hate speech within social media, the unjustly accused 15-year-old deleted his profile picture and several posts on his Facebook timeline. And yet, months later and despite the facts that Bachmann's tweet is obviously a lie and the police are investigating him for it, the false accusations, full name and pictures of the 15-year-old still circulate online, accessible to everyone. Political actors like Lutz Bachmann aim to fabricate assumed truths in service of their own agenda. Bachmann's own reaction, once his tweet had been uncovered as fake, also reflects this. In response to critical posts he merely replied with several smilies and insisted that what he wrote, "*seems to be* official" (Wienand 2018). He then deleted his posts. Any sign of regret for wrongfully accuFsing a high school student is missing.

The police also reacted to Bachmann's posts, trying to quell the rumors spreading within the alternative right's echo chambers. Berlin's police department published a screenshot of Bachmann's post crossed by red, bold letters spelling "FAKE" on Facebook and Twitter. The pictures of the student had been pixelated to prevent identification. In the post, police officers stated that "willful misinformation regarding the suspect's background and citizenship" circulated online. They demanded: "Please, do not take part in speculation and agitating speech and please do not

share FAKES". In another post, the department explained potential consequences of sharing misinformation: "Do not partake in inciting speech.
[...] Report every user who shares such pictures on Facebook. Those who
publish may be punishable by law".

In the police post's comment section, several users demanded that the
suspect's 'cultural background' should be made public. According to a racist world-view, German citizenship is not sufficient proof that someone is
'truly' German. One Facebook user wrote: "Obviously it was a PASSPORT
German". Eventually, the Berlin police department reacted to the ceaseless
requests: "Regrettable that this question is an issue at all. The suspect is
German and has no migratory background (if such a thing can be defined
at all)", retorted the officers.

CHALLENGING THE EXTREME RIGHT ONLINE: COUNTER-STRATEGIES FOR THE DIGITAL CIVIL SOCIETY

The far-right comments surrounding the Keira case demonstrate how
hate speech, misinformation, and rumors are used intentionally to reinforce narratives within right-wing echo chambers. Apparently, to the Alternative Right and its actors hate speech and intentional manipulation
are legitimate tool to compete politically. Germany's federal government
has its eye on hate speech and intends to oppose it. On January 1, 2018 the
so-called "Network Enforcement Act" (Netzwerkdurchsetzungsgesetz,
NetzDG) went into effect.[5] From an international perspective this legislation constitutes a novel and aggressive approach to force social media companies to crack down on hateful, slanderous, or racist posts. At the heart
of the law lies the obligation on the companies to register user complaints
immediately and to delete "content obviously punishable by law" within
24 hours or seven days in less clear incidents. Additionally, social media
providers have to report their resources, teams, and measures dedicated to
deleting hateful and punishable content every three months. From a civil
society perspective, the new legislation's biggest benefit is an increase in
transparency with regard to the companies' curating practices. But there

---

5 | The German Federal Ministry of Justice and for Consumer Protection provides
an English translation of the act, 30 May 2018 (http://www.bmjv.de/DE/Themen/
FokusThemen/NetzDG/NetzDG_EN_node.html).

is much to be lamented. First and foremost, NetzDG shifts the decision about whether or not certain contents are illegal and therefore actionable on to the employees of private companies. NGOs and experts issued a *Declaration of Freedom of Expression* criticizing this transfer of responsibilities as an unfortunate privatization of law enforcement.[6] They are also concerned that the high fines threatened by the German government might lead to so called 'overblocking', which entails the excessive deletion of contents that are not unlawful. The legislation misses the point that most hate speech comments and strategic communications within and from right-wing echo chambers are not punishable by law but are covered by the very freedom of expression activists try to preserve. To be successful in fighting right-wing extremism, -populism, and hate speech online, the combined efforts of civil society actors, social media providers, and national legislators are required. A digital civil society should pursue three goals:

1. Support and protect victims of hate speech.
2. Visualize, repel, and counter intolerance and group-focused enmity.
3. Strengthen a democratic culture of debate.

1) Hate speech usually targets people that are already discriminated against. All users can help: by standing in solidarity with affected individuals; by resolutely contradicting hostile comments; by reporting offensive content to social media providers or the authorities. Like all users, hosts of large Facebook pages, e.g. media companies or publishers, should be interested in pluralistic debates free from discrimination in their comments sections. To enable such a debate, resources for community management need to be allocated to utilize all tools of moderation available. According to a study by the London-based Institute for Strategic Dialogue, a proactive moderation of websites is essential: sites without moderators are up to 100 per cent more likely to be commented on by right-wing extremist. Enmity and hate speech can prosper wherever they remain unopposed. The internet's old words of wisdom – 'don't feed the troll' – seem refuted. Furthermore, the study shows that hate speech is proliferated and supported by very few users – yet they still have a dominant impact on debates. Accor-

---

6 | Declaration on Freedom of Expressionon Freedom of Expression (5 April 2017). Online: (https://deklaration-fuer-meinungsfreiheit.de/en/).

ding to the authors, only one per cent of all users generate 25 per cent of all likes for hateful comments. Despite their small numbers, these users act jointly and express their views aggressively (Kreißel et al. 2018: 12).

2) Right-wing extremist media and their accounts that propagate hate speech regard themselves both as being in the right and untouchable when they do not have to fear dissent or repercussions. This means, in turn, that a digital civil society needs to contradict them within these spaces. Before becoming active, users interested in opposing enmity online should think first of self-preservation and check what kind of private details about them are available online through their profiles. Posts can go viral or at least have a surprising reach. Far-right extremists or other hateful communities might use publicly accessible information against those who challenge them. It can be meaningful and sensitive to contradict contemptuous, inhuman posts. One should not expect, however, to convince determined haters of an opposite worldview. This will happen very rarely. This limit should not ennoble racist or slanderous positions as legitimate arguments worth considering. One should rather aim to address and convince the part of the silent reading majority that is open to argument. Eventually one can help minimize the influence of hate speech and its proponents and to protect those targeted by them. Those who do not want to contradict hate speech actively could instead like, and thus support, arguments that do. Additionally, all users can launch interventions, websites, campaigns, or hashtags for equality and against enmity – either alone or with the help of allies. A variety of tools are at their disposal: websites or campaigns can provide information on far-right actors and document their activities; one can work with humor or polemics, or provide arguments, knowledge, and facts to those willing to take a pro-equality position within debates. All of the approaches above are useful and can cross-fertilize each other in their plurality.

3) Advocates of a democratic civil society, who build alliances, organize counter-protests against Neo-Nazis, or welcome refugees in the real world, still act too timidly in the virtual realm. To spread their approaches to the online world, they should cooperate with digital activists. As of now, there are too few democratic counter-narratives that celebrate diversity, equality, and human rights online. To spread these positive narratives, democrats should not reject emotional approaches. State institutions, in turn, should not rest on the laurels of the NetzDG legislation, whose impact remains

marginal so far.[7] A more effective way would be to sponsor youth and adult programs that strengthen competencies in using different media. As a consequence, users can spot intentional misinformation more easily. Finally, victims of hate speech and cyberbullying need support and places to which they can turn, online and in real life.

REFERENCES

Amadeu Antonio Foundation (2017): Toxic Narratives – Monitoring Alternative-Right Actors, Berlin: Amadeu Antonio Foundation.

Amadeu Antonio Foundation (2016a): Das Bild des 'Übergriffigen Fremden' – Warum Ist es ein Mythos? Wenn mit Lügen über Sexualisierte Gewalt Hass Geschürt Wird, Berlin: Amadeu Antonio Foundation.

Amadeu Antonio Foundation (2016b): Peggy War Da! Social Media als Kitt Rechtspopulistischer Bewegungen, Berlin: Amadeu Antonio Foundation.

Brodnig, Ingrid (2017): Lügen im Netz – Wie Fake News, Populisten und Unkontrollierte Technik uns Manipulieren, Wien: Brandstätter Verlag.

Brodnig, Ingrid (2016): Hass im Netz, Wien: Brandstätter Verlag.

Caiani, Manuela/Parenti, Linda (2013): European and American Extreme Right Groups and the Internet, London: Routledge.

Committee of Ministers (2016 [1997]): "Recommendation No.R (97) 20 of the Commitee of Ministers to Member States on "Hate Speech." In: Recommendations and Declarations of the Committee of Ministers of the Council of Europe in the Field of Media and Information Society, Straßbourg: Media and Internet Division Directorate General of Human Rights and Rule of Law, pp. 76–79.

Dinar, Christina/Heyken, Cornelia (2017): "Rechte Propaganda im Internet und in den Sozialen Netzwerken des Web 2.0." In: Nerdinger, Winfried (eds.), Nie wieder. Schon wieder. Immer noch. Rechtsextremismus in Deutschland seit 1945, Berlin: Metropol, pp. 41–54.

Kreißel, Philip/Ebner, Julia/Urban, Alexander/Guhl, Jakob (2018): "Hass Auf Knopfdruck. Rechtsextreme Trollfabriken und das Ökosystem

---

7 | Tagesschau.de (2018): "Weniger Beschwerden als erwartet", 03 March 2018 (https://www.tagesschau.de/inland/hassimnetz-101.html).

Koordinierter Hasskampagnen im Netz." Institute for Strategic Dialogue (https://www.isdglobal.org/wp-content/uploads/2018/07/ISD_Ich_Bin_Hier_2.pdf).

Nagle, Angela (2017): Kill All Normies. The Online Culture Wars from Tumblr and 4chan to the Alt-Right and Trump, Winchester and Washington: Zero Books.

Rafael, Simone/Ritzmann, Alexander (2018): "Hintergrund: Das ABC des Problemkomplexes Hassrede, Extremismus und NetzDG." In: Baldauf, Johannes/Ebner, Julia/Guhl, Jakob (eds.): Hassrede und Radikalisierung im Netz. Der OCCI-Forschungsbericht, pp. 11–19.

Sängerlaub, Alexander/Meier, Miriam/Rühl, Wolf-Dieter (2018): Fakten statt Fakes. Verursacher, Verbreitungswege und Wirkungen von Fake News im Bundestagswahlkampf 2017, Berlin: Stiftung Neue Verantwortung.

Schade, Marvin (2017): "Diskriminierungsrichtlinie zur Täterherkunft: Presserat Überarbeitet Viel Diskutierten Kodex-Paragrafen 12.1", 22 March 2017 (https://meedia.de/2017/03/22/diskriminierungsrichtlinie-zur-taeterherkunft-presserat-ueberarbeitet-viel-diskutierten-kodex-paragrafen-12-1/).

Vorreyer, Thomas (2018): "So Erfindet die AfD Messer-Attacken durch Ausländer", 14 March 2018 (https://www.vice.com/de/article/j5bym7/so-erfindet-die-afd-messer-attacken-durch-auslander).

Wienand, Lars (2018): "Getötete Keira: Bachmann Stellt Unschuldigen an den Pranger", 13 March 2018 (https://www.t-online.de/nachrichten/panorama/kriminalitaet/id_83381986/erstochene-keira-lka-prueft-hetztweet-von-lutz-bachmann-.html).

Zick, Andreas/Krause, Daniela/Berghan, Wilhelm/Küpper, Beate (2016): "Gruppenbezogene Menschenfeindlichkeit in Deutschland 2002–2016." In: Zick, Andreas/Küpper, Beate/Krause, Daniela (eds.), Gespaltene Mitte – Feindselige Zustände. Rechtsextreme Einstellungen in Deutschland 2016, Bonn: Dietz, pp. 33–82.

Counter-Creativity

Innovative Ways to Counter
Far-Right Communication Tactics

Julia Ebner

"The left can't meme", is a common saying among the Alt-Right. Far-right efforts to mock the political correctness of the liberal left – who they call "libtards"[1] – and ridicule the conservative mainstream – in their words, "cuckservatives"[2] – have relied on transgressive jokes and funny visuals. In an unexpectedly inventive fashion, the far right has pioneered a new wave of taboo-breaking and controlled provocation, which they call 'triggering'. "We use the tactics of the left against them", many of them would say. Ironically taking inspiration from the civil rights youth revolts, their biggest scapegoat for everything they deem wrong in today's society, the far right has been imitating 1960's counter-culture strategies to protest against establishment politics. Their focus on lifestyle, youth culture and the arts can be seen as an attempt to reach the critical mass needed for any counterculture movement: in their case, this paradoxically takes the shape of a globalized counterculture that is opposed to 'globalism', and uses modern communication tools to spread anti-modern ideas.

While one can argue whether offensive Pepe the Frog memes (the symbol co-opted by the Alt-Right) and racist Synthwave tracks (the favorite music genre of white nationalists) qualify as art, it is self-evident that this new far-right counter-culture has successfully galvanized young people worldwide into supporting often openly racist and dangerous groups.

---

1 | "Libtard" is a derogatory term used by the Alt-Right – combining the words liberal and retard – to describe left-leaning liberals.
2 | "Cuckservative" is a derogatory term used by the Alt-Right – combining the words cuckold and conservative – to describe center-right conservatives.

Has their offer for a collective identity that rejects the political, economic and societal status quo been sexier, faster and more innovative than the voices trying to counter it? Many counterspeech efforts against the Alt-Right have been declared ineffective or even counter-productive. Two major stumbling blocks for those of us who care about countering the far-right's growth have been our limited understanding of emerging subcultures on the internet coupled with a lack of creative and proactive approaches. Researchers, artists and concerned citizens can play a huge role in filling these gaps.

This chapter will outline a strategy to replace, optimize and complement current approaches to prevent, disrupt and counter online far-right activities. First, it will analyze the set of post-digital tactics employed by the far right when targeting different audiences and assess its current comparative advantages. In a next step, it will then suggest solutions to counter far-right post-internet campaigns, drawing on insights from research and evaluation projects that measured the effectiveness of different counter speech and interruption approaches. Furthermore, it will discuss a range of novel, experimental approaches that could potentially add to the range of current attempts being made to counter far-right activities in cyberspace.

FRAMING THE CHALLENGE

Over the past few years, far-right actors have been successful at exploiting windows of opportunity offered by the emergence of new media ecosystems and the novel interconnected information and communication cycles they afford. More specifically, they have leveraged the digital space for three different types of campaigns to reach their key audiences: radicalization campaigns targeting sympathizers, manipulation campaigns targeting the mainstream, and intimidation campaigns targeting political opponents.

Radicalization campaigns aimed at sympathizers involve the sophisticated use of micro-targeting, the hijacking of youth culture and the exploitation of tabooed and under-addressed grievances, fears and identity crises, which have enabled far-right actors to lure vulnerable internet users into their networks. Andrew Anglin, founder of the world's biggest neo-Nazi website Daily Stormer, which is now banned across the world, has pioneered some of these tactics. By using troll armies and far-right influencers with large followerships as mouthpieces, Anglin has managed to inject his propaganda pieces into mainstream social media channels. His antisemitic conspiracy theories and neo-Nazi ideologies often come under the disguise of satire and transgressive internet culture (O'Brien 2017; Feinberg 2017; Marantz 2017).

Increasingly, far-right groups have learnt to segment their audiences, using micro-targeting tactics and tailoring their language to the different sub-cultures they want to reach. For example, the organizers of the white supremacist Charlottesville protest used entirely different sets of memes[3] and propaganda pieces for the different communication channels they targeted. Their rally trailers on fringe neo-Nazi websites and forums were much more explicitly racist and antisemitic than their propaganda contents on Twitter and Facebook. While the former featured Swastikas and called for the annihilation of Jews, the latter focused on topics such as freedom of speech and Southern heritage and addressed fears of immigration and the loss of cultural identity. The aim of these hyper-targeted campaigns was to appeal to different online communities along the far-right ideological spectrum and eventually 'unite the right' on the basis of their lowest common denominators (Davey/Ebner 2017).

Manipulation campaigns aimed at the 'greyzones' involve the creation, planting and dissemination of disinformation and the use of psy-ops style online campaigns, which have allowed far-right actors to influence mainstream discussions. Manuals circulated in American Alt-Right networks and their European equivalents include detailed instructions on how to 'redpill the normies' – a euphemism for hacking the minds of average users. Their strategy documents include guidelines on how to initiate conversations, build trust, exploit common grievances and tailor the language to the person they seek to bring closer to their ideologies. Generation Identity highlights that family members and friends might be the easiest target groups to start with (Generation D. 2017). The New Right Network has even hosted tutorials on Youtube, explaining step by step how to "redpill your girlfriend/wife".[4]

---

3 | Memes are graphics of visual and textual remixes shared and widely distributed in online spaces.

4 | New Right Network (2018): "How to Red-Pill your Woman/Girlfriend/Wife or ANY woman PARTII", 26 June 2018 (https://www.youtube.com/watch?v=Cdv1yDJfH_g).

Manipulation campaigns seeking to provoke the 'greyzones' to pick a side have become a particular priority for the international Alt-Right in the run-up to elections. 'Strategic polarization' is a concept the far right uses to deliberately sow discord, divide communities and spread binary world views. Its goal is to force the moderate middle to choose a side in order to expand the influence of the political fringes. At the Institute for Strategic Dialogue (ISD), we have monitored far-right trolling armies who sought to influence the elections in favor of far-right populist parties in the US, France, Germany, Italy and Sweden and found that the tactics they employed, their language and media ecosystems all followed roughly the same pattern (see graphic below). The campaigns usually start with Alt-Right users trying to mobilize and recruit sympathizers on messaging platforms such as 4chan and 8chan in English. Their next step has been to shift those conversations into encrypted applications such as Telegram and Discord, where they collect materials in the local language and plan campaigns that they can then launch on mainstream social media platforms like Facebook, Twitter and Instagram. Their aim is to shape the online discourse, set the agenda for discussions and put pressure on politicians to ultimately persuade the mainstream to support their parties of choice (Ebner/Davey 2018).

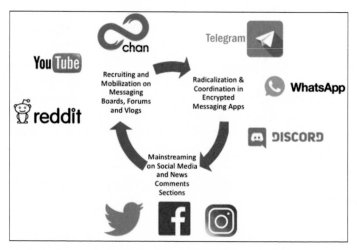

Author's visualization of far-right online influence ecosystems.

Intimidation campaigns aimed at opponents involve trolling and coordinated hate campaigns have enabled far-right actors to harass, silence and publicly discredit critical voices and political opponents including journalists, activists and politicians (Kreißel et al. 2018). Doxxing has been a particularly popular tactic among Alt-Right actors who want to take revenge on individuals who openly criticized them or simply don not share their opinions. The Crash Override Network, an organization made up of former cyber-bullying victims, defines doxxing as "a common first-stage tactic of mobs of anonymous online groups looking to intimidate you and start digging up information on your life".[5] Campaigns that involve the leaking of an individual's address and phone number, do not just fuel online hate but also increase the likelihood that these people are attacked in real life. In the US, activists, journalists and even academics have become increasingly frequent targets of doxing campaigns and cyber-harassment. At least 250 university professors reportedly became victims of right-wing online campaigns between early 2017 and mid-2018 (Kamenetz 2018). For example, Joshua Cuevas, a psychology professor at the University of North Georgia received racist and threatening private messages and was targeted in a sophisticated public doxxing campaign for his liberal leanings. "Those of us in higher education increasingly find ourselves the target of hostilities" (Cuevas 2018), he reflected in a firsthand account for the American Association of University Professors.

Ultimately, all three types of campaigns – radicalization, manipulation and intimidation – are designed to maximize the far right's online and offline influence by provoking overreactions on a political and societal level, which can set in motion profound systemic change.

The far right currently holds a number of comparative advantages in the realm of strategic communications: First of all, its campaigns have benefitted from the significant time lag in the responses given by policy makers, tech firms and civil society. Not only were the prevention and countering efforts often reactive but they also tended to be inward-looking and generic. Far-right activists are currently ahead of those trying to counter their activities on at least three levels: they have been better at

---

5 | Crash Override (2018): *Preventing Doxing: "A Primer on Removing your Personal Information from the most Commonly Exploited Places"*, (http://www.cra shoverridenetwork.com/preventingdoxing.html).

exploiting new technologies, at fostering international ties and synergies, and at appealing to young audiences.

Far-right extremists, as early adopters of new technology, have been particularly apt at spotting and exploiting infrastructural loopholes and socio-psychological weaknesses that social media have unleashed within our societies. By coordinating slick campaigns in encrypted channels and then propagating these on mainstream social media platforms, far-right groups have managed to conquer entire online spaces, leveraging the traditional media's growing pressure to compete for clicks and baits with their faster online counterparts (Kreißel et al. 2018).

Yet, far-right extremist efforts and effects are by no means limited to cyberspace. Many fringe groups have built powerful online-offline hybrid strategies to maximize their real-world impact. By sharing knowledge and experience across borders, far-right movements in Europe and the US have been able to learn from each other. "We've mastered the online activism, you've mastered the in-real-life activism", said American far-right activist Brittany Pettibone in a filmed conversation with European Identitiarian figurehead Martin Sellner in 2017 (Sellner 2017).

The pan-European white nationalist group Generation Identity as well as American Alt-Right influencers frequently stage carefully planned media stunts on the street, which they then livestream to social media (Hentges et al. 2014). By combining sharable – often shocking – contents with credible messengers – often charismatic influencers with massive followerships – their slick social media campaigns are easily turned viral. The result is a wide online reach that goes beyond their own fanbase, which in turn forces traditional news outlets to report about them. This is particularly true once a tipping point is reached, where fringe groups make hashtags and their content trends in numbers significantly large enough to penetrate mainstream audiences (Philips 2018).

The creation of transnational and cross-ideological alliances, and exploitation of international synergies, are a second area where the far right seem to have gained a 'first mover' advantage. Over the past few years the phenomenon of "networked nationalism" (Donovan et al. 2018) has become a growing aspect of far-right movements. Increasingly, far-right groups and actors put aside ideological differences and historic sources of in-fighting. For instance, the Defend Europe mission in the summer of 2017, which sought to prevent NGOs from rescuing drowning refugees in the Mediterranean Sea, received social media support and donations from across the world (Davey/Ebner 2017). Cases such as the Defend Europe campaign, the Charlottesville rally and multi-group mobilisiations in the run-up to elections, are examples of such explicit efforts to cross borders and overcome ideological differences for the sake of maximizing collective impact. To act as agents of change they opportunistically join forces, focusing on the lowest common denominator: their shared enemies and their shared goals. These are most commonly their aversion to multiculturalism, their opposition to 'establishment' politics, their hatred of the left, and their fear that cultural-ethnic identity is being eroded. All three, and others, have become a bridge that has brought together far-right groups who traditionally did not cooperate.

The targeting of young people through the creation of counter-culture movements and the use of gamification in their communication and recruiting strategies have given far-right activists a third advantage. "Politics is downstream from culture. I want to change the cultural narrative", said Andrew Breitbart, the creator of the website that has become the premier source of information and commentary for today's far right (Poniewozig 2012). Based on Breitbart's philosophy of changing politics by altering culture, far-right movements and influencers have placed their bets on developing a strategy that has the potential to bring about drastic attitudinal and behavioral changes within large sections of society. In their positioning against the political establishment and in satirical fashion their messaging has resonated well with a range of sub-cultures such as online gamers, anti-feminists and conspiracy theorists who now coalesce around common themes, grievances and online meeting points. The development of a shared set of insider jokes, references and even a common playbook for online campaigns has created a strong sense of in- and out-group thinking.

The online far-right's successes in reaching young digital natives have been particularly striking. Their use of computer game references, anti-establishment rhetoric and exciting counter-culture activities has allowed them to appeal to large proportions of Generation Z and the millennials. By hiding racial slurs behind funny memes and jokes, and by replacing traditional swastika-ridden attire with cool jeans and Ray Ban sunglasses, the far right has increasingly polished its image among younger generations.

DEVELOPING THE RESPONSE

An international framework to protect those targeted by radicalization, manipulation and intimidation campaigns should be based on a collaborative, integrated approach that builds on the following pillars: Predicting the trends, understanding the audiences, building an anti-hate coalition, and testing new intervention approaches.

Many of the response systems in place have been too slow to be effective as a result of a failure to predict new trends in the use of new technology and communication strategies by far-right activists. Research is needed to understand the emerging new media ecosystems, their internal dynamics as well as their influence on mainstream platforms. Over the last couple of years, far-right campaigners have increasingly moved their operations to so-called 'Alt-Tech platforms' (see Donovan et al. in this book), reacting to the introduction of stricter anti-hate speech measures across major Silicon Valley companies like Facebook, Twitter and Google. Alt-Tech safe havens for far-right extremists include, for instance, Alt-Right social media like Gab and Minds, the far-right's Youtube equivalent Pewtube, and the white supremacist crowdsourcing website Hatreon. These virtual migration streams demonstrate that a static, linear perspective will fail to reflect the changes in the fast-paced online universe of far-right extremists. It is therefore necessary to look at how different platforms interact with each other and are used as part of an information and communication ecosystem that runs in parallel to that of the political mainstream.

Some of the measures undertaken to prevent or disrupt far-right mobilization proved ineffective or even counter-productive due to an insufficient understanding of the far-right's support base, its key target audiences and the characteristics of their various sub-cultures. Furthermore, neglecting the high degree of interconnectedness among far-right networks can restrict the desired effect of counterspeech campaigns or even backfire.

A case in point is the #MoreThanARefugee video, which told the stories of individuals who had to flee their countries and was featured on Youtube Spotlight in June 2017 as part of the Creators for Change initiative. The campaign focused on maximizing its visibility and reach among a general audience but experienced a significant backlash from far-right communities on 4chan and Reddit, who launched a so-called 'dislike raid' on a massive scale. Their reframing and mockery of the original message allowed them to spread their campaign on Twitter, where they were able to encourage even moderate users to participate. A month after #More-ThanARefugee was published, the video counted over 450,000 dislikes, compared to just 144,000 likes. The vast majority of its 80,000 comments were negative or contained hateful speech and threatening language. For example, ISD's analysis of a sample of 239 of the 80,000 comments revealed that just 4 percent held positive sentiment.

Raids like these expose the need to significantly step up our efforts to comprehend how far-right subcultures take shape in online spaces, as well as their grievances, language, insider jokes and reference points. Only a handful of institutes are currently focused on the far-right's use of new media. For example, MIT's Center for Civic Media, the Oxford Internet Institute and Data & Society Foundation have released seminal studies that can lay the foundation for further research. The University of Amsterdam's Alt-Right Open Intelligence Initiative has released the first comprehensive taxonomy of trolls and far-right online communities. Using Google's BigQuery Tool, the researchers conducted a linguistic analysis of 3 billion Reddit comments.[6] Likewise, scholars at University College London have developed a way to measure how memes spread across the web and have identified the most influential groups in the creation and dissemination of memetic contents. Their study shows how far-right actors have weaponized neutral memes such as Pepe the Frog to spread politically loaded, racist and antisemitic messages.[7]

However, online sub-cultures and different parts of the online far-right networks remain underexplored. Their audiences are often misunderstood by outsider commentators. Only by studying their narratives and language can we get to the core of their motivations, ideologies and identity perceptions. These insights could then serve as a basis to develop adequate intervention approaches to debunk, discredit and counter their messages.

The creation of a global multi-agent coalition against far-right campaigns in the digital space could be the starting point for coordinating

---

6 | Alt-Right Open Intelligence Initiative (2017): "Mapping the Alt-Right: US Alternative Right across the Atlantic", 18 July 2017 (https://wiki.digitalmethods.net/Dmi/AltRightOpenIntelligenceInitiative).

7 | MIT Technology Review (2018): "This is where Internet Memes Come from", 11 June 2018 (https://www.technologyreview.com/s/611332/this-is-where-internet-memes-come-from/).

such intervention efforts, as well as a massive step towards reducing the comparative advantages held by the far right. The goal should be to foster closer cooperation between researchers, policymakers, the private sector and civil society. Concerted efforts led by stakeholders on all levels could help to develop and scale novel approaches to prevent, disrupt and counter far-right campaigns.

Ideally, an integrated intervention model would combine proactive counterspeech and rapid reaction systems that make use of international, cross-sector synergies and explore innovative methods for audience analysis, segmentation and micro-targeting. The development of counter-speech or disruption campaigns should be based on in-depth research of the new trends and the target audiences. The first step in the development of effective response mechanisms is audience segmentation. Once the different sub-audiences as well as their preferred communication medium have been identified, messages that use credible messengers should be tailored to the different specifics of the different sub-cultures then tested across different platforms (Tuck/Silverman 2016).[8]

Most counterspeech and intervention approaches do come with a certain degree of risk. For example, harmful side effects may include causing unintended exposure to extremist propaganda, provoking negative belief reinforcement, setting off cumulative extremism dynamics, or triggering a backlash from fringe communities as in the case of the #MoreThanARefugee dislike raid. ISD has developed a risk framework that can serve as a guide to categorize and minimize many of these problems. Building resilience, raising awareness and offering hate aid can reduce the risks associated with anti-hate-speech campaigns. The Online Civil Courage Initiative, which ISD founded in cooperation with Facebook, or networks such as the German organization das NETTZ, can help to connect and empower young activists and NGOs and offer advice and safety nets to those that are at risk of receiving abuse as a result of their anti-hate campaigns.

Although risk mitigation is important, it should not prevent intervention providers from taking entirely novel approaches. The self-imposed limits of counter-speech should be reconsidered, and new prevention and

---

8 | RAN (2017): "RAN Guidelines for Effective Alternative and Counter-Narrative Campaigns", (https://ec.europa.eu/home-affairs/sites/homeaffairs/files/docs/pages/201702_ran_how_to_measure_impact_of_online_campaign_en.pdf).

disruption approaches tested as a process of constant improvement. Initiatives such as #ichbinhier, an anti-hate community that counters coordinated trolling and hateful commentary on Facebook, and the No Hatespeech Movement, a campaign that mobilizes young people to speak up against hate speech, are excellent examples for new models that have effectively disrupted and reduced online far-right activities. Counterspeech needs to become more dynamic, more innovative and bolder to reach some of the obscure and self-absorbed internet cultures as well as those in the greyzones. Our future efforts need to be:

- Dynamic: Involving both proactive communication and rapid response systems to react to spontaneous far-right campaigns. Pro-active efforts need a significantly more nuanced method of choosing their messages, messengers and medium based on the target audience that the campaign seeks to reach. On the other hand, rapid ad-hoc interventions require the pooling of resources and linking of networks, so that these can quickly be leveraged and adapted to different contexts. Whenever an incident or news event triggers a far-right reaction, this kind of collective synchronicity would allow for immediate civic responses.
- Innovative: Developing creative messages could be done in cooperation with artists, scientists or even trolling communities. Furthermore, it may be worth testing experimental approaches, using for example video games and app games (Ament 2017; Bogost 2006), interactive videos and music. Out-of-the-box thinking will be essential to penetrate new audiences and offer appealing alternatives to those provided by extremists.
- Bold: Sexy counterspeech needs to develop bolder and funnier contents. It needs to dare to break taboos, transcend the limits of conventional debates and present issues from entirely new perspectives. While the use of sarcasm and humor can be an immensely powerful tool to establish sympathy, our research at ISD showed that it can also render counter-narrative campaigns counter-productive if it devalues or mocks the target audience. However, for example, self-ironizing can act as a formidable icebreaker.

To conclude, more research into the different online sub-cultures targeted by far-right campaigns will be needed to engage with them in a constructive way. Without a more thorough understanding of their grievances, language, insider jokes and reference points that are galvanizing, far-right communities, counterspeech efforts are likely to miss their objective. Moreover, a strong coalition of researchers, policy makers, the tech sector, artists and voluntary activists will be necessary to pilot new, innovative bottom-up approaches to countering far-right campaigns. A counter-culture to extremist counter-cultures can only be led by civil society itself. The Online Civil Courage Initiative (OCCI) is one of many initiatives that provide an infrastructure and support network for civil society activists fighting at the frontlines to counter online radicalization and hate speech. No doubt the challenges are growing in scope and sophistication, but so are the response mechanisms.

REFERENCES

Ament, Rachel (2017): "Screen Saviors: Can Activism-Focused Games Change Our Behavior?", 23 July 2017 (https://www.npr.org/sections/alltechconsidered/2017/07/23/538617205/screen-saviors-can-activism-focused-games-change-our-behavior).

Bogost, Ian (2006): "Playing Politics: Videogames for Politics, Activism and Advocacy", 25 August 2006 (http://firstmonday.org/article/view/1617/1532).

Cuevas, Joshua (2018): "A New Reality? The Far Right's Use of Cyberharassment Against Academics. American Association of University Professors", 9 February 2018 (https://www.aaup.org/article/new-reality-far-rights-use-cyberharassment-against-academics#.WoGsdSBofN).

Davey, Jacob/Ebner, Julia (2017): "The Fringe Insurgency. Connectivity, Convergence and Mainstreaming of the Extreme Right". Institute for Strategic Dialogue (http://www.isdglobal.org/wp-content/uploads/2017/10/The-Fringe-Insurgency-221017.pdf).

Donovan, Joan/Lewis, Rebecca/Friedberg, Brian (2018): "Networked Nationalisms", 11 July 2018 (https://medium.com/@MediaManipulation/networked-nationalisms-2983deae5620).

Ebner, Julia/Davey, Jacob (2018): "Mainstreaming Mussolini: How the Extreme Right Attempted to 'Make Italy Great Again' in the 2018 Italian Election." Institute for Strategic Dialogue (http://www.isdglobal.org/wp-content/uploads/2018/03/Mainstreaming-Mussolini-Report-28.03.18.pdf).

Feinberg, Ashley (2017). "This is the Daily Stormer's Playbook. Huffington Post", 13 December 2017 (https://www.huffingtonpost.com/entry/daily-stormer-nazi-style-guide_us_5a2ece19e4b0ce3b344492f2).

Generation D. (2017): "Handbuch Für Medienguerillas: Teil I. Shitposting 1x1", (https://www.hogesatzbau.de/wp-content/uploads/2018/01/HANDBUCH-F%c3%9cR-MEDIENGUERILLAS.pdf).

Hentges, Gudrun/Kökgiran, Gürcan/Nottbohm, Kristina. (2014): "Die Identitäre Bewegung Deutschland (IBD): Bewegung oder Virtuelles Phänomen?", (http://forschungsjournal.de/sites/default/files/fjsb plus/fjsb-plus_2014-3_hentges_koekgiran_nottbohm_x.pdf).

Kamenetz, Anya (2018): "Professors Are Targets in Online Culture Wars; Some Fight Back. National Public Radio", 4 April 2018 (https://www.npr.org/sections/ed/2018/04/04/590928008/professor-harassment).

Kreißel, Philip/Ebner, Julia/Urban, Alexander/Guhl, Jakob (2018): "Hass Auf Knopfdruck. Rechtsextreme Trollfabriken und das Ökosystem Koordinierter Hasskampagnen im Netz." Institute for Strategic Dialogue (https://www.isdglobal.org/wp-content/uploads/2018/07/ISD_Ich_Bin_Hier_2.pdf).

Marantz, Andrew (2017): "Inside the Daily Stormer's Style Guide. New Yorker", 15 January 2018 (https://www.newyorker.com/magazine/2018/01/15/inside-the-daily-stormers-style-guide).

O'Brien, Luke (2017): "The Making of an American Nazi", (https://www.theatlantic.com/magazine/archive/2017/12/the-making-of-an-american-nazi/544119/).

Philips, Whitney (2018): "The Oxygen of Amplification: Better Practices for Reporting on Extremists, Antagonists, and Manipulators Online", 22 May 2018 (https://datasociety.net/output/oxygen-of-amplification/).

Poniewozig, Jamie (2012): "Andrew Breitbart 1969–2012", 1 March 2012 (http://entertainment.time.com/2012/03/01/andrew-breitbart-1969-2012/).

Sellner, Martin (2017): "The American and European Right – Lauren Southern, Brittany Pettibone & Martin Sellner", 29 September 2017 (https://www.youtube.com/watch?v=cgwerO355to).

Tuck, Henry/Silverman, Tanya (2016): "The Counter-Narrative Handbook." Institute for Strategic Dialogue (http://www.isdglobal.org/wp-content/uploads/2016/06/Counter-narrative-Handbook_1.pdf).

Activating the Archive From Below at a Moment of Cultural and Political Crisis

Gregory Sholette

The delirium and crisis of capitalism – as well as of art – is now the delirium and crisis of liberal democracy. From India and Turkey to the Philippines and the Gulf region, from Hungary to Austria and Italy, from the US to parts of Central America and the UK, it appears that both developed and developing nations are being equally afflicted with a global contagion of nationalistic and authoritarian sentiment grounded in fear, hatred, and above all, pessimism about any government's or any politician's promise to provide a stable and secure future. Neoliberalism's postponement of crisis through consumer credit expansion has run its course. In its place we find a narrative invoking wealthy male leadership, military capacity and warnings of retribution towards one's perceived competitors as well as certain targeted minorities, be they other states, refugees, precarious and paperless migrant workers or even the disaffected surplus populace of one's own nation. On the positive side, the proponents of this toxic worldview who may previously have been hiding in the bushes have no more need for camouflage. The stakes for liberal civil societies have become much clearer and more urgent.[1]

Meanwhile, art's mythical quarantine from everyday life, already made improbable under the conditions of what I call *bare art*, is clearly no longer viable in light of the gestating political and economic crisis we now face. A 'bare art world' has emerged, one in which art's mystique and romance have boiled away, and where its imagined historical autonomy from the

---

1 | Some parts of this essay initially appeared in the Postscript and other sections of my (2017) book *Delirium and Resistance: Activist Art and the Crisis of Capitalism.*

market place has collapsed to such a degree that the laws of supply and demand can be invoked about cultural production without irony. We see this nakedness at work when artworks are blatantly transformed into an investment instrument, making our nostalgic belief that creative work is inherently antithetical to capital vanish into thin air. As one senior manager of the global financial consulting firm Deloitte enthusiastically puts it, when the complete monetization of art takes hold its:

"financial activities will have ripple effects on other sectors of the economy. This evolution should create a new era for the art markets and for the benefit of the society as a whole by fostering culture, knowledge and creativity" (Picinatti di Tocello 2010: 23).

However, this state of cultural ultra-reification is not the end of art's subversive potential. This process of reification has both positive and negative effects. For example, being subjected to the delusion that capitalism is an ahistorical inevitability is a negative deformation caused by reification, but confronting our bare art world without illusions is a potentially positive way of utilizing objectification, a chance to see our conditions clearly. The only catch is that the 'real' we perceive so plainly is itself delirious. In short, we have entered what Rebecca Bryant calls the "uncanny present", which is a shorthand way to say that we seem to be experiencing the present as if it were unfamiliar and the future as a mere repetition of the present – known and unknown, anticipated and unanticipated, all at the same time (Bryant 2016: 27). This surreal feeling of displacement in an ersatz reality was neatly summed up by journalist Matthew Yglesias: "We're living through a weird and disturbing dream and we don't seem able to wake up" (Yglesias 2018).

That said, from this moment forwards, culture no longer serves as a salve for nervous souls. Art's freedom – as long as it lasts – its peculiar license to speak up, to misbehave, mock and imitate reality, to blur genres and disciplines, must be deployed to prevent the normalization of the emerging authoritarian paradigm. And if it is blocked, it must then move underground to continue its mission as what I call a form of "artistic dark matter" (Sholette 2010).

Artistic dark matter refers to the marginalized and systematically underdeveloped aggregate of creative productivity that nonetheless reproduces the material and symbolic economy of high art. Think of the way the majority of art school graduates will, ten years after graduating, find themselves working as exhibition installers or art fabricators, rather than living off the sales of their own art (that is, if they are still making art at all). Or similarly, the way countless collectives and interventionist art practitioners add energy and ideas to the overall art world from the margins, while only a few ever gain recognition within the white citadels of that same world. Instead, most participants in high art – the sphere of museums and galleries and international biennials – make up a necessarily redundant economy of artistic labor. Think of this as a residual agency that operates out of sight and from below, somewhere within a surplus archive of artistic hopes, possibilities, failures and alternative practices. I call that surplus archive, the *archive from below*. How this underground archive is continually developed and expressed against the force of repressive powers is central to my argument here, just as it is essential to the development of socially-engaged art practices that can offer any counter-culture to the growing authoritarian mainstream culture.

NEOLIBERALISM, COMPLICITY AND RESISTANCE

How art got to this juncture is politically and art-historically significant. In the 1990s, a fresh wave of activist art and cultural collectivism emerged to immediately challenge many key assumptions held by an earlier generation of politically engaged artists still linked to the rebellions of May 1968. Dovetailing with the rise of the counter, or 'alt' globalization movement (not to be confused with the more recent term 'Alt-Right'), this new cultural activism was less concerned with demystifying ideology than creatively disrupting it. Unlike most of the critical art practices of the 1970s and 1980s, in which dominant representational forms were systematically analyzed through a variety of methods ranging from Semiotics to Marxism, Feminism and Psychoanalysis, the new approach plowed directly and some would say gleefully into what Guy Debord described as "the society of the spectacle" in 1967 (Debord 1994). Groups such as RTmark, The Yes Men, Yomango, Electronic Disturbance Theater, Nettime, and Critical Art Ensemble, among other artists' collectives, took full advantage of increasingly widespread and affordable digital communication networks in order to practice what was often referred to as "tactical media", a concept inspired as much by the Zapatista rebellion as it was by the Situationist International. According to key theorists of tactical media David Garcia and Geert Lovink, the practice involved the appropriation of cheap, available technologies for the purpose of engendering political resistance amongst socially disenfranchised populations.[2]

What was unique to these 1990s antagonistic practices was the way technology-based artists took advantage of post-Fordist capital's distributed communicative networks in order to generate acts of disruption within its very structure. Tactical media did this by mobilizing those 'surplus' practices and practitioners of the archive from below. Though only informally structured, this 'secondary economy' of informal dark matter productivity functioned in cellular fashion, much like a social club or rock band. Sometimes it even established its own ersatz institutions, or mockstitutions, with intentionally unstable public identities (Robert 2015). This marginal agency was also structurally entangled with, or parasitic upon, the existing mainstream art world and mass media sector as well as (to some degree) their cultural markets, hence the term 'secondary economy'. In this way, tactical media practitioners diverged even further from the somewhat more hierarchically structured art activism of the 1960s-80s, with its vision of an entirely autonomous political cultural sphere.[3] Instead, the cultural interventionists of the 1990s and 2000s championed small-scale, in-between spaces and ephemeral gestures for their work, often illegally infiltrating public squares, corporate websites, libraries, flea markets, housing projects and local political machines in ways that were not intended to recover a specific meaning or use-value for either art world discourse or private interests. And yet, this emerging interventionist culture also revealed certain definite similarities with the anarcho-entrepreneurial spirit of the neoliberal enterprise, including its highly plastic sense of organizational identity and a romantic distrust of comprehensive administrative structures, a propensity that simultaneously energized and deflated Occupy Wall Street (OWS) for instance.[4]

---

2 | For a guide to Tactical Media in the visual arts see Thompson/Sholette 2014.

3 | See for example the 1982 mission statement of art Political Art Documentation/Distribution, "PAD [/D] can not serve as a means of advancement within the art world structure of museums and galleries. Rather, we have to develop new forms of distribution economy as well as art" (Sholette 2011).

4 | Writing brilliantly about the rise of neoliberalism and Alt-Globalization politics before the emergence of Occupy Wall Street or Arab Spring was theorist Brian

WHITHER TACTICAL MEDIA?

Since roughly the second decade of the 21st century, contemporary socially engaged art has taken shape in the wake of these widespread, entre-
preneurial tendencies, which coincide with the normalization and mainstreaming of the Internet as a full-on capitalist marketplace. Therefore,
what I am describing as the raw condition of bare art is a state of affairs
fully entwined with the dominance of a hyper-financialized and spectac-
ularized society. Paradoxically, bare art also generates an increasingly
politicized art world, perhaps because its participants cannot ignore the
obvious collusion between art and capital or the fragility of the social reality that it has sprung from. This is the greatest contradiction that activist artists must now come to terms with at the theoretical, political,
and artistic levels: How to invent, or how to reinvent, a partisan art praxis
when deregulated capitalism has become a dead weight, and its social and
political forms are imploding across the globe. We might think of this as
an *urguard,* a self-appointed primitive rebelliousness that denounces contemporary society while purporting to belong to the cutting edge of the
future. We have seen this outlook on the anarchist Left, but today witness
it welling up within the far right. This far-right version is typified by raw
and frequently barbaric language and opinion, including promoting racialized privilege and anti-feminist ideologies. These affects are then amplified by sophisticated communication networks (ironically a technology
that is very much a part of the contemporary world being denounced) to
generate an eerie, yet also farcical echo of the early-20th century avant-garde movement known as Italian Futurism, which infamously celebrated
militarism, technology and machismo. As one of its key figures insisted,
Futurists would be defined by their "aggression, feverish sleeplessness,
the double march, the perilous leap, the slap and the blow with the fist".[5]

Holmes (2011), whose essays such as *The Flexible Personality*, substantially inform my analysis here.

5 | Excerpt from Filippo Tommaso Marinetti's, *The Manifesto of Futurism* (1909).
For an extended discussion about this assertion see my essay "Confronting Fascist Banalities on the Centenary of the Futurist Manifesto", in which I propose that
Trump and the Alt-Right are not genuine cultural radicals, but instead a "bathetic,
bargain basement version of Futurism redux, more like an *astroturf* reinterpreta-

Perhaps this paradox is most apparent if we contrast the surreal authoritarian right-wing culture that surrounds the current US president,
with the spread of a generalized oppositional activism that takes on public
forms of creative resistance such as legions of 'Pussyhats' or a giant in-
flatable caricature of Donald Trump floating above thousands of London
protesters during his visit there in July 2018.

Even before Brexit, and the September 2016 US elections, or even
President Trump's startling travel ban and various videos showing police
brutality towards unarmed African Americans, we had already witnessed
swarms of bodies mobilized with the assistance of modern communications technology erupt into public spaces, actively interrupting automobile
traffic flows and deregulating barricades and ordinances that segregate
those who have access to visibility from those who have little or none.
Think of groups such as Black Lives Matter (BLM), Occupy Wall Street
(OWS) the Indignados in Spain, or the so-called Arab Spring and other
self-organized forms of resistance, all of which are evidence that what I
call marginalized dark matter resistance is no longer dark – that invisible
peoples, labor and networks have been demanding recognition for several
decades. After Brexit and Trump, these forces have become even more em-
phatic, and yet more than one paradox arises here. Along with the social
antagonism that fully networked culture fosters with its panoptic vulner-
ability to surveillance and self-obsessive tendencies (such as sharing one's
privacy with thousands of others as well as corporate marketing specialists), there are also no barricades or prohibitions that prevent assemblies
of authoritarian and white supremacist bodies from similarly using networked culture to assemble in an effort to eclipse (or to affirm) their own
dark matter obscurity. And this is precisely what we have seen over the
past few years across the globe, at an accelerating pace.

Anti-abortion activists, Tea-Party Loyalists, right-wing Brexiteers,
Movement for a Better Hungary, Serbian ultra-nationalists, and of course
Alt-Right Trump supporters are taking full advantage of inexpensive media tech and tactics borrowed from the playbook of 1960s counter-culture
to assert their ideology within our uncanny present. Nonetheless, what
these typically rigid bodies framed by authoritarian doctrine cannot conceal is their fidelity to dogmatic first principles and fundamentally un-

---

tion of the notorious avant-garde faction than a "roaring motor car which seems to
run on machine-gun fire" to cite Marinetti again.

democratic ideas of racial sovereignty. Whether it is a Tea Party Loyalist dressed as George Washington or a neo-National Socialist wearing a 1930's swastika armband, the Right's mimesis is administered by a second-rate, Hollywood version of history filled with cardboard cut-outs of a highly mediated and phantasmagoric notion of the past. In contrast, movements such as BLM, OWS, 15-M/Los Indignados, and Take the Square celebrate a critical plurality and the essential uncertainty of an archive from below: a communal repository of innumerable attempts at resistance against authority, patriarchy, capitalism, now and then made concrete through the collective labors of mass protest, no matter how motley, ungainly or informal in appearance.

CLASH OF 21ˢᵀ CENTURY REBEL CULTURES

Thus, today, two essentially contrasting dissident impulses confront one another, and in turn produce contrasting corporeal, visual and narrative public manifestations. One, exemplified by the Alt-Right, understands history and 'whiteness' as a rigid and unchanging guarantee of their own longed-for political dominance. That they dress this belief up in a narrative about white people as victims of liberal conspiracy, or even appropriate the hoodies and bandanas of Antifa or hipster fashion, only conceals the fact that neo-fascist acolytes are fundamentally attached to the construction of a homogeneous identity – one might even say to narcissistic self-representation – in ways that shallowly pastiche pop culture.[6]

The other rebel impulse recognizes the lacuna of the archive as its inheritance: a non-legacy in which the long-term struggle from below has no inventory to check-off, and no authoritative catalog of ideal prototypes to emulate. This elliptical uncertainty opens up a crucial space for an entirely different social horizon, one that not only resists the mainstreaming of far-right politics, but that can also situate its collective resistance within a broader socio-political struggle against inequality and exploitation. Thus, the surplus *archive from below* is about the politics of memory, as opposed to the memory of politics that a Right-leaning imaginary posits as a history of obedience and servility towards authority and mythical origins, such

---

6 | An excellent source of detailed reporting on the Alt-Right is found in Angela Nagle's book *Kill All Normies* (2017).

as whiteness. By embracing this overabundant surplus – this dark matter archive from below with its ambitions, meanderings, resentments, and uncertainties – rather than limiting access to it, or curating it into one or other official cannon, that critical openness has become the very quality that holds out hope for a radically heterodox socially-engaged art practice.

The task that stands before the forces of progressive culture involves *not* eliminating ambiguity and ellipsis from the historical imagination in the way we see neo-fascists and the Alt-Right push for. And perhaps this defence is *the* pivotal task, one that every progressive artist is called upon to carry out, lest, as Walter Benjamin somberly maintained, "not even the dead will be safe from the enemy, if he is victorious" (Benjamin 1969). Therefore, what is called for is a grammar of cultural dissent which does not turn innocently away from the chaotic and delirious state of contemporary social realities, or the contradictions of bare art, but recognizes this moment, this very dangerous moment, as ultimately historical in nature, and therefore also as a time and conflict that will one day be displaced, as all such moments are. One weapon in this battle is the difficult and continuous collective development of the archive from below, that activated space of surplus memories, marginalized hopes, as well as defeats, that the dead have passed to us, and we must pass on to future generations.

References

Benjamin, Walter (1969): Thesis on the Philosophy of History, New York: Schocken Books.

Bryant, Rebecca (2016): "On Critical Times: Return, Repetition, and the Uncanny Present", History and Anthropology 27/1, pp. 19–31.

Debord, Guy (1994): The Society of the Spectacle, New York: Zone Books.

Holmes, Brian (2011): "The Flexible Personality", (http://transform.eipcp.net/transversal/1106/holmes/en).

Nagle, Angela (2017): Kill All Normies. The Online Culture Wars from Tumblr and 4chan to the Alt-Right and Trump, Winchester and Washington: Zero Books.

Picinati di Torcello, Adriano (2010): "Why Should Art Be Considered as an Asset Class?", (www.deloitte.com/lu/en/pages/art-finance/articles/art-as-investment.html).

Robert, John (2015): Revolutionary Time and the Avant-Garde, London and New York: Verso.

Sholette, Gregory (2010): Dark Matter: Art and Politics in the Age of Enterprise Culture, London: Pluto Press.

Sholette, Gregory (2011): "A Collectography of PAD/D", (http://www.gregorysholette.com/wp-content/uploads/2011/04/14_collecto graphy1.pdf).

Sholette, Gregory (2017): Delirium and Resistance: Activist Art and the Crisis of Capitalism, London: Pluto Press.

Thompson, Nato/Sholette, Gregory (2004): The Interventionists: Users' Manual for the Creative Disruption of Everyday Life, North Adams: Mass MoCA Publications & MIT Press.

Yglesias, Matthew 2018: "Trump-Era Politics is a Surreal Nightmare and we Can't Wake Up", 30 March 2018 (https://www.vox.com/policy-and-politics/2018/3/30/17170716/trump-surreal-nightmare).

Back to Front Truths

Hate Library

Nick Thurston

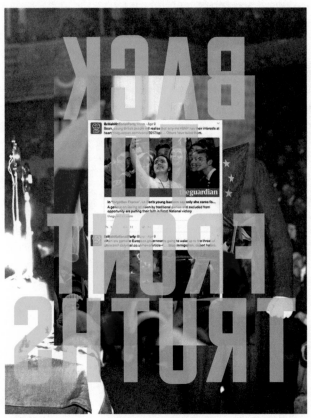

Montaged poster poem (English version) from Nick Thurston,
Hate Library (2017). Photo: Courtesy of the artist.

'Hate' means different things to different people in different circumstances. Inevitably those different communities and their interpretations sometimes overlap and come into conflict. Even if, in theory, a general concept of hatred can be agreed, real life tends to complicate its applicability as an underwriter for anything like legal action. What exactly constitutes hate speech, or indeed a *Hate Library*, is therefore deceptively complicated. Various derivative concepts are already in use to filter the kinds of expressions and intentions we might gather under the umbrella of hate speech, to establish more specific and applicable categories like incitement or dangerous speech. For example, Susan Benesch and her team at the Dangerous Speech Project distinguish hate speech, which is hateful to some, from dangerous speech, which motivates an endangerment of that group because it inspires violence against them (Benesch 2018).

Images and ideas about activist violence have been popularly fixated on Islamic extremism in the wake of 9/11, with representations defaulting time and again to the cliché of Jihadist propaganda. The growing use of dangerous speech tactics by far-right activists has been either downplayed as a traditional conservative entitlement to free speech or ignored completely because its motives seem entangled with the disgruntlement of white customers and voters. Yet hateful rhetoric and victimization methods, charged by the positive and negative effects of the growing importance of identity politics and its offshoots like call-out culture, seem to flood the expanding archives of images and text that far-right groups are creating via public peer-to-peer networks like social media feeds and web forums. There, the evidence of hate and dangerous speech is publicly available to readers everywhere, and "to make public", from the Latin *publicare*, is the root meaning of 'publish'. Yet in that same fluid digital sphere of publishing, those expressions and their effects do not seem to have become *public knowledge* in any strong sense of that phrase. How do we learn to see it, hear it, read it and so get to know it, so that we can do something about its base causes? Making offline repositories that re-contextualize such material, making it accessible to audiences who would never enter those online bubbles, is one answer this essay explores through the case-study of my artwork *Hate Library*.

I am not going to suggest that art is the solution to the very real and current problem propelling this flood, or indeed any other real world problem. This book is testament to the fact that there are lots of amazing activists and research groups who do grounded social and policy work in the spirit of what we might call 'language critique' or even 'counter speech' – the best of them proving well aware that the status of free speech is a contested, even gray issue. For example, in Germany there is the dedicated work done by the Amadeu Antonio Foundation's Debate-Dehate project, and in the UK there is the committed anti-fascist action group HOPE Not Hate.

In the fourth section of this essay I describe some the gestures that went in to the making of *Hate Library,* which was commissioned by Katarzyna Krysiak for the Foksal Gallery in Warsaw where it was first shown in summer 2017. In the second and third sections I explain why I think radically public forums for sociable reading – for reading together, as epitomized by libraries – are something that can be made *as art* and could be one type of space where a politics of thought and counter-thought, speech and counter-speech, can be productively held together. Underpinning that discussion is my belief that the arts might be able to make some, maybe unique, contribution to broad and collective forms of counter-action against aggressively singular visions for what the world should be, by embracing the eternal contest over the concept of what art is. Rather than prescribe that art must be a mirror as William Shakespeare did, or a hammer as Bertold Brecht declared, or a speculative act of worlding as Ernst Cassirer proposed, I am interested in the idea that it could be all of those things and more, all held together by a society as a web of productive contradictions. I am invested in the idea that art is one form of culture that can hold things open, in public, as a specific, experienceable yet contestable knot of materials and gestures and concepts.

Nonetheless, the kind of art that I find particularly interesting, and of which *Hate Library* is just one example, tends to display a certain set of commitments: First, this kind of work treats languages as contextually-specific and necessary lies – not a "noble lie" in the Platonic sense, but a present mark or utterance (a gesture) whose primary purpose is to represent something it is not. Second, this kind of work understands poetics as a committed exploration of the compositional and sociological potential of those lies when stretched to the limit of their primary purpose and acknowledged as present gestures. Third, it leans on documentary modes of art-making to deploy, at one of its extremes, the relatively simple practice of reproducing and sharing documents – effectively, of publishing or re-publishing or *making language public* – as a mode of documentary practice in itself (Thurston 2018a).

THE NEARING RIGHT

Before all that, I want to begin by borrowing an observation made to me by my collaborator on the *Hate Library* project, Matthew Feldman, who is the founding Director of the Centre for Analysis of the Radical Right.[1] It is a corrective that might help us to see why and how issues of right-wing populism, ethno-nationalism and even fascism are coming back into view but are doing so out of focus. As someone who cares but is not a social scientist, I have found it a helpful way of understanding why our apprehension of these ideologies remains relatively blurry because of our out-of-date figures of speech.

Most of us still use the spatial metaphor of a spectrum to describe political positions, stretching from a left to a right. That metaphor triangulates a center, the point between those poles, which then centers or anchors political viewpoints and discourse. All non-centrist political positions are judged by their distance from the center, left or right, from the near to the far. It is easy to forget that where the center is at any one time on that spectrum can change. The window constituting the center or mainstream is not a static point nor singular, unlike the center-point of, say, a circle. The range of ideas open for debate that a society will tolerate, what we could call the window of mainstream discourse, can move and the direction of its movement can be strategically influenced. This political center is more like the contingent concentration of power in a particular socio-historic moment and place. And if the center moves, then so too does its proximity to the spectrum's poles, left and right.

The center-ground of contemporary mainstream politics in Europe has lurched rightwards, and the radical right has become more culturally and politically active, managing to acculturate previously unacceptable extremist terms for public discourse as new norms. Simply put, the 'far right' is no longer very far away from the political center, and it is the center-ground that hedges most of our everyday experiences. We have a nearing extreme right and continuing to call it 'far' encourages a false sense

---

1 | Matthew Feldman has since developed this observation in *Between Alt-Right and Mainstream Conservatism: The 'Near Right' in Contemporary American Politics and Culture* (Feldman 2017) and *Islam and the Far Right: Is Bigotry Back?* (Feldman 2016).

of safe distance. I am not disputing its accuracy and value as a technical term, just flagging the risk encoded in its phrasing.

Whether the blame for that lays with a lack of liberal resilience or whatever else, we do need to adjust our metaphors. If the far right is getting closer then we should be figuring out how to see it and hear it and read it, and to say so more clearly. It should be coming into view and we should be sharpening our blurred focus. At the moment, too often, it seems we are trying to use a telescope when we really need a pair of reading glasses. We need to learn to look in appropriate ways and in the appropriate places, which means that we have to re-imagine where and how we look. This will require us to nuance a better common-sense grasp of the specific and general features of this renewed radical-right energy as well as its diverse cultures, which develop with transnational features and local differences. To do so, we need access to its manifestations, the literacies to engage with them, and for those experiences to be contextualized through informed discourses. That is a cocktail of needs that are paradoxically made both easier and harder to fulfil in our age of fluid public language and pluralized centers of power and community.

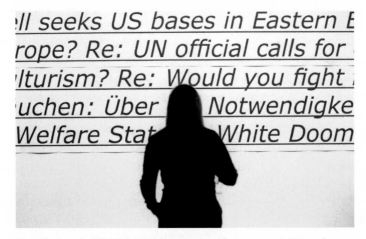

Installation detail: Nick Thurston, Hate Library (2017), Haus der Kulturen der Welt, Berlin, 2018. Photo: Adam Berry, transmediale, CC BY NC-SA 4.0.

POST-DIGITAL PUBLISHING AND READING

We all know that the way we live is being radically transformed by the augmented interaction of digital networked technologies, which largely do their work under the surface of daily life (invisibly) while their effects and applications work on its surface (visibly or not).[2] The recent successes of the Alternative for Germany party (AfD) are a good example of how this combination works in terms of our topic: Under the surface, they have tapped in to the proliferation of user-driven online activism; and on the surface of everyday life, they have had unprecedented electoral success. I am not saying that the correlation is simple, just that digitally-led mobilization is already recognized widely enough to merit general public attention – what we might call *citizen* or even *civil* interest – on more subtle terms than those set by Cold War shock stories about Russian Fancy Bear hack attacks.

Developing that kind of sophisticated common interest – the basis for a stronger sense of what I called 'public knowledge' above – will depend in part on civil societies cultivating an appropriate level of media literacy. The ability to understand and use media, new and old, often in combination, requires a technical and conceptual understanding of how networked media work in different ways yet inter-effectively. Any such understanding would help us to realize that our literacies will only be appropriate if they are multilayered and keep tow with technological change. To take responsibility for the augmented online-offline lives we lead, we have to first accept that the "mediascapes" we inhabit are expansive and our relationships with them are active and generative (Appadurai 1990: 298–299). The concept of the 'post-digital' can be a crucial part of that toolkit because it names the socio-historical condition wherein the distinction between digital and non-digital are blurred beyond separation – after the advent of digitization yet constitutively altered by it.

To even recognize the connections between our post-digital mediascapes and contemporary far-right activism, let alone robustly critique how and why they are entwined, we have to make their interactions legible. We have to see it and hear it and read it to comprehend it. One imperfect way of doing so is to say it again yet differently, even if we disagree with its con-

---

2 | For further discussion of this topic, see my essay *The Mediatization of Contemporary Writing* (Thurston 2016).

tent. Saying it again is the easy bit: You repeat it, and that has never been simpler than digital capture and copy-and-paste allow. Saying it differently – so that you do not just reinforce or monumentalize its significances – is trickier: It is not, necessarily, about changing the content, but it is always about re-contextualizing both that content's legibility and the experiences of reading it that others might have. Put simply, a documentary method of saying it again yet differently hinges upon changing the mode of attention not the testimony (Weizman 2017: 80–84).

When it comes to making legible the specific interaction between net-worked activism under the surface of life and its effects on the surface of lived experience, I think such re-contextualizations can be relatively simple but potentially transformative. They involve shifting the manifes-tations of post-digital activism from the seemingly private circuits of in-dividuals and their web-enabled devices into unavoidably social situations where the largely private mental experience of reading is done in relation to other people. Reading is, after all, a fundamentally embodied practice; and a group of readers can collectively become a (secondary and minor) body politic – a network of actors capable of developing a civil discourse based on their shared readings. We need to be reminded as we read, as Étienne Balibar so painstakingly manages, that all of our personas and avatars are anchored by our actual-world status as political subjects.[3] Read-ing like that keeps the content we are attending to in the same view as, in the same earshot as, in relation with, our senses of social justice, of our social contracts, and of being-with.

Reading in communal situations – what Abigail Williams calls "so-ciable reading" or simply "reading together" – tends to be conducive to discussing content rather than just commenting on it (Williams 2017: 3). When that content is potentially contentious, like all of the expressions that would fall under the umbrella of hate speech, those conversations may lead to civil debate, maybe even legal action, and maybe forms of counter-speech. But how and where they are read makes a significant dif-ference. Context, form and content all matter, inter-effectively, in ways that late-modern and contemporary art can do a good job of reminding us.

---

3 | For the most extensive account of this connection, see Étienne Balibar's *Citi-zen Subject: Foundations for Philosophical Antropology* (Balibar 2016).

"Merely Civil" Libraries

Spaces for reading and discussing communally, without pressure to be a customer but with the freedom to listen and speak closely, are rare. You need a space that can hold that contentious content together and welcome competing readings – it needs to hold those ideas and people together, but also hold them open. Public libraries can be one such rare platform for doing just that, and not because of some regressive model of civic nostalgia. Rather, when it comes to the value of the civic or civil, I find Teresa Bejan's concept of "mere civility" really useful. For Bejan, "mere civility" describes a minimal and imperfect sense of respectful engagement with our conversants and what they have to say. What she calls "civility skeptics" tend to flatten the concept's range, conflating all forms of civil discussion with being polite, presuming it to be necessarily deferential or even a kind of suppression of one's right to speak freely. But what free-speech absolutists often misassume is that there is a flat equality of opportunity in public discourse, as if everyone has equal means and chance to speak freely, as if intersecting inequalities never matter and are not precoded in our languages. As Bejan points out, if there is no baseline for public discourse that can allow its participants to *sustain* an honest conversation, then those who disagree are more likely to force their position upon others and/or retreat into bubbles of the like-minded (Bejan 2017). "Merely civil" libraries could be one such space for readers where the questions of public-ness, public knowledge and shared literacies are all sustained in non-violent discourse by an open yet respectful archive of ideas – ideas that we can disagree about together.

Making temporary public libraries as artworks brings the qualities I described in the opening section – of keeping productive contradictions open – to this "merely civil" reference resource. It allows us to *compose* libraries beyond their conventional norms, focussing on the inter-connection of specific contents, specific forms of sharing and specific contextual conditions, with care for both the practical and symbolic value of our decisions. It is the speculative yet specific act of composition, of art-making, which can enable this different kind of library-making. This different kind of public library is partial, in the sense of incomplete and biased, yet open to contested engagements and readings, maybe even "merely civil" disobedience.

HATE LIBRARY

For about seven years I have been trying to bring together my literary and editorial work with my interests in the sociology of reading and public art by doing exactly this: Making temporary functioning public libraries as artworks. These artworks treat the gallery as a specific place with specific conventions, fill it with specific published holdings, and contextualize the audience's access to them in specific ways. It is the most boiled-down recipe for a public library, and very different from the quiet, neo-classical conventional civic model most people are more familiar with. These spaces should be noisy and temporary, and make unusual literatures available to be read and responded to on "merely civil" terms.

Installation detail: Nick Thurston, Hate Library (2017), Haus der Kulturen der Welt, Berlin, 2018. Photo: Adam Berry, transmediale, CC BY NC-SA 4.0.

Hate Library is a public reference resource in this mold and has five components with a very particular choreography. In a ring in the middle are twelve blue orchestra stands, spaced according to the design of the EU flag with a diameter calculated according to the proportions of the room, but all turned inwards as communal reading lecterns. On each stand is one of twelve free-to-handle, comb-bound volumes. Each of these 500–700-page books is a tiny sample of the on-going public discussions between supporters of twelve of the most significant far-right groups from European nations, which have been exported from their original digital platforms and re-materialized here as history books. Each of these unedited volumes pauses one far-right national conversation, repeating it offline by using simple data-gathering and print-on-demand processes.

Two of the three components on the walls repeat a different, lateral chain of conversation. The continuous lines of over-sized blue text are a single poem made entirely of buttressed hyperlinks. Each hyperlink or phrase included is the title of a thread from a public web forum on Storm-front, the world's largest white supremacist discussion platform, kept in the order they were found with only duplicated titles removed. Around the walls, encircling the history books, runs a frieze of paper columns. Each digitally-tiled sheet is one page of results returned by searching for the word "truth" across the European sections of Stormfront, ordered chronologically until three of those walls are full. Together, this frieze and thread-name poem are backdrops that signal the vexing growth of transnational cooperation between radical, extreme and far-right groups, as enabled by digital networked technology.

The final component is a montaged poster poem that occupies the fourth surrounding wall. It condenses the sharpening problems of civic cohesion and free speech at the heart of this project. Inside its frame – frames inside frames that brace one another conceptually to form what Walter Benjamin called a "dialectical image" (Benjamin 1999: 460–461) – from back to front and past to present yet big to small, are an iconic photograph of Oswald Mosley addressing a fascist rally in 1930s London and a screen grab of the British National Party's Twitter feed sandwiching a news media image of pro-EU liberals marching in Warsaw. The slogan printed over the top in translucent mirror writing, "BACK TO FRONT TRUTHS", remixes a pair of colloquial English wordplays with a drama-turgical metaphor famously borrowed by the sociologist Erving Goff-man in his influential 1956 book *The Presentation of Self in Everyday Life*. Through its combination of text and image, this poster tries to juxtapose the confusing overlap between the public 'frontstage' and online activist 'backstage' behavior by far-right groups and parties, as well as their mobi-lization of PR-friendly strategies to conceal and legitimate the beliefs that unify their memberships.

In ways that are blunt – maybe even too blunt – a contest over truths and truth-claims are at the heart of this library, all of which is obviously skewed by my subjective concerns as its librarian and composer. It is partial, in the sense of both incomplete and biased. The potential I see in this kind of speculative public library is that it eschews the supposed neutrality of the conventional civic model. It is *too public* or excessively public, from its catalogue to its cheaply reproduced contents: It hinges upon my personal concerns and my small portion of finds; and it amplifies the semi-discrete personal discussions of registered community members into printed testimonies – it exports them into testimonies said 'on the (old media) record'.

At the heart of the project is the idea of taking responsibility for a public language act as, in itself, an authorial act and a key gesture in contemporary poetics (Thurston 2018b). But that same idea is the basis for on-going international legal debates about liability: Are online platforms neutral hosts or responsible publishers? *Hate Library* tries to open up that central issue by very simply documenting just a few of stances adopted by nearing-right and right-wing fringe communities, in ways that are too partial to be conventionally civic but frank enough to be merely civil. Neither the dataset nor its collection are robust enough to be evidence for any kind of lazy generalizations. It is just a lumpen slice of real communication, lyrically selected in the spirit of the long history of documentary poetry as something that works by playing with an odd mix of literalism and allegory. For me, what readers do with it is what matters.

REFERENCES

Appadurai, Arjun (1990): "Disjuncture and Difference in the Global Cultural Economy." In: Public Culture 2/2, pp. 295–310.

Balibar, Étienne (2016): Citizen Subject: Foundations for Philosophical Antropology, New York: Fordham University Press.

Bejan, Teresa (2017): Mere Civility: Disagreement and the Limits of Toleration, Cambridge: Harvard University Press.

Benesch, Susan (2018): "What is Dangerous Speech?", 28 August 2018 (https://dangerousspeech.org/the-dangerous-speech-project-preventing-mass-violence/).

Benjamin, Walter (1999): The Arcades Project, Cambridge and London: Belknap Press.

Feldman, Matthew (2017): "Between Alt-Right and Mainstream Conservatism: The 'Near Right' in Contemporary American Politics and Culture", Unpublished Manuscript.

Feldman, Matthew (2016): "Islam and the Fair Right: Is Bigotry Back", 28 November 2016 (https://www.fairobserver.com/region/europe/islam-far-right-racism-terrorism-news-headlines-90662/).

Thurston, Nick (2016): "The Mediatization of Contemporary Writing." In: Gilbert, Annette (ed.), Publishing As Artistic Practice, Berlin: Sternberg Press, pp. 90–99.

Thurston, Nick (2018a): "Document Practices", 28 August 2018 (https://transmediale.de/content/document-practices).

Thurston, Nick (2018b): "What Was Conceptual Writing?" In: Andersson, Andrea (ed.), Postscript: Writing After Conceptual Art, Toronto: University of Toronto Press, pp. 260–269.

Weizman, Eyal (2017): Forensic Architecture: Violence at the Threshold of Detectability, New York: Zone Books.

Williams, Abigail (2017): The Social Life of Books, New Haven: Yale University Pres.

Biographical Notes

Stephen Albrecht is a student research assistant at the Institute for Peace Research and Security Policy at the University of Hamburg where he studies History. His special interest is far-right extremism, in particular its connections to online activism in Germany.

Lynn Berg is the scientific coordinator for Right-wing Populism, Social Question and Democracy at the Research Institute for Societal Development. She is co-editor of *Populär – Extrem – Normal: Zur Debatte über Rechten Populismus* together with Andreas Zick. Her work focuses on gender and gender relations in right-wing populism, modern anti-feminism and image analysis.

Lisa Bogerts is a research fellow at the Freie Universität Berlin and project manager at a Berlin-based NGO for conflict transformation. She obtained her PhD from Goethe University Frankfurt and was a visiting scholar at the New School for Social Research, New York City. Her research focuses on visual culture, power relations and political protest.

Alina Darmstadt is an education consultant for the Berlin-based Amadeu Antonio Foundation. She studied Philosophy and Fine Art Education at Goethe University Frankfurt. At the Amadeu Antonio Foundation, she provides training about online strategies to counter hate speech for organizations and citizens' initiatives.

Joan Donovan is lead researcher on media manipulation and platform accountability at the Data & Society research institute in New York City. After completing her PhD in Sociology and Science Studies at the University of California San Diego, Joan was a postdoctoral fellow at the UCLA Institute for Society and Genetics. Joan has conducted action research with different networked social movements in order to map and improve their communication infrastructure.

Julia Ebner is a research fellow at the London-based Institute for Strategic Dialogue, where she leads research projects on online radicalization, disinformation and hate speech and advises governments and tech firms. She is author of *The Rage: The Vicious Circle of Islamist and Far-Right Extremism* and regularly writes for *The Guardian* and *The Independent*.

Matthew Feldman is Emeritus Professor at the University of Teesside, Visiting Professor at the American University in London and a Professorial Fellow at the University of York. He is the author or editor of more than 20 books, including three monographs, and most recently became Director of the world's largest research unit on far-right extremism, the Centre for Analysis of the Radical Right.

Maik Fielitz is a research associate at the Institute for Peace Research and Security Policy at the University of Hamburg and a PhD Candidate at Goethe University Frankfurt. He works on far-right extremism and social movements in Europe and is a Fellow at the Centre for Analysis of the Radical Right.

Brian Friedberg is a researcher at the Data & Society research institute in New York City. He conducts digital ethnographic research on networked social movements, online political communication, and fringe subcultures.

Caterina Froio is an Assistant Professor in Political Science at Sciences Po, Centre for European Studies and Comparative Politics (CEE), and an affiliate researcher to the Center for Research on Extremism, University of Oslo. Her research focusses on political parties, agenda-setting dynamics, e-politics, right-wing extremism, radicalism and populism in Europe. Since 2016 she has been a joint convenor of the ECPR Standing Group on Extremism & Democracy.

Bharath Ganesh is a researcher at the Oxford Internet Institute, University of Oxford. He completed a PhD in Geography at University College London. His work focuses on online hate speech and right-wing extremism in the United States and Western Europe. Bharath is a member of the VOX-Pol Network of Excellence and a Senior Fellow at the Centre for Analysis of the Radical Right.

Philipp Karl obtained a PhD from Andrássy University Budapest and is a political scientist. His main topics of research are social movements, the radical right, social media, network and content analysis. He has been a visiting researcher at the European University Viadrina in Frankfurt and a fellow at the Central European University in Budapest and the Institute for Peace Research and Security Policy in Hamburg.

Becca Lewis is a researcher at the Data & Society research institute in New York City and a PhD student at Stanford in the Communications Department. She researches online political subcultures and grassroots media movements, with a focus on influence-building, media manipulation, and disinformation efforts among these groups. She holds an MSc in Social Science from the Oxford Internet Institute.

Kaja Marczewska is a Research Fellow at the Centre for Postdigital Cultures, Coventry University and a member of the Information as Material editorial collective. Her research is positioned at the intersection of cultural studies, publishing, and art history and theory. She is the author of *This is Not a Copy* (Bloomsbury, 2018).

Rob May is a doctoral researcher who focuses on the radical right. He has written for academic journals, newsletters and organizations, such as the European International Tolerance Centre. He is a Fellow at the Centre for Analysis of the Radical Right and a monthly contributor to its website.

Cynthia Miller-Idriss is Professor of Education and Sociology at the American University in Washington, DC. Her most recent books are *The Extreme Gone Mainstream: Commercialization and Far Right Youth Culture in Germany* and *Seeing the World: How Universities Make Knowledge in a Global Era* (with co-authors Mitchell Stevens and Seteney Shami), both published by Princeton University Press in 2018.

Mick Prinz is head of the project Civic.net – Aktiv gegen Hass im Netz at the Amadeu Antonio Foundation in Berlin. He started at the foundation in public relations and now offers social media workshops for organizations and civil society. He studied Social Sciences at the University of Siegen.

Oliver Saal is a social media consultant at the Amadeu Antonio Foundation in Berlin. He studied History at Freie Universität Berlin and has published on the far right in Germany. He started at the foundation as a social media editor and now offers social media training for organizations and citizens' initiatives.

Gregory Sholette is Professor at Queens College, CUNY, where he co-directs the Social Practice Queens program. He co-founded the groups Political Art Documentation/Distribution, REPOhistory, and the Gulf Labor Coalition. He curates the Imaginary Archive and is author of *Dark Matter* (Pluto, 2010), *Delirium and Resistance: Activist Art and the Crisis of Capitalism* (Pluto, 2017), and *Art As Social Action* (with Chloë Bass, SPQ, 2018).

Nick Thurston is Associate Professor in the School of Fine Art, History of Art and Cultural Studies at the University of Leeds. He publishes regularly on the connections between contemporary art, literature and media studies in relation to issues of public language, publishing cultures and innovative writing. His artworks have been exhibited in Europe and North America and are held in public and private collections.

Marc Tuters is a Senior Lecturer in New Media and Digital Culture at the University of Amsterdam and has a background in media arts. As a researcher affiliated with the Digital Methods Initiative (DMI) and as the director of the Open Intelligence Lab (OILab), his current work focuses on how online subcultures constitute themselves as political movements, with a particular interest in the reactionary right.

Essays

Carlo Bordoni
Interregnum
Beyond Liquid Modernity

2016, 136 p., pb.
19,99 € (DE), 978-3-8376-3515-7
E-Book
PDF: 17,99 € (DE), ISBN 978-3-8394-3515-1
EPUB: 17,99 € (DE), ISBN 978-3-7328-3515-7

Maik Fielitz, Laura Lotte Laloire (eds.)
Trouble on the Far Right
Contemporary Right-Wing Strategies
and Practices in Europe

2016, 208 p., pb.
19,99 € (DE), 978-3-8376-3720-5
E-Book
PDF: 17,99 € (DE), ISBN 978-3-8394-3720-9
EPUB: 17,99 € (DE), ISBN 978-3-7328-3720-5

European Alternatives, Daphne Büllesbach,
Marta Cillero, Lukas Stolz (eds.)
Shifting Baselines of Europe
New Perspectives beyond Neoliberalism and Nationalism

2017, 212 p., pb.
19,99 € (DE), 978-3-8376-3954-4
E-Book available as free open access publication
ISBN 978-3-8394-3954-8

**All print, e-book and open access versions of the titles in our list
are available in our online shop www.transcript-verlag.de/en!**

Essays

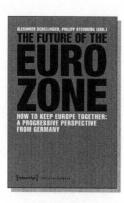

Alexander Schellinger, Philipp Steinberg (eds.)
The Future of the Eurozone
How to Keep Europe Together:
A Progressive Perspective from Germany

2017, 202 p., pb.
29,99 € (DE), 978-3-8376-4081-6
E-Book
PDF: 26,99 € (DE), ISBN 978-3-8394-4081-0
EPUB: 26,99 € (DE), ISBN 978-3-7328-4081-6

Ilker Ataç, Gerda Heck, Sabine Hess, Zeynep Kasli,
Philipp Ratfisch, Cavidan Soykan, Bediz Yilmaz (eds.)
**movements. Journal for Critical Migration and
Border Regime Studies**
Vol. 3, Issue 2/2017: Turkey's Changing Migration Regime
and its Global and Regional Dynamics

2017, 230 p., pb.
24,99 € (DE), 978-3-8376-3719-9

Ramón Reichert, Annika Richterich, Pablo Abend,
Mathias Fuchs, Karin Wenz (eds.)
Digital Culture & Society (DCS)
Vol. 1, Issue 1 – Digital Material/ism

2015, 242 p., pb.
29,99 € (DE), 978-3-8376-3153-1
E-Book: 29,99 € (DE), ISBN 978-3-8394-3153-5

**All print, e-book and open access versions of the titles in our list
are available in our online shop www.transcript-verlag.de/en!**